I0763883

THE

SPECTATOR.

RELIGIOUS, MORAL, HUMOROUS
SATIRICAL, AND CRITICAL
ESSAYS.

A New Edition.

VOL. II.

NEW YORK:
GEO. A. LEAVITT, PUBLISHER,
No. 8 HOWARD STREET.

CONTENTS TO VOLUME II.

WITH THE NAMES (WHEN KNOWN) OF THE AUTHORS OF THE VARIOUS ESSAYS.

THE

LIFE

OF

SIR RICHARD STEELE.

Caput domina venalo sub hasta.

JUVENAL.

His fortune ruin'd, and himself a slave.

Richard Steele, whose father was a counsellor at law, and private secretary to James, first Duke of Ormond, was at an early age carried over from Dublin* to England; and placed, by the influence of his father's patron, at the Charter House school in London, where he gave proofs of great quickness of apprehension, and made very considerable progress in classical learning. There he became intimate with Addison.

Steele was afterward removed to Merton College, in Oxford, where he applied himself chiefly to polite literature, discovered an inclination to become a dramatic author, and actually wrote a comedy which has never been published.†

His first appearance in print was in a poem, entitled *The Funeral Procession*, on the Death of Queen Mary. This effusoin, though not highly poetical, con-

* *Steele* was born in Dublin about the year 1675; his parents were English, of a good family.

† *Steele* showed it to one of his friends, who advised him to suppress it, as not worthy of his genius.

tains animated pictures of the benevolence of that amiable princess.

Our author early entertained a predilection for the army; and deaf to the remonstrances of his friends, who refused to assist him in applying for a commission, he left the college without taking a degree, and enlisted as a private soldier in the horse guards. This imprudent step was more hurtful to STEELE in life, than even the loss of an estate in the county of Wexford he expected to inherit from a relation, who henceforth looking upon him as a reprobate, a disgrace to his family, left the estate to another. A disregard for his interest, whenever it interfered with his inclination, uniformly marked his conduct, and was the cause of the endless pecuniary embarrassments in which he was involved. His disposition however was so happy, that in his so often perplexed and humble station, he was perfectly cheerful; and among his comrades gave full vent to his sprightliness and vivacity. Thus, he not only became the delight of the soldiers, but gained also the regard of the officers, who wishing to have so pleasant a fellow as their companion, exerted their interest, and procured him an ensign's commission.

Now, become an officer, STEELE gave himself up to every pleasurable excess; but his debaucheries were not uninterrupted by serious reflections on their destructive tendency: it was during some intervals of sober meditation, that he wrote his little treatise, entitled *The Christian Hero*, which he dedicated to Lord CULLS, who appointed him his own private secretary, and procured him a company in Lord LUCAS's fusileers. Though, as he himself tells us, he wrote this short treatise for his own private use, and to fix on his mind a strong impression of virtue and religion, Sir RICHARD still went on in his old course. In the midst of his follies, however, a friendly disposition and great goodness of heart were in him eminently conspicuous; and his writings were always conducive to virtue. He continued his intimacy with ADDISON who though he regretted the excesses of STEELE, esteemed his talents, and endeavoured to check his irregularities.* Both were of the Whig party; ADDISON, with the calmness of a philosopher; STEELE, with the violence of a partisan.

Whilst STEELE continued in the army, he wrote his comedy, called, *The Funeral, or Grief-a-la-mode*:† a performance whose plot wants unity, but which abounds in bustle and incident, and possesses a considerable portion of humour. Its object is to expose the enormities of the undertakers,‡ to ridicule the barbarous tautology of the lawyers, and to exhibit the wickedness of young women, who insinuate themselves in the affections of weak and doating old men, to the prejudice of their families.

Recommended by his friend ADDISON to Lord HALIFAX, the Mæcenas of the age, STEELE obtained, by the interest of that nobleman, and of Lord SUNDERLAND, the post of editor of the Gazette, whose duties he performed with the most exact fidelity.

He brought forward soon after§ a comedy very friendly to morality, and written with considerable humour, entitled, *The Tender Husband, or the Accomplished Fools*, which greatly increased his literary reputation. The comedy which succeeded

* *Steele*, in one of his pecuniary difficulties, borrowed an hundred guineas from that gentleman, who insisted on repayment, which circumstance much afflicted *Steele*. *Addison* has been blamed for this proceeding, but we think unjustly; for if *Steele* could raise the sum, why was *Addison* wrong to reclaim that, which his debtor would, most probably, from his extravagance, have applied to his pleasures. He who supplies a profuse man with money, is often the minister of the vices of his friend, rather than his real benefactor.

† It was brought on the stage in the winter of 1701.

‡ These enormities they painted admirably themselves:

Steele says in his preface, "On a door I just now pass'd by a great artist informs us of his cure upon the dead."

'Mr. W. known and approved of for the art of embalming, having preserved the corpse of a gentlewoman sweet and entire, without embowelling, and has reduced the bodies of several persons of quality to sweetness, in Flanders and in Ireland, after nine months under ground, and they were known by their friends in England. No man performeth the like.'

§ In 1704.

was that of *The Lying Lover*, written in the most severe moral rigidity; it was damned: an unfortunate circumstance which determined STEELE, who represented himself as a martyr of the church and morality, to turn his talents into another channel.

STEELE then, taking the name of ISAAC BICKERSTAFF,* began *The Tatler* in concert with SWIFT, with whom at this time he was in habits of intimacy. The professed intention of this periodical paper, whose gay essays are very pleasant, and its serious very instructive, was, to expose the false arts of life, to pull off the disguises of cunning, vanity, and ostentation; and to recommend simplicity in dress, discourse, and behaviour. STEELE himself produced the greatest part of this performance; and in his excellent essays upon domestic happiness, finely illustrated the relative duties of husband and wife. In his account of gamesters and sharpers, who call forth the severest animadversions of our author, he mixes with serious exhortations, much humorous and just satire. Duelling is one of the principal objects of his attack in the *Tatler*; STEELE, who from his earliest years had reprobated this practice,† combats it by authority, from the example of the most polished nations; shows the frivolity of its usual causes; proves its folly and bar-

* *Steele* took that name because his friend *Swift* had published under it his celebrated prediction for 1708, in which he ridicules the absurd prophecies of judicial astrologers. *Swift's* writings under that assumed denomination created in the town an inclination to peruse any which should appear in the same disguise.

† When in the Cold-stream Regiment, *Steele* was forced by a wrong-headed youth to go to the field. In endeavouring to disarm and chastise his rash antagonist, without endangering his life, he aimed at his arm, but, by the turning of the young man to parry the thrust, he ran him through the body. The young officer was for a long time in great danger from the wound, but fortunately at length recovered. The grief and anxiety this affair caused to *Steele* rendered him a most determined enemy to duelling.

barity; enlarges on the miseries it has so often caused to individuals and families; and fully demonstrates its inconsistency with the Christian religion.

About two months after the *Tattler* ended,* STEELE, in conjunction with ADDISON, began the *Spectator*, in which both generally forbore interfering in politics. The essays of STEELE, in this celebrated work, are by no means so generally read as they deserve. In their eagerness to peruse the most entertaining and instructive essayist, ADDISON, many readers overlook STEELE's papers, which are nevertheless worthy not only of being read, but also of being examined with accurate attention, though by no means without defects. His language is perspicuous, natural, and often animated; but it frequently shows marks of haste and carelessness. The construction of his sentences is sufficiently clear, but often defective. His periods are sometimes musical; but their harmony seems more the result of accident than of intended arrangement. On the whole, STEELE's *Spectators* are vehicles of agreeable amusement, and of useful instruction.

Encouraged by the celebrity and the extensive sale of that performance, our author began a new paper on the same plan, in the character, and under the title of *Guardian*. The *Guardian* was to have nothing to manage with any person or party, but he was to make the pulpit, the stage, and the bar, all act in concert, in the cause of piety, justice, and virtue. Calling wit and humour as auxiliaries to the execution, the *Guardian* adhered during the first forty papers to his plan; but in his forty-first number he commenced a political contest with the Tory paper, entitled *The Examiner*.

Adopting an opinion generally prevailing among the Whigs, that the ministry had agreed with France, on the death of QUEEN ANNE, of establishing the Pretender! SIR RICHARD was much disaffected towards a ministry whom he believed capable of betraying the liberties and religion of their country. He then warmly

* January 2, 1711.

engaged in party politics, and openly avowed his determination to procure a seat in parliament, that he might oppose the ministers more effectually. Apprehending a forcible dismission from the Stamp-office, he anticipated compulsion by a voluntary resignation. At the same time he renounced a pension, which had been hitherto paid him by the Queen, as one of the household of her deceased husband, Prince GEORGE of DENMARK.

The most illiberal, virulent, and the bitterest of STEELE's antagonists, was the *Examiner*. It attacked his private character, and still more his circumstances. The whole of his wit and humour consists in the description of the poverty of STEELE, his being arrested, and carried to a spunging-house, &c. When we see the elegance of an ATTERBURY, the splendour of a BOLINGBROKE, and the wit of a SWIFT, employed in such illiberal personalities, how much are we not disposed to lament the contracting spirit of party malevolence! Though violent, STEELE was not malignant, and he never suffered his warmth to transport him into those invectives, which so much disgrace the writings of his opponents.

When the *Guardian* ceased, our author began the *Englishman*,* the professed advocate of Whig principles and of the Protestant succession. He wrote also, during the continuance of that publication, the *Crisis*, dedicated to the clergy, whom he exhorts to be zealous in promoting the cause of civil and religious liberty, by teaching the people to support the House of Hanover, and to dread the evils of a Popish successor, whom, he says, many endeavour to establish on the throne. This paper excited a most furious rage amongst the friends of the ministry. It was branded with the epithets of seditious and inflammatory; and on March 12, 1714, a complaint was laid before the house of commons against certain paragraphs of it and of the *Englishman*, said to be written by RICHARD STEELE, as reflecting on her Majesty, arraign-

* It was published three days in the week.

ing her administra ion, and tending to excite sedition. STEELE was ordered to attend. He did so; and heard the various paragraphs complained of read. After which, desiring time to prepare his defence, it was granted till the 18th. STEELE on that day made a very eloquent defence, which however was ineffectual with the house of commons, though supported by ADDISON, WALPOLE, and other members of the highest talents. After a warm debate, the majority declared for his expulsion. Whether the pamphlets contained ideas dangerous to the public, or only inimical to the administration and its friends, is a point on which we will remain silent. It belongs only to historians to investigate STEELE's political conduct; and to us, his literary biographers, to consider its motives. They appear to have been truly patriotic; and the morality of his intention cannot be doubted.

Though abused by the Tory writers, STEELE persevered in his resolution of abstaining from personalities. He was in high favour with the Whigs, who considered him as a martyr for the cause of freedom; and he continued, to the Queen's death, writing against her ministers. At that time he began the *Spinster*, and the *Reader*, in which he gives an account of his plan for writing a history of the Duke of MARLBOROUGH, which was never executed.

STEELE's dread of LEWIS's machinations in favour of the Pretender, made him write a pamphlet, called *French Faith*. He wrote also one entitled *A Letter to a Member of Parliament*, against a bill, which passed both houses of parliament, and received the royal assent, prohibiting dissenters from teaching in schools and academies. STEELE showed that bill as originating in bigotry, and tending to produce pernicious effects; as a violation of natural justice; as contrary to the precepts of the gospel; and at last, as inconsistent with the spirit of the British constitution. The death of the Queen rendered it ineffectual.

On the arrival of King GEORGE in England, the monarch being informed of STEELE's zeal in favour of his illustrious house, appointed him surveyor to the royal stables of Hampton Court, and made him justice of the peace for the county of Middlesex. The theatre had from the beginning of his literary career been much obliged to our author. His dramatic writings had not only filled the house, but his periodical papers had pointed out the merit of the performers. He was then, justly, appointed chief manager of Drury-lane, whose license had expired at the Queen's death, and whose renewal he had obtained by his interest. From the moment that he became a joint proprietor in the theatre, his income amounted from it to a thousand a year. He stood candidate for representing Boroughbridge, in parliament; and he was successful. The King, in 1715, conferred on him the honour of knighthood. He was now in a very prosperous situation. He had a large income derived from sources which did not appear precarious. He had by his wife* an estate in Wales, and a considerable sum of money. His own literary talents enabled him to add to his fame and to his fortune. He was esteemed and caressed at court: he might expect to be promoted to higher and more lucrative employments. Such an expectation was certainly justifiable :—the event, however, was totally different. The extravagance and indiscretion of Sir RICHARD blasted the fair prospect.†

* *Steele* was twice married; first to a lady of the island of Barbadoes, sister to a rich planter, who, taken by the French on his coming to England, died in France. On his death, *Steele* succeeded to his plantation and effects. His first wife died without issue. He married afterward *Mary*, the daughter of *Jonathan Scurlock*, Esq. of Languanor, in Caermarthenshire; by her he had four children: a boy who died in his infancy, a second son named *Eugene*, after the renowned Prince, an amiable and ingenious youth, who fell early into a consumption and died: he had also two daughters, *Mary*, who died young, and *Elizabeth*, who was married, in 1731, to the Honourable *John Trevor*, one of the Welsh Judges.

† The following is one instance among many of *Steele's* inattention to pecuniary concerns. Without considering if his finances could bear the expenses, he had a splendid theatre constructed and finished, in a part of his house under his direction. *Steele* was delighted with the ap-

He was appointed, in 1717, one of the commissioners for inquiring into the estates forfeited by the late rebellion in Scotland. He set out for the northern part of the United Kingdom, was welcomed with cordiality and respect by the nobility and gentry attached to the court; and kindly by the clergy of that country, who have always distinguished themselves for their zeal in favour of the House of Hanover, and of civil and religious liberty. During his stay in Scotland, he indulged his taste for humour, by searching into the manners of low life. With this view, he prepared a splendid entertainment at Edinburgh, and ordered his servants to pick up all the beggars and poor people they could find in the streets as his guests. Whatever humour our author may have learned from these poor people, he never made use of it in any comedy.

Soon after his return to England, Sir Richard lost his second wife: neither the fortune which she had brought to him, nor his other emoluments, were sufficient to supply the demands of his extravagance. To recruit his exhausted finances, he became projector.* He invented a vessel for carrying fish alive, and without wasting, from any part of the kingdom to another, and procured a patent for his invention. The commercial projects of genius are rarely advantageous to the projector. Genius, frequently, like Moses, guides others to that object which it never reaches itself. Thus Steele's scheme, promising enough in theory, like

pearance of the place; and, to know if it was equally fitted for pleasing the ear as the eye, he desired the carpenter to go to one end of the room, and from thence to pronounce some sentences, whilst he himself, at the other, should judge of the effect. The carpenter, thus directed, in a distinct and audible voice, called out, "Sir Richard Steele, here has I, and these here men, been doing our work for three months, and never seen the colour of your money. When are you to pay us? I cannot pay my journeymen without money, and money I must have." Sir *Richard* replied, "that he was delighted with the oratory, but by no means approved of the subject."

* In 1718.

many other plausible speculations, was found not to be successful in practice, and proved pernicious to its inventor.*

In the year 1719, STEELE lost a considerable part of his income by his violent oppositions, not only in his legislative capacity, but also in political pamphlets, to the peerage bill;† to the rejection of it his publications contributed powerfully. His license for acting plays was revoked, and his patent rendered ineffectual. He set on foot a paper entitled *The Theatre*, where he endeavoured to convince the public that he and his brother-managers had been very unjustly treated. His application, however, for the restoration of the license was rendered hopeless by the disgrace of his friend Mr. Walpole. Groaning under the persecution o power, the natural gayety of our author was nearly overwhelmed, when to complete his misery, DENNIS attacked him in a pamphlet.‡ The face and figure of a writer were favourite subjects of this despicable assailant's criticisms. STEELE had an expressive manly countenance, and a good figure, but a dark complexion, and wore a black peruke. Those two circumstances made a part of DENNIS's attack: such scurrilous abuse deserved no serious answer, and from STEELE it received none.§

* The fish, though supplied by the contrivance with a continual stream of water, yet not brooking the confinement, battered themselves to pieces against the sides of the pool. Thus, when they were brought to market, they were so damaged that they fetched very little money.

† The scope of the bill was this, that instead of the sixteen Scotch peers, there were for the future to be twenty-five hereditary peers of Scotland; and the crown to be restrained from creating new peers, except on the extinction of an old family.

‡ It was entitled, *The Character and Conduct of Sir John Edgar, &c.*

§ *Steele* only entered into a humorous defence of his own beauty; and published the following ludicrous advertisement:—"An eminent Turkey merchant, and an ingenious foreigner, do hereby give notice, that if any person will discover the libeller or libellers who has or have falsely and maliciously insinuated in his or their

From the failure of his scheme, and other misfortunes, arising from his indiscretion and extravagance, STEELE was now in very distressed circumstances. He was burdened with debts, and had nothing to trust to but his pen. Thus he was often under the necessity of exerting his ingenuity in eluding or quieting his creditors.* It was remarked, however, that in all his difficulties he never lost the gayety of his temper; a circumstance which by no means forebodes amendment.

In April, 1721, STEELE's friend, Mr. WALPOLE, was appointed chancellor of the exchequer, in the room of Mr. AISLABIE, disgraced and prosecuted as a sharer in the fraud and profits of the South Sea ruinous project, against which our author had written two pamphlets, *The Crisis of Property;* and *The Nation, a Family.* Through WALPOLE's influence, he was

writings that Sir *Richard Steele* is ugly, so that he or they may be prosecuted by law, shall have all fitting encouragements; the said gentlemen having lost considerable matches by reason of the similitude of their persons to the said injured knight."

* *Steele* one day invited several persons of rank and quality to dine at his house. The company was surprised to see the number of footmen which surrounded the table. Being asked after dinner, when wine had dispelled ceremony, by a nobleman, how so expensive a train of domestics accorded with his fortune? Sir *Richard* replied, they were fellows of whom he would very willingly be rid; and confessed they were bailiffs who *had* introduced themselves with an execution, and whom, since he could not send them away, he had thought it convenient to embellish with liveries, that they might do him honour whilst they stayed.

Steele had one day dined with *Savage*, whom he long patronised, at a petty tavern near Hyde Park Gate, where he had dictated to him a pamphlet. In the evening he told *Savage* he had not a farthing in his pocket, that he must go and sell the pamphlet to discharge the reckoning. *Savage* went out to offer this new production to sale, and obtained two guineas for it. Sir *Richard* then returned home, having retired that day only to avoid his creditors, and composed the pamphlet to discharge the reckoning.

restored to his office and authority in the play-house; and soon after brought out his comedy of *The Conscious Lovers*, in the fable of which he is a close imitator of TERENCE, whilst he has displayed very great originality in the characters, sentiments, and incidents. This play abounds in pathos; its sentiments are those of the most refined morality; and as honest parson ADAMS very justly observes, there are many things in it that would do vastly well in a sermon. It was acted with very great success. STEELE's profits from the representation were considerable; and he was presented with five hundred pounds by his Majesty.

The profusion however of STEELE was too great for him to be long benefited by the success of *The Conscious Lovers*. Being reduced to great extremity, he sold, a year after, his share in the play-house. He soon after commenced a law suit with the managers, which was determined to his disadvantage. When Sir RICHARD threw his affairs into the hands of lawyers and trustees, the friend and gentleman had nothing more to do in the matter. It can be no wonder, then, that a flaw was found in the conduct of him who acted no longer for himself. The loss of this cause, together with his profusion, which still continued unabated, plunged our author in the utmost extremity of poverty. Old age was fast approaching on him now, without any means of supporting himself and his children, but the exertion of his literary talents. Gloomy is the prospect in declining years, of genius compelled to write for daily bread, when the powers begin to be impaired, when the impression of objects begins to grow faint, when the fancy becomes inanimate and feeble, and sensibility cold and languid; when even reason, if she preserves the force, loses the quickness of her operations. Aged genius then sees the time drawing near, when it will depend for sustenance on the precarious benefactions of individuals, or on the galling provisions of benevolent institutions.

This melancholy prospect was, without doubt, aggravated for STEELE, by the consciousness that he owed his distresses not to misfortunes, but to imprudence and folly. His distressed situation was soon increased by a paralytic disorder, which rendered him utterly incapable of further literary efforts. In these unhappy circumstances he bid adieu to London: he retired first to Hertfordshire, then to Wales, to live as cheaply as possible, and so be less burdensome to his friends. He took up his abode at Languanor, near Caermarthen, a seat he retained by the permission of the mortgagee. His pecuniary distresses having never subverted his principles of conduct, he had, before he left London, surrendered all his property to his creditors. To their benevolence he was in the end of his life principally indebted for his maintenance. He lingered out near two years in Wales, in the melancholy contemplation of what he might have been, and what he was; and Sept. 21st, 1729, paid the last debt to nature. He was privately interred, according to his own desire, in Caermarthen church.

Among his papers were found the manuscripts of two plays almost finished. The one was entitled *The Gentleman*, founded on *The Eunuch* of TERENCE, the other *The School of Action*.

STEELE was a man endued by nature with superior talents. His understanding was quick, acute, and vigorous: his imagination was fertile, and his memory retentive. He had received a good education; and although not very learned, he possessed a considerable share of knowledge. He was acquainted with the Latin classics, but not conversant in Grecian literature. As an author, he must be acknowledged to have made a considerable addition to the general mass of pleasing and useful literature. Quick and penetrating, his genius was well fitted for diving into the human mind. He had studied man as he found him in society, not in books; and, with an humour lively and versatile, he could paint him, as a comic writer, justly and agreeably as he saw him. His characters are natural, well drawn, and well supported. The sentiments and observations are suitable to the characters. In moral tendency, his comedies are unexceptionable. Virtue excites esteem and admiration; vice contempt and hatred. Rectitude is shown to be true wisdom. Intemperance and profligacy are never varnished with agreeable colours, but exhibited in their real deformity. Purity of expression accompanies purity of sentiment. Nothing is introduced which can inflame or corrupt youth. Wit and humour minister to wisdom and morality. Tenderness is the quality the most eminently conspicuous in some of STEELE's comedies, which please us by powerfully moving our best affections. As a political writer, STEELE, who had acquired a just knowledge of the principles of government, and diligently attended to the history and constitution of his country, shows general, liberal, and enlarged views. He was warm, but always candid. His political pamphlets afford considerable information concerning the state of affairs in his time.

As an essayist, STEELE is an able and agreeable describer of life and manners; a strenuous and persuasive supporter of religion and virtue.

In his moral character, STEELE was a man of upright principles, though he deviated from the paths of prudence. He was a man of great and extensive benevolence; the reliever of the distressed, the protector of the helpless, and the encourager of merit. In his transaction of business he was fair and equitable; in his opinions of mankind candid and liberal. He allowed those who were above him the due superiority. He treated his equals with ease and cordiality. He behaved to his inferiors with affability, without the arrogant insolence of familiarity, or the ostentatious parade of condescension. He was, by his benevolent disposition, and by his sprightly talents, a most agreeable companion, desirous of pleasing, possessing a great flow of spirits, and abounding in lively repartees.

With such talents and with such virtues, the question naturally arises, how came STEELE to be so distressed and miserable? By his violence, his indiscretion, his extravagance. The superiority ascribed by the Satirist* to prudence over fortune, was never more manifest than in the life of STEELE. Fortune held out her favours to him, but not courting the assistance of discretion, he was unable to keep them from vanishing for ever. In his lamentable fate is strikingly exhibited the important truth, that great talents, benevolent and mild disposition, and amiable manners, cannot secure happiness, without the co-operation of self-command and of prudence.

* *Juvenal*, conclusion of Satire x

dies, that "you may trace him;" which I look upon as a good funeral oration at the death of an honest husbandman, who hath left the impressions of his industry behind him in the place where he has lived.

Upon the foregoing considerations, I can scarce forbear representing the subject of this essay as a kind of moral virtue; which, as I have already shown, recommends itself likewise by the pleasure that attends it. It must be confessed that this is none of those turbulent pleasures which is apt to gratify a man in the heat of youth; but if it be not so tumultuous, it is more lasting. Nothing can be more delightful than to entertain ourselves with prospects of our own making, and to walk under those shades which our own industry has raised. Amusements of this nature compose the mind, and lay at rest all those passions which are uneasy to the soul of man, besides that they naturally engender good thoughts, and dispose us to laudable contemplations. Many of the old philosophers passed away the greatest part of their lives in their gardens. Epicurus himself could not think sensual pleasure attainable in any other scene. Every reader who is acquainted with Homer, Virgil, and Horace, the greatest geniuses of all antiquity, knows very well with how much rapture they have spoken on this subject: and that Virgil in particular has written a whole book on the art of planting.

This art seems to have been more especially adapted to the nature of man in his primeval state, when he had life enough to see his productions flourish in their utmost beauty, and gradually decay with him. One who lived before the flood might have seen a wood of the tallest oaks in the acorn.

* * * *

Persequitur scelus ille suum: labefactaque tandem
Ictibus innumeris adductaque funibus arbor
Corruit———

The impious axe he plies; loud strokes resound;
Till dragg'd with ropes, and fell'd with many a wound,
The loosen'd tree comes rushing to the ground.

It is not without the utmost indignation, that I observe several prodigal young heirs felling down the most glorious monuments of their ancestors' industry, and ruining in a day the product of ages.

Looking into my books, I find some account of the veneration the ancients had for trees. There is an old tradition, that Abraham planted a cypress, a pine, and a cedar, and that these three incorporated into one tree, which was cut down for the building of the temple of Solomon.

Isidorus who lived in the reign of Constantius, assures us, that he saw, even in his time, that famous oak in the plains of Mamre, under which Abraham is reported to have dwelt, and adds, that the people looked upon it with a great veneration, and preserved it as a sacred tree.

The heathens still went farther, and regarded it as the highest piece of sacrilege to injure certain trees which they took to be protected by some deity. The story of Erisicthon, the grove at Dodona, and that at Delphi, are all instances of this kind.

If we consider the machine in Virgil, so much blamed by several critics, in this light, we shall hardly think it too violent.

Æneas, when he built his fleet in order to sail for Italy, was obliged to cut down the grove on Mount Ida, which however he durst not do until he had obtained leave from Cybele, to whom it was dedicated. The goddess could not but think herself obliged to protect these ships, which were made of consecrated timber, after a very extraordinary manner, and therefore desired Jupiter, that they might not be obnoxious to the power of waves or winds. Jupiter would not grant this, but promised her, that as many as came safe to Italy should be transformed into goddesses of the sea; which the poet tells us was accordingly executed.

"And now at length the number'd hours were come,
Prefix'd by Fate's irrevocable doom,
When the great mother of the gods was free
To save her ships, and finish Jove's decree.

First, from the quarter of the morn there sprung
A light that sing'd the heavens, and shot along;
Then from a cloud, fring'd round with golden fires,
Were timbrels heard, and Berecynthian quires:
And last a voice, with more than mortal sounds,
Both hosts in arms oppos'd with equal horror wounds.
"O Trojan race, your needless aid forbear;
And know my ships are my peculiar care,
With greater ease the bold Rutulian may,
With hissing brands, attempt to burn the sea,
Than singe my sacred pines. But you, my charge,
Loos'd from your crooked anchors launch at large,
Exalted each a nymph: forsake the sand,
And swim the seas at Cybele's command.
No sooner had the goddess ceas'd to speak,
When lo, th' obedient ships their hawsers break;
And strange to tell, like dolphins in the main,
They plunge their prows, and dive, and spring again:
As many beauteous maids the billows sweep,
As rode before tall vessels on the deep."

DRYDEN'S VIRG.

The common opinion concerning the nymphs, whom the ancients called Hamadryads, is more to the honour of trees than any thing yet mentioned. It was thought the fate of these nymphs had so near a dependence on some trees, more especially oaks, that they lived and died together. For this reason they were extremely grateful to such persons who preserved those trees with which their being subsisted. Apollonius tells us a very remarkable story to this purpose.

"A certain man, called Rhæcus, observing an old oak ready to fall, and being moved with a sort of compassion towards the tree, ordered his servants to pour in fresh earth at the roots of it, and set it upright. The Hamadryad, or nymph, who must necessarily have perished with the tree, appeared to him the next day, and after having returned him her thanks, told him she was ready to grant whatever he should ask. As she was extremely beautiful, Rhæcus desired he might be entertained as her lover. The Hamadryad, not much displeased with the request, promised to give him a meeting, but commanded him for some days to abstain from the embraces of all other women, adding that she would send a bee to him, to let him know when he was to be happy. Rhæcus was, it seems, too much addicted to gaming, and happened to be in a run of ill-luck when the faithful bee came buzzing about him; so that instead of minding his kind invitation, he had like to have killed him for his pains. The Hamadryad was so provoked at her own disappointment, and the ill-usage of her messenger, that she deprived Rhæcus of the use of his limbs. However, says the story, he was not so much a cripple, but he made a shift to cut down the tree, and consequently to fell his mistress.

THE PASSIONATE, THE PEEVISH, AND THE SNARLISH TEMPER, CENSURED.

——*Animum rege, qui nisi paret*
Imperat——

HOR.

————————Curb thy soul,
And check thy rage, which must be rul'd or rule.

CREECH.

It is a very common expression that such-a-one is very good natured, but very passionate. The expression, indeed, is very good-natured to allow passionate people so much quarter: But I think a passionate man deserves the least indulgence imaginable. It is said, it is soon over; that is, all the mischief he does is quickly despatched, which, I think, is no great recommendation to favour. I have known one of these good-natured passionate men say in a mixed company, even to his own wife or child, such things as the most inveterate enemy of his family would not have spoke, even in imagination. It is certain that quick sensibility is inseparable from a ready understanding; but why should not that good understanding call to itself all its force on such occasions, to master that sudden inclination to anger? To contain the spirit of anger, is the worthiest discipline we can put ourselves to

When a man has made any progress this way, a frivolous fellow in a passion is to him as contemptible as a froward child. It ought to be the study of every man, for his own quiet and peace. When he stands combustible, and ready to flame upon every thing that touches him, life is as uneasy to himself as it is to all about him. Syncropius leads, of all men living, the most ridiculous life; he is ever offending, and begging pardon. If his man enters the room without what he sent for, "That blockhead," begins he—"Gentlemen, I ask your pardon, but servants now-a-days"—The wrong plates are laid, they are thrown into the middle of the room; his wife stands by in pain for him, which he sees in her face, and answers as if he had heard all she was thinking; "Why, what the devil! Why don't you take care to give orders in these things?" His friends sit down to a tasteless plenty of every thing, every minute expecting new insults from his impertinent passions. In a word, to eat with, or visit Syncropius, is no other than going to see him exercise his family, exercise their patience, and his own anger.

It is monstrous that the shame and confusion in which this good-natured angry man must needs behold his friends while he thus lays about him, does not give him so much reflection as to create an amendment. This is the most scandalous disuse of reason imaginable; all the harmless part of him is no more than that of a bull-dog, they are tame no longer than they are not offended. One of these good-natured angry men shall, in an instant, assemble together so many allusions to secret circumstances, as are enough to dissolve the peace of all the families and friends he is acquainted with, in a quarter of an hour, and yet the next moment be the best-natured man in the whole world. If you would see passion in its purity, without mixture of reason, behold it represented in a mad hero, drawn by a mad poet. Nat. Lee makes his Alexander say thus:

"Away, begone, and give a whirlwind room,
Or I will blow you up like dust! Avaunt;

Madness but meanly represents my toil,
Eternal discord!
Fury! revenge! disdain and indignation
Tear my swollen breast, make way for fire and tempest.
My brain is burst, debate and reason quench'd;
The storm is up, and my hot bleeding heart
Splits with the rack, while passions, like the wind,
Rise up to heav'n, and put out all the stars."

Every passionate fellow in town talks half the day with as little consistency, and threatens things as much out of his power.

The next disagreeable person to the outrageous gentleman, is one of a much lower order of anger, and he is what we commonly call a peevish fellow. A peevish fellow is one who has some reason in himself for being out of humour, or has a natural incapacity for delight, and therefore disturbs all who are happier than himself with pishes and pshaws, or other well-bred interjections, at every thing that is said or done in his presence. There should be physic mixed in the food of all which these fellows eat in good company. This degree of anger passes, forsooth, for a delicacy of judgment, that won't admit of being easily pleased: but none above the character of wearing a peevish man's livery, ought to bear with his ill manners. All things among men of sense and condition should pass the censure, and have the protection of the eye of reason.

No man ought to be tolerated in an habitual humour, whim, or particularity of behaviour, by any who do not wait upon him for bread. Next to the peevish fellow is the snarler. This gentleman deals mightily in what we call the irony, and as these sort of people exert themselves most against those below them, you see their humour best in their talk to their servants. That is so like you, you are a fine fellow, thou art the quickest head-piece, and the like. One would think the hectoring, the storming, the sullen, and all the different species and subordinations of the angry should be cured, by knowing they live only as pardoned men, and how pitiful is the condition of being only suffered?

But I am interrupted by the pleasantest scene of anger and the disappointment of it that I have ever known, which happened while I was yet writing, and I overheard as I sat in a back room at a French booksellers'. There came into the shop a very learned man with an erect solemn air, and though a person of great parts otherwise, slow in understanding any thing which makes against himself. The composure of the faulty man, and the whimsical perplexity of him that was justly angry, is perfectly new. After turning over many volumes, said the seller to the buyer, "Sir, you know I have long asked you to send me back the first volume of French Sermons I formerly lent you."—"Sir," said the chapman, "I have often looked for it, but cannot find it; it is certainly lost, and I know not to whom I lent it, it is so many years ago."—"Then, Sir, here is the other volume, I'll send you home that, and please to pay for both."—"My friend," replied he, "canst thou be so senseless as not to know that one volume is as imperfect in my library as your shop?"—"Yes, Sir, but it is you have lost the first volume, and, to be short, I will be paid."—"Sir," answered the chapman, "you are a young man, your book is lost, and learn by this little loss to bear much greater adversities, which you must expect to meet with."—"Yes, Sir, I'll bear when I must, but I have not lost now, for I say you have it and shall pay me."—"Friend, you grow warm, I tell you the book is lost, and I foresee in the course even of a prosperous life, that you will meet afflictions to make you mad, if you cannot bear this trifle."—"Sir, there is in this case no need of bearing, for you have the book."—"I say, Sir, I have not the book. But your passion will not let you hear enough to be informed that I have it not. Learn resignation of yourself to the distresses of this life: nay, do not fret and fume, it is my duty to tell you that you are of an impatient spirit, and an impatient spirit is never without wo."—"Was ever any thing like this?"—"Yes, Sir, there have been many things like this. The loss is but a trifle, but your temper is wanton, and incapable of the least pain; therefore let me advise you, be patient, the book is lost, but do not you for that reason lose yourself.' T.

PRONUNCIATION AND ACTION.

Format enim Natura prius non intus ad omnem
Fortunarum habitum; juvat, aut impellit ad iram.
Aut ad humum mœrore gravi deducit et angit;
Post effert animi motus interprete lingua.
HOR. Ars. Poet. v. 108.

For nature forms and softens us within,
And writes our fortune's changes in our face:
Pleasure enchants, impetuous rage transports,
And grief dejects, and wrings the tortur'd soul;
And these are all interpreted by speech.
ROSCOMMON.

CICERO concludes his celebrated books *de Oratore* with some precepts for pronunciation and action, without which parts he affirms that the best orator in the world can never succeed; and an indifferent one, who is master of this, shall gain much greater applause. What could make a stronger impression, says he, than those exclamations of Gracchus, "Whither shall I turn? Wretch that I am! to what place betake myself? Shall I go to the Capitol? Alas! it is overflowed with my brother's blood. Or shall I retire to my house? Yet there I behold my mother plunged in misery, weeping and despairing!" These breaks and turns of passion, it seems, were so enforced by the eyes, voice, and gesture of the speaker that his very enemies could not refrain from tears. insist, says Tully, upon this, the rather because our orators, who are as it were actors of the truth itself, have quitted this manner of speaking; and the players, who are but the imitators of truth, have taken it up.

I shall therefore pursue the hint he has here given me, and for the service of the British stage I shall copy some of the rules which this great Roman master has laid down; yet, without confining myself wholly to his thoughts or words; and to adapt this essay the more to the purpose for which I intend it, instead of the examples he has inserted in this discourse, out of the ancient tragedies, I shall make use of parallel passages out of the most celebrated of our own.

The design of art is to assist action as much as possible in the representation of nature; for the appearance of reality is that which moves us in all representations, and these have always the greater force, the nearer they approach to nature, and the less they show of imitation.

Nature herself has assigned, to every emotion of the soul, its peculiar cast of the countenance, tone of voice, and manner of gesture; and the whole person, all the features of the face and tones of the voice, answer, like strings upon musical instruments, to the impressions made on them by the mind. Thus the sounds of the voice, according to the various touches which raise them, form themselves into an acute or grave, quick or slow, loud or soft tone. These too may be subdivided into various kinds of tones, as the gentle, the rough, the contracted, the diffuse, the continued, the intermitted, the broken, abrupt, winding, softened, or elevated. Every one of these may be employed with art and judgment: and all supply the actor, as colours do the painter, with an expressive variety.

Anger exerts its peculiar voice in an acute, raised and hurrying sound. The passionate character of King Lear, as it is admirably drawn by Shakspeare, abounds with the strongest instances of this kind.

"——— Death! Confusion!
Fiery!——what quality?——why Gloster! Gloster!
I'd speak with the Duke of Cornwall and his wife,
Are they inform'd of this? my breath and blood!
Fiery! the fiery duke!"——&c.

Sorrow and complaint demand a voice quite different, flexible, slow, interrupted, and modulated in a mournful tone; as in that pathetical soliloquy of Cardinal Wolsey on his fall.

"Farewell!——a long farewell to all my greatness!
This is the state of man!——to-day he puts forth
The tender leaves of hope; to-morrow blossoms,
And bears his blushing honours thick upon him.
The third day comes a frost, a killing frost,
And when he thinks, good easy man, full surely
His greatness is a ripening, nips his root,
And then he falls as I do."

We have likewise a fine example of this in the whole part of Andromache in the Distrest Mother, particularly in these lines:

"I'll go, and in the anguish of my heart
Weep o'er my child——If he must die, my life
Is wrapt in his, I shall not long survive.
'Tis for his sake that I have suffer'd life,
Groan'd in captivity, and out-liv'd Hector.
Yes, my Astyanax, we'll go together!
Together to the realms of night we'll go:
There to thy ravish'd eyes thy sire I'll show,
And point him out among the shades below."

Fear expresses itself in a low, hesitating, and abject sound. If the reader considers the following speech of Lady Macbeth, while her husband is about the murder of Duncan and his grooms, he will imagine her even affrighted with the sound of her own voice while she is speaking it.

"Alas! I am afraid they have awak'd,
And 'tis not done; th' attempt, and not the deed,
Confounds us—Hark!—I laid the daggers ready,
He could not miss them. Had he not resembled
My father as he slept, I had done it."

Courage assumes a louder tone, as in that speech of Don Sebastian.

"Here satiate all your fury;
Let fortune empty her whole quiver on me,
I have a soul that like an ample shield
Can take in all, and verge enough for more."

Pleasure dissolves into a luxurious, mild, tender and joyous modulation; as in the following lines of Caius Marius.

"Lavinia! O there's music in the name,
That soft'ning me to infant tenderness,
Makes my heart spring, like the first leaps of life.

And perplexity is different from all these; grave, but not bemoaning, with an earnest uniform sound of voice; as in that celebrated speech of Hamlet.

"To be, or not to be?——that is the question:
Whether 'tis nobler in the mind to suffer
The stings and arrows of outrageous Fortune
Or to take arms against a sea of troubles,
And by opposing end them. To die, to sleep;
No more; and by a sleep to say we end
The heart-ach, and the thousand natural shocks
That flesh is heir to; 'tis a consummation
Devoutly to be wish'd. To die, to sleep——
To sleep! perchance to dream! Ay, there's the rub,
For in that sleep of death what dreams may come,
When we have shuffled off this mortal coil,
Must give us pause——There's the respect
That makes calamity of so long life:
For who would bear the whips and scorns of time,
Th' oppressor's wrongs, the proud man's contumely,
The pangs of despised love, the law's delay,
The insolence of office, and the spurns
That patient merit of th' unworthy takes,
When he himself might his quietus make
With a bare bodkin? Who would fardles bear,
To groan and sweat under a weary life?
But that the dread of something after death,
The undiscover'd country, from whose bourn
No traveller returns, puzzles the will,
And makes us rather choose those ills we have,
Than fly to others that we know not of."

As all these varieties of voice are to be directed by the sense, so the action is to be directed by the voice, and with a beautiful propriety, as it were to enforce it. The arm, which, by a strong figure, Tully calls the Orator's weapon, is to be sometimes raised and extended; and the hand, by its motion, sometimes, to lead, and sometimes to follow the words as they are uttered. The stamping of the foot too has its proper expression in contention, anger, or absolute command. But the face is the epitome of the whole man, and the eyes are, as it were, the epitome of the face; for which reason, he says, the best judges among the Romans were not extremely pleased, even with Roscius himself, in his mask. No part of the body, besides the face, is capable of so many changes as there are different emotions in the mind, and of expressing them all by those changes. Nor is this to be done without the freedom of the eyes; therefore Theophrastus called one, who barely rehearsed his speech with his eyes fixed, an absent actor.

As the countenance admits of so great variety, it requires also great judgment to govern it. Not that the form of the face is to be shifted on every occasion, lest it turn to farce and buffoonery; but it is certain that the eyes have a wonderful power of marking the emotions of the mind, sometimes by a steadfast look, sometimes by a careless one, now by a sudden regard, then by a joyful sparkling, as the sense of of the words is diversified: for action is, as it were, the speech of the features and limbs, and must therefore conform itself always to the sentiments of the soul. And it may be observed, that in all which relates to the gesture, there is a wonderful force implanted by nature, since the vulgar, the unskilful, and even the most barbarous, are chiefly affected by this. None are moved by the sound of words, but those who understand the language; and the sense of many things is lost upon men of dull apprehension; but action is a kind of universal tongue; all men are subject to the same passions, and consequently know the same marks of them in others, by which they themselves express them.

Perhaps some of my readers may be of opinion, that the hints I have here made use of, out of Cicero, are somewhat too refined for the players on our theatre: in answer to which, I venture to lay it down as a maxim, that without good sense no one can be a good player, and that he is very unfit to personate the dignity of a Roman hero, who cannot enter into the rules for pronunciation and gesture delivered by a Roman orator.

There is another thing which the author does not think too minute to insist on, though it is purely mechanical; and that is the right pitching of the voice. On this occasion, he tells the story of Gracchus, who employed a servant with a little ivory pipe, to stand behind him, and give him the right pitch, as often as he wandered too far from the proper modulation. Every voice, says Tully, has its particular medium and compass, and the sweetness of speech consists in leading it through all the variety of tones naturally, and without touching any extreme. Therefore, says he, leave the pipe at home, but carry the sense of this custom with you.

HOW TO ENJOY LIFE.

Non est vivere sed valere vita. **MAR.**

To breathe is not to live; but to be well.

It is an unreasonable thing some men expect of their acquaintance. They are ever complaining that they are out of order, or displeased, or they know not how, and are so far from letting that be a reason for retiring to their own homes, that they make it their argument for coming into company. What has any body to do with accounts of a man's being indisposed but his physician? If a man laments in company, where the rest are in humour enough to enjoy themselves, he should not take it ill if a servant is ordered to present him with a porringer of caudle or posset drink, by way of admonition that he go home to bed. That part of life which we ordinarily understand by the word conversation, is an indulgence to the sociable part of our make; and should incline us to bring our proportion of good-will or good-humour among the friends we meet with, and not to trouble them with relations which must of necessity oblige them to a real or feigned affliction. Cares, distresses, diseases, uneasiness, and dislikes of our own, are by no means to be obtruded upon our friends. If we would consider how little of this vicissitude of motion and rest, which we call life, is spent with satisfaction, we should be more tender of our friends, than to bring them little sorrows which do not belong to them. There is no real life but cheerful life; therefore valetudinarians should be sworn before they enter into company, not to say a word of themselves until the meeting breaks up. It is not here pretended, that we should be always sitting with chaplets of flowers round our heads, or be crowned with roses in order to make our entertainment agreeable to us: but if, as it is usually observed, they who resolve to be merry, seldom are so; it will be much more unlikely for us to be well pleased, if they are admitted who are always complaining they are sad. Whatever we do we should keep up the cheerfulness of our spirits, and never let them sink below an inclination at least to be well pleased: the way to this, is to keep our bodies in exercise, our minds at ease. That insipid state wherein neither are in vigour, is not to be accounted any part of our portion of being. When we are in the satisfaction of some innocent pleasure, or pursuit of some laudable design, we are in the possession of life, of human life. Fortune will give us disappointments enough, and nature is attended with infirmities enough, without our adding to the unhappy side of our account by our spleen or ill-humour. Poor Cottilus, among so many real evils, a chronical distemper and a narrow fortune, is never heard to complain: that equal spirit of his, which any man may have, that, like him, will conquer pride, vanity, and affectation, and follow nature, is not to be broken, because it has no points to contend for. To be anxious for nothing, but what nature demands as necessary, if it is not the way to an estate, is the way to what men aim at by getting an estate. This temper will preserve health in the body, as well as tranquillity in the mind. Cottilus sees the world in a hurry with the same scorn that a sober person sees a man drunk. Had he been contented with what he ought to have been, how could, says he, such-a-one have met with such a disappointment? If another had valued his mistress for what he ought to have loved her, he had not been in her power: if her virtue had a part of his passion, her levity had been his cure; she could not then have been false and amiable at the same time.

Since we cannot promise ourselves constant health, let us endeavour at such a temper as may be our best support in the decay of it. Uranius has arrived at that composure of soul, and wrought himself up to such a neglect of every thing with which the generality of mankind is enchanted, that nothing but acute pains can give him disturbance, and, against those too he will tell his intimate friends he has a secret which gives him present ease. Uranius is so thoroughly persuaded of another life, and endeavours so sincerely to secure an interest in it, that he looks upon pain but as a quickening of his pace to an home, were he shall be better provided for than in his present apartment. Instead of the melancholy views which others are apt to give themselves, he will tell you that he has forgot he is mortal, nor will he think of himself as such. He thinks at the time of his birth he entered into an eternal being; and the short article of death he will not allow an interruption of life; since that moment is not of half the duration as is his ordinary sleep. Thus is his being one uniform and consistent series of cheerful diversions, and moderate cares, without fear or hope of futurity. Health to him is more than pleasure to another man, and sickness less affecting to him than indisposition is to others.

I must confess, if one does not regard life after this manner, none but idiots can pass it away with any tolerable patience. Take a fine lady who is of a delicate frame, and you may observe from the hour she rises a certain weariness of all that passes about her. I know more than one who is much too nice to be quite alive. They are sick of such strange frightful people that they meet; one is so awkward, and another so disagreeable, that it looks like a penance to breathe the same air with them. You see this is so very true, that a great part of ceremony and good-breeding among the ladies turns upon their uneasiness; and I will undertake, if the how d'ye servants of our women were to make a weekly bill of sickness, as the parish clerks do of mortality, you would not find in an account of seven days, one in thirty that was not downright sick or indisposed, or but a very little better than she was, and so forth.

It is certain that to enjoy life and health as a constant feast, we should not think pleasure necessary; but, if possible, to arrive at an equality of mind. It is as mean to be overjoyed upon occasions of good fortune, as to be dejected in circumstances of distress. Laughter in one condition is as unmanly as weeping in the other. We should not form our minds to expect transport on every occasion, but know how to make it enjoyment to be out of pain. Ambition, envy, vagrant desire, or impertinent mirth, will take up our minds, without we can possess ourselves in that sobriety of heart which is above all pleasures, and can be felt much better than described, but the ready way, I believe, to the right enjoyment of life, is, by a prospect towards another to have but a very mean opinion of it. A great author of our time has set this in an excellent light, when with a philosophic pity of human life, he spoke of it in his Theory of the Earth in the following manner:

"For what is this life but a circulation of little mean actions? We lie down and rise again, dress and undress, feed and wax hungry, work or play, and are weary, and then we lie down again, and the circle returns. We spend the day in trifles, and when the night comes, we throw ourselves into the bed of folly amongst dreams and broken thoughts and wild imaginations. Our reason lies asleep by us, and we are for the time as errant brutes as those that sleep in the stalls or in the field. Are not the capacities of man higher than these? And ought not his ambition and expectations to be greater? Let us be adventurers for another world: it is at least a fair and noble chance; and there is nothing in this worth our thoughts or our passions. If we should be disappointed, we are still no worse than the rest of our fellow-mortals; and if we succeed in our expectations, we are eternally happy." T.

NOBLE PRIDE.

——Postquam se lumine puro
Implevit stellasque vagas miratur et astra
Fixa polis, vidit quanta sub nocte jaceret
Nostra dies, risitque sui ludibria——

LUCAN.

Now to the blest abode, with wonder fill'd,
The sun and moving planets he beheld;
Then looking down on the sun's feeble ray,
Survey'd our dusky, faint, imperfect day,
And under what a cloud of night we lay

ROWE.

The common topics against the pride of man, which are laboured by florid and declamatory writers, are taken from the baseness of his original, the imperfections of his nature, or the short duration of those goods in which he makes his boast. Though it be true that we can have nothing in us that ought to raise our vanity, yet a consciousness of our own merit may be sometimes laudable. The folly therefore lies here; we are apt to pride ourselves in worthless or perhaps shameful things; and on the other hand, count that disgraceful which is our truest glory.

Hence it is, that the lovers of praise take wrong measures to attain it. Would a vain man consult his own heart, he would find that if others knew his weaknesses as well as he himself doth, he could not have the impudence to expect the public esteem. Pride therefore flows from want of reflection, and ignorance of ourselves. Knowledge and humility come upon us together.

The proper way to make an estimate of ourselves, is to consider seriously what it is we value or despise in others. A man who boasts of the goods of fortune, a gay dress, or a new title, is generally the mark of ridicule. We ought therefore not to admire in ourselves, what we are so ready to laugh at in other men.

Much less can we with reason pride ourselves in those things, which at some time of our life we shall certainly despise. And yet, if we will give ourselves the trouble of looking backward and forward on the several changes which we have already undergone and hereafter must try, we shall find that the greater degrees of knowledge and wisdom, serve only to show us our own imperfections.

As we rise from childhood to youth, we look with contempt on the toys and trifles which our hearts have hitherto been set upon. When we advance to manhood, we are held wise in proportion to our shame and regret for the rashness and extravagance of youth. Old age fills us with mortifying reflections upon a life misspent in the pursuit of anxious wealth or uncertain honour. Agreeable to this gradation of thought in this life, it may be reasonably supposed, that in a future state, the wisdom, the experience, and the maxims of old age, will be looked upon by a separate spirit in much the same light as an ancient man now sees the little follies and toyings of infants. The pomps, the honours, the policies, and arts of mortal men, will be thought as trifling as hobby-horses, mock-battles, or any other sports that now employ all the cunning, and strength, and ambition of rational beings from four years old to nine or ten.

If the notion of a gradual rise in beings from the meanest to the most high, be not a vain imagination, it is not improbable that an angel looks down upon a man, as a man doth upon a creature which approaches nearest to the rational nature. By the same rule, if I may indulge my fancy in this particular, a superior brute looks with a kind of pride on one of an inferior species. If they could reflect, we might imagine from the gestures of some of them that they think themselves the sovereigns of the world, and that all things were made for them. Such a thought would not be more absurd in brute creatures, than one which men are apt to entertain, namely, that all the stars in the firmament were created only to please their eyes and amuse their imaginations. Mr. Dryden, in his fable of the Cock and the Fox, makes a speech for his hero the cock, which is a pretty instance for this purpose.

Then turning, said to Partlet, see, my dear,
How lavish nature hath adorn'd the year;
How the pale primrose and the violet spring,
And birds essay their throats, disus'd to sing:
All these are ours, and I with pleasure see
Man strutting on two legs, and aping me."

What I would observe from the whole is this, that we ought to value ourselves upon those things only which superior beings think valuable, since that is the only way for us not to sink in our esteem hereafter.

HANDSOME WOMEN.

——Noris quam elegans formarum spectator sum.
TER.

You shall see how nice a judge of beauty I am.

THERE is something irresistible in a beauteous form; the most severe will not pretend, that they do not feel an immediate prepossession in favour of the handsome. No one denies them the privilege of being first heard, and being regarded before others in matters of ordinary consideration. At the same time the handsome should consider that it is a possession, as it were, foreign to them. No one can give it himself, or preserve it when they have it. Yet so it is, that people can bear any quality in the world better than beauty. It is the consolation of all who are naturally too much affected with the force of it, that a little attention, if a man can attend with judgment, will cure them. Handsome people are usually so fantastically pleased with themselves, that if they do not kill at first sight, as the phrase is, a second interview disarms them of all their power. I shall make this essay rather a warning-piece to give notice where the danger is, than to propose instructions how to avoid it when you have fallen in the way of it. Handsome women shall take up the present discourse.

Amaryllis, who has been in town but one winter, is extremely improved with the arts of good breeding, without leaving nature. She has not lost the native simplicity of her aspect, to substitute that patience of being stared at, which is the usual triumph and distinction of a town-lady. In public assemblies you meet her careless eye diverting itself with the objects around her, insensible that she herself is one of the brightest in the place.

Dulcissa is quite of another make, she is almost a beauty by nature, but more than one by art. If it were possible for her to let her fan or any limb about her rest, she would do some part of the execution she meditates; but though she designs herself a prey, she will not stay to be taken. No painter can give you words for the different aspects of Dulcissa in half a moment, wherever she appears: so little does she accomplish what she takes so much pains for, to be gay and careless.

Merah is attended with all the charms of woman and accomplishments of man. It is not to be doubted but she has a great deal of wit, if she were not such a beauty; and she would have more beauty had she not so much wit. Affectation prevents her excellencies from walking together. If she has a mind to speak such a thing, it must be done with such an air of her body; and if she has an inclination to look very careless, there is such a smart thing to be said at the same time, that the design of being admired destroys itself. Thus the unhappy Merah, though a wit and beauty, is allowed to be neither, because she will always be both.

Albacinda has the skill as well as power of pleasing. Her form is majestic, but her aspect humble. All good men should beware of the destroyer. She will speak to you like your sister until she has you sure; but is the most vexatious of tyrants when you are so. Her familiarity of behaviour, her indifferent questions and general conversation, make the silly part of her votaries full of hopes, while the wise fly from the power. She well knows she is too beautiful and to witty to be indifferent to any who converse with her, and therefore knows she does not lessen herself by familiarity, but gains occasions of admiration, by a seeming ignorance of her perfections.

Eudosia adds to the height of her stature a nobility of spirit, which still distinguishes her above the rest of her sex. Beauty in others is lovely, in others agreeable, in others attractive; but in Eudosia it is commanding; Love towards Eudosia is a sentiment like the love of glory. The lovers of other women are softened into fondness, the admirers of Eudosia exalted into ambition.

Eucratia presents herself to the imagination with a more kindly pleasure, and as she is woman, her praise is wholly feminine. If we were to form an image of dignity in a man, we should give him wisdom and valour, as being essential to the character of manhood. In like manner, if you describe a right woman in a laudable sense, she should have gentle softness, tender fear, and all those parts of life which distinguish her from the other sex: with some subordination to it, but such an inferiority that makes her still more lovely. Eucratia is that creature, she is all over woman, kindness is all her art, and beauty all her arms. Her look, her voice, her gesture, and whole behaviour is truly feminine. A goodness mixed with fear, gives a tincture to all her behaviour. It would be savage to offend her, and cruelty to use art to gain her. Others are beautiful, but Eucratia, thou art beauty!

Omnamante is made for deceit, she has an aspect as innocent as the famed Lucrece, but a mind as wild as the more famed Cleopatra. Her face speaks a vestal, but her heart a Messalina. Who that beheld Omnamante's negligent unobserving air, would believe that she hid under that regardless manner the witty prostitute, the rapacious wench, the prodigal courtezan?

She can, when she pleases, adorn those eyes with tears like an infant that is chid: she can cast down that pretty face in confusion, while you rage with jealousy, and storm at her perfidiousness; she can wipe her eyes, tremble and look frighted, until you think yourself a brute for your rage, own yourself an offender, beg pardon, and make her new presents.

But I go too far in reporting only the dangers in beholding the beauteous, wihch I design for the instruction of the fair as well as their beholders; and shall end this rhapsody with mentioning what I thought was well enough said of an ancient sage to a beautiful youth, whom he saw admiring his own figure in brass. "What," said the philosopher, "could that image of yours say for itself if it could speak,"—"It might say," answered the youth, "that it is very beautiful."—"And are not you ashamed," replied the cynic, "to value yourself upon that only of which a piece of brass is capable?"

T

INSTINCT OF IMMORTALITY.

Τȣ μεν γαρ γενος εσεμν. ARAT.
For we are his offspring. ACTS.

THAT sublime manner of salutation with which the Jews approached their kings,

"O king, live for ever!"

may be addressed to the lowest and most despised mortal among us, under all the infirmities and distresses with which we see him surrounded. And whoever believes the immortality of the soul, will not need a better argument for the dignity of his nature, nor a stronger incitement to action suitable to it.

I cannot without pleasure call to mind the thoughts of Cicero to this purpose, in the close of his book concerning old age. Every one who is acquainted with his writings, will remember that the elder Cato is introduced in that discourse as the speaker, and Scipio and Lelius as his auditors. This venerable person is represented looking forward as it were from the verge of extreme old age into a future state, and rising into contemplation on the unperishable part of his nature, and its existence after death. I shall collect part of his discourse. And as you have formerly offered some arguments for the soul's immortality, agreeable both to reason and the Christian doctrine, I believe your readers will not be displeased to see how the same great truth shines in the pomp of the Roman eloquence.

"This," says Cato, "is my firm persuasion, that since the human soul exerts itself with so great activity, since it has such a remembrance of the past, such a concern for the future, since it is enriched with so many arts, sciences, and discoveries, it is impossible but the Being which contains all these must be immortal.

"The elder Cyrus, just before his death, is represented by Xenophon speaking after this manner: 'Think not, my dearest children, that when I depart from you I shall be no more; but remember, that my soul, even while I lived among you, was invisible to you; yet by my actions you were sensible it existed in this body. Believe it therefore existing still, though it be still unseen. How quickly would the honours of illustrious men perish after death, if their souls performed nothing to preserve their fame? For my own part, I never could think that the soul, while in a mortal body, lives, but when departed out of it, dies; or that its consciousness is lost when it is discharged out of an unconscious habitation. But when it is freed from all corporeal alliance, then it truly exists. Further, since the human frame is broken by death, tell us what becomes of its parts? It is visible whither the materials of other beings are translated, namely, to the source from whence they had their birth. The soul alone, neither present or departed, is the object of our eyes.'

"Thus Cyrus. But to proceed. No one shall persuade me, Scipio, that your worthy father, or your grandfathers Paulus and Africanus, or Africanus his father or uncle, or many other excellent men whom I need not name, performed so many actions to be remembered by posterity, without being sensible that futurity was their right. And, if I may be allowed an old man's privilege, to speak of myself, do you think I would have endured the fatigue of so many wearisome days and nights, both at home and abroad if I imagined that the same boundary which is set to my life must terminate my glory? Were it not more desirable to have worn out my days in ease and tranquillity, free from labour, and without emulation? But I know not how, my soul has always raised itself, and looked forward on futurity, in this view and expectation, that when it shall depart out of life, it shall then live for ever; and if this were not true, that the mind is immortal, the souls of the most worthy would not, above all others, have the strongest impulse to glory.

"What besides this is the cause that the wisest men die with the greatest equanimity, the ignorant with the greatest concern? Does it not seem that those minds which have the most extensive views, foresee they are removing to a happier condition, which those of a narrower sight do not perceive? I, for my part, am transported with the hope of seeing your ancestors, whom I have honoured and loved, and am earnestly desirous of meeting not only those excellent persons whom I have known, but those too of whom I have heard and read, and of whom I myself have written; nor would I be detained from so pleasing a journey. O happy day, when I shall escape from this crowd, this heap of pollution, and be admitted to that divine assembly of exalted spirits! When I shall go not only to those great persons I have named, but to my Cato, my son, than whom a better man was never born, and whose funeral rites I myself performed, whereas he ought rather to have attended mine. Yet has not his soul deserted me, but seeming to cast back a look on me, is gone before to those habitations to which it was sensible I should soon follow him. And though I might appear to have borne my loss with courage, I was not unaffected with it, but I comforted myself in the assurance that it would not be long before we should meet again, and be divorced no more."

HEEDLESS PROMISERS CENSURED

Fadius hoc aliquid quandoque audebis.

JUV.

In time to greater baseness you'll proceed.

The first steps toward ill are very carefully to be avoided, for men insensibly go on when they are once entered, and do not keep up a lively abhorrence of the least unworthiness. There is a certain frivolous falsehood that people indulge themselves in, which ought to be had in greater detestation than it commonly meets with: what I mean is a neglect of promises made on small and indifferent occasions, such as parties of pleasure, entertainments, and sometimes meetings out of curiosity in men of like faculties to be in each other's company. There are many causes to which one may assign this light infidelity. Jack Sippet never keeps the hour he has appointed to come to a friend's to dinner, but he is an insignificant fellow who does it out of vanity. He could never, he knows, make any figure in company, but by giving a little disturbance at his entry, and therefore takes care to drop in when he thinks you are just seated. He takes his place after having discomposed every body, and desires there may be no ceremony: then does he begin to call himself the saddest fellow, in disappointing so many places as he was invited to elsewhere. It is the fop's vanity to name houses of better cheer, and to acquaint you that he chose yours out of ten dinners, which he was obliged to be at that day The last time I had the fortune to eat with him, he was imagining how very fat he should have been had he eaten all he had ever been invited to. But it is impertinent to dwell upon the manners of such a wretch as obliges all whom he disappoints, though his circumstances constrain them to be civil to him. But there are those that every one would be glad to see, who fall into the same detestable habit. It is a merciless thing, that any one can be at ease, and suppose a set of people who have a kindness for him, at that moment waiting out of respect to him, and refusing to taste their food or conversation with the utmost impatience One of these promisers sometimes shall make his excuses for not coming at all, so late that half the company have only to lament, that they have neglected matters of moment to meet him whom they find a trifler. They immediately repent of the value they had for him; and such treatment repeated, makes company never depend upon his promise any more; so that he often comes at the middle of a meal, where he is secretly slighted by the persons with whom he eats, and cursed by the servants, whose dinner is delayed by his prolonging their master's entertainment. It is wonderful, that men guilty this way could never have observed, that the whiling time, the gathering together, and waiting a little before dinner, is the most awkwardly passed away of any part in the four-and-twenty hours. If they did think at all, they would reflect upon their guilt, in lengthening such a suspension of agreeable life. The constant offending this way has, in a degree, an effect upon the honesty of his mind who is guilty of it, as common swearing is a kind of habitual perjury: it makes the soul unattentive to what an oath is, even while it utters it at the lips. Phocion beholding a wordy orator while he was making a magnificent speech to the people full of vain promises, "Methinks," said he, "I am now fixing my eyes upon a cypress tree; it has a.: the pomp and beauty imaginable in its branches, leaves, and height, but, alas! it bears no fruit."

Though the expectation which is raised by impertinent promisers is thus barren, their confidence, even after failures, is so great, that they subsist by still promising on. Indeed I cannot let heedless promisers, though in the most minute circumstances, pass without a censure. If a man should take a resolution to pay only sums above an hundred pounds, and yet contract with different people debts of five and ten, how long can we suppose he will keep his credit? This man will as long support his good name in business, as he will in conversation, who without difficulty makes assignations which he is indifferent whether he keeps or not.

This fault is sometimes to be accounted for, when desirable people are fearful of appearing precious and reserved by denials; but they will find the apprehension of that imputation will betray them into a childish impotence of mind, and make them promise all who are so kind to ask it of them. This leads such soft creatures into the misfortune of seeming to return overtures of good-will with ingratitude. The first steps in the breach of a man's integrity are much more important than men are aware of. The man who scruples breaking his word in little things would not suffer in his own conscience so great pain for failures of consequence, as he who thinks every little offence against truth and justice a disparagement. We should not make any thing we ourselves disapprove habitual to us if we would be sure of our integrity

T.

A DETRACTING CIRCLE.

Invidiam placare paras virtute relicta?
HOR. Sat. iii. l. 2. v. 13.

To shun detraction would'st thou virtue fly?

I AM extremely discomposed when I hear scandal, and am an utter enemy to all manner of detraction, and think it the greatest meanness that people of distinction can be guily of: however, it is hardly possible to come into company, where you do not find them pulling one another to pieces, and that from no other provocation but that of hearing any one commended. Merit, both as to wit and beauty, is become no other than the possession of a few trifling people's favour, which you cannot possibly arive at, if you have really any thing in you that is deserving. What they would bring to pass, is, to make all good and evil consist in report, and with whispers, calumnies, and impertinencies, to have the conduct of those reports. By this means innocents are blasted upon their first appearance in town; and there is nothing more required to make a young woman the object of envy and hatred, than to deserve love and admiration. This abominable endeavour to suppress or lessen every thing that is praiseworthy, is as frequent among the men as the women. If I can remember what passed at a visit last night, it will serve as an instance that the sexes are equally inclined to defamation, with equal malice, with equal impotence. Jack Triplett came into my Lady Airy's about eight of the clock. You know the manner we sit at a visit, and I need not describe the circle; but Mr. Triplett came in introduced by two tapers, supported by a spruce servant, whose hair is under a cap till my lady's candles are all lighted up, and the hour of ceremony begins: I say, Jack Triplett came in, and singing (for he is really good company) "Every feature, charming creature,"——he went on, "It is a most unreasonable thing that people cannot go peaceably to see their friends, but these murderers are let loose. Such a shape! such an air! what a glance was that as her chariot passed by mine"——My lady herself interrupted him; "Pray who is this fine thing?"—"I warrant," says another, "'tis the creature I was telling your ladyship of just now." "You were telling of!" says Jack; "I wish I had been so happy as to have come in and heard you, for I have not words to say what she is; but, if an agreeable height, a modest air, a virgin shame, an impatience of being beheld, amidst a blaze of ten thousand charms"——The whole room flew out, "Oh Mr. Triplett!" When

Miss Lofty, a known prude, said she believed she knew whom the gentleman meant; but she was indeed, as he civilly represented her, impatient of being beheld. Then turning to the lady next to her, "The most unbred creature you ever saw." Another pursued the discourse; "As unbred, madam, as you may think her, she is extremely belied if she is the novice she appears; she was last week at a ball till two in the morning; Mr. Triplett knows whether he was the happy man that took care of her home: but" ——This was followed by some particular exception that each woman in the room made to some peculiar grace or advantage: so that Mr. Triplett was beaten from one limb and feature to another, till he was forced to resign the whole woman. In the end, I took notice Triplett recorded all this malice in his heart; and saw in his countenance, and a certain waggish shrug, that he designed to repeat the conversation; I therefore let the discourse die, and soon after took an occasion to commend a certain gentleman of my acquaintance for a person of singular modesty, courage, integrity, and withal as a man of an entertaining conversation, to which advantages he had a shape and manner peculiarly graceful. Mr. Triplett, who is a woman's man, seemed to hear me with patience enough commend the qualities of his mind: he never heard indeed but that he was a very honest man and no fool; but for a fine gentleman, he must ask pardon. Upon no other foundation than this, Mr. Triplett took occasion to give the gentleman's pedigree, by what methods some part of the estate was acquired, how much it was beholden to a marriage for the present circumstances of it: after all, he could see nothing but a common man in his person, his breeding, or understanding.

Thus this impertinent humour of diminishing every one who is produced in conversation to their advantage, runs through the world; and I am, I confess, so fearful of the force of ill tongues, that I have begged of all those who are my well-wishers never to commend me, for it will but bring my frailties into examination, and I had rather be unobserved, than conspicuous, for disputed perfections. I am confident a thousand young people, who would have been ornaments to society, have, from fear of scandal, never dared to exert themselves in the polite arts of life. Their lives have passed away in an odious rusticity, in spite of great advantages of person, genius, and fortune. There is a vicious terror of being blamed in some well-inclined people, and a wicked pleasure in suppressing them in others; both which are to be animadverted upon. T.

METAPHORS.

——*Non ut placidis coeant immitia, non ut*
Serpentes avibus geminentur, tigribus agni.

——Nature, and the common laws of sense,
Forbids to reconcile antipathies;
Or make a snake engender with a dove,
And hungry tigers court the tender lambs.
ROSCOMMON.

If ordinary authors would condescend to write as they think, they would at least be allowed the praise of being intelligible, but they really take pains to be ridiculous; and by the studied ornament of style, perfectly disguise the little sense they aim at. There is a grievance of that sort in the commonwealth of letters, which I have for some time resolved to redress, and accordingly I have set this day apart for justice. What I mean is the mixture of inconsistent metaphors, which is a fault but too often found in learned writers, but in all the unlearned without exception.

In order to set this matter in a clear light to every reader, I shall in the first place observe, that a metaphor is a simile in one word, which serves to convey the thoughts of the mind under resemblances and images which affect the senses. There is not any thing in the world, which may not be compared to several things, if considered in several distinct lights; or, in other words, the same thing may be expressed by different metaphors. But the mischief is, that an unskilful author shall run their metaphors so absurdly into one another, that there shall be no simile, no agreeable picture, no apt resemblance, but confusion, obscurity, and noise. Thus I have known a hero compared to a thunderbolt, a lion, and the sea; all and each of them proper metaphors for impetuosity, courage, or force. But by bad management it hath so happened, that the thunderbolt hath overflowed its banks; the lion hath been darted through the skies, and the billows have rolled out of the Lybian desert.

The absurdity in this instance is obvious. And yet every time that clashing metaphors are put together, the fault is committed more or less. It hath already been said, that metaphors are images of things which affect the senses. An image, therefore, taken from what acts upon the sight, cannot, without violence, be applied to the hearing; and so of the rest. It is no less an impropriety to make any being in nature or art to do things in its metaphorical state, which it could not do in its original. I shall illustrate what I have said by an instance which I have read more than once in controversial writers. "The heavy lashes," saith a celebrated author, "that have dropt from your pen," &c. I suppose this gentleman having frequently heard of "gall dropping from a pen, and being lashed in a satire," he was resolved to have them both at any rate, and so uttered this complete piece of nonsense. It will most effectually discover the absurdity of these monstrous unions, if we will suppose these metaphors or images actually painted. Imagine then a hand holding a pen, and several lashes of whip-cord falling from it, and you have the true representation of this sort of eloquence. I believe, by this very rule, a reader may be able to judge of the union of all metaphors whatsoever, and determine which are homogeneous, and which heterogeneous; or, to speak more plainly, which are consistent, and which inconsistent.

There is yet one evil more which I must take no

tice of, and that is the running of metaphors into tedious allegories; which, though an error on the better hand, causes confusion as much as the other. This becomes abominable, when the lustre of one word leads a writer out of his road, and makes him wander from his subject for a page together. I remember a young fellow, of this turn, who having said by chance that his mistress had a world of charms, thereupon took occasion to consider her as one possessed of frigid and torrid zones, and pursued her from the one pole to the other.

I shall conclude this paper with a letter written in that enormous style, which I hope my reader hath by this time set his heart against. The epistle hath heretofore received great applause; but after what hath been said, let any man commend it if he dare.

"Sir,

"After the many heavy lashes that have fallen from your pen, you may justly expect in return all the load that my ink can lay upon your shoulders. You have quartered all the foul language upon me, that could be raked out of the air of Billingsgate, without knowing who I am, or whether I deserve to be cupped and scarified at this rate. I tell you once for all, turn your eyes where you please, you shall never smell me out. Do you think that the panics, which you sow about the parish, will ever build a monument to your glory? No, sir, you may fight these battles as long as you will, but when you come to balance the account, you will find that you have been fishing in troubled waters, and that an *ignis fatuus* hath bewildered you, and that indeed you have built upon a sandy foundation, and brought your hogs to a poor market

"I am, Sir,

"Yours, &c.

RELIGIOUS GRATITUDE.

Non usitata nec tenui ferar
Penna—— HOR

No weak, no common wing shall bear
My rising body through the air. CREECH.

THERE is not a more pleasing exercise of the mind than gratitude. It is accompanied with such an inward satisfaction, that the duty is sufficiently rewarded by the performance. It is not like the practice of many other virtues, difficult and painful, but attended with so much pleasure, that were there no positive command which enjoined it, nor any recompense laid up for it hereafter, a generous mind would indulge in it, for the natural gratification that accompanies it.

If gratitude is due from man to man, how much more from man to his Maker? The Supreme Being does not only confer upon us those bounties which proceed more immediately from his hand, but even those benefits which are conveyed to us by others. Every blessing we enjoy, by what means soever it may be derived upon us, is the gift of him who is the great Author of good, and Father of mercies,

If gratitude, when exerted toward one another, naturally produce a very pleasing sensation in the mind of a grateful man; it exalts the soul into rapture, when it is employed on this great object of gratitude; on this beneficent Being who has given us every thing we already possess, and from whom we expect every thing we yet hope for.

Most of the works of the pagan poets were either direct hymns to their deities, or tended indirectly to the celebration of their respective attributes and perfections. Those who are acquainted with the works of the Greek and Latin poets which are still extant, will upon reflection find this observation so true, that I shall not enlarge upon it. One would wonder that more of our Christian poets have not turned their thoughts this way, especially, if we consider, that our idea of the Supreme Being is not only infinitely more great and noble than what could possibly enter into the heart of a heathen, but filled with every thing that can raise the imagination, and give an opportunity for the sublimest thoughts and conceptions.

Plutarch tells us of a heathen who was singing a hymn to Diana, in which he celebrated her for her delight in human sacrifices, and other instances of cruelty and revenge; upon which a poet who was present at this piece of devotion, and seems to have had a truer idea of the Divine Nature, told the votary by way of reproof, that in recompense for his hymn, he heartily wished he might have a daughter of the same temper with the goddess he celebrated. It was indeed impossible to write the praises of one of those false deities, according to the pagan creed, without a mixture of impertinence and absurdity.

The Jews, who before the times of Christianity were the only people that had the knowledge of the true God, have set the Christian world an example how they ought to employ this divine talent of which I am speaking. As that nation produced men of great genius, without considering them as inspired writers, they have transmitted to us many hymns and divine odes, which excel those that are delivered down to us by the ancient Greeks and Romans, in the poetry, as much as in the subject to which it was consecrated. This I think might easily be shown, if there were occasion for it.

I shall end this essay by the following piece of divine poetry, sacred to graitude.

"When all thy mercies, O my God,
My rising soul surveys;
Transported with the view, I'm lost
In wonder, love and praise:

"O how shall words with equal warmth
The gratitude declare,
That glows within my ravish'd heart!
But thou can'st read it there.

"Thy Providence my life sustain'd,
And all my wants redress'd,

When in the silent womb I lay,
And hung upon the breast.

"To all my weak complaints and cries
Thy mercy lent an ear,
Ere yet my feeble thoughts had learnt
To form themselves in pray'r.

"Unnumber'd comforts to my soul
Thy tender care bestow'd,
Before my infant heart conceiv'd
From whom those comforts flow'd

"When in the slipp'ry paths of youth
With heedless steps I ran,
Thine arm unseen convey'd me safe,
And led me up to man;

'Through hidden dangers, toils and deaths,
It gently clear'd my way,
And through the pleasing snares of vice,
More to be fear'd than they.

'When worn with sickness oft hast Thou
With health renew'd my face,
And when in sins and sorrows sunk
Reviv'd my soul with grace.

Thy bounteous hand with worldly bliss,
Has made my cup run o'er,
And in a kind and faithful friend
Has doubled all my store.

"Ten thousand thousand precious gifts
My daily thanks employ,
Nor is the least a cheerful heart,
That tastes those gifts with joy

"Through every period of my life
Thy goodness I'll pursue,
And after death in distant worlds
The glorious theme renew.

"When Nature fails, and day and night
Divide thy works no more,
My ever grateful heart, O Lord,
Thy mercy shall adore.

"Through all eternity to Thee
A joyful song I'll raise,
For oh! eternity's too short
To utter all thy praise."

THE THEATRE

SHOULD BE A SCHOOL OF MORALITY.

Quid deceat, quid non; quo virtus, quo ferat error.
HOR.

What fit, what not; what excellent or ill.
ROSCOMMON.

SINCE two or three writers of comedy who are now living have taken their farewell of the stage, those who succeed them finding themselves incapable of rising up to their wit, humour, and good sense, have only imitated them in some of those loose unguarded strokes in which they complied with the corrupt taste of the more vicious part of their audience. When persons of a low genius attempt this kind of writing, they know no difference between being merry and being lewd. It is with an eye to some of these degenerate compositions that I have written the following discourse.

Were our English stage but half so virtuous as that of the Greeks or Romans, we should quickly see the influence of it in the behaviour of all the politer part of mankind. It would not be fashionable to ridicule religion, or its professors; the man of pleasure would not be the complete gentleman; vanity would be out of countenance, and every quality which is ornamental to human nature, would meet with that esteem which is due to it.

If the English stage were under the same regulations the Athenian was formerly, it would have the same effect that had, in recommending the religion, the government, and public worship of its country. Were our plays subject to proper inspections and limitations, we might not only pass away several of our vacant hours in the highest entertainments; but should always rise from them wiser and better than we sat down to them.

It is one of the most unaccountable things in our age that the lewdness of our theatre should be so much complained of, so well exposed, and so little redressed. It is to be hoped, that some time or other we may be at leisure to restrain the licentiousness of the theatre, and make it contribute its assistance to the advancement of morality, and to the reformation of the age. As matters stand at present, multitudes are shut out from this noble diversion, by reason of those abuses and corruptions that accompany it. A father is often afraid that his daughter should be ruined by those entertainments, which were invented for the accomplishment and refining of human nature. The Athenian and Roman plays were written with such a regard to morality, that Socrates used to frequent the one, and Cicero the other.

It happened once indeed, that Cato dropped into the Roman theatre, when the Floralia were to be represented; and as in that performance, which was a kind of religious ceremony, there were several indecent parts to be acted, the people refused to see them whilst Cato was present. Martial on this hint made the following epigram, which we must suppose was applied to some grave friend of his, that had been accidentally present at some such entertainment.

Nosses jocosæ dulce cum sacrum Floræ,
Festosque lusus, et licentiam vulgi,
Cur in theatrum Cato severe venisti?
An ideo tantum veneras, ut exires?

Why dost thou come, great censor of thy age,
To see the loose diversions of the stage?
With awful countenance and brow severe,
What in the name of goodness dost thou here?
See the mix'd crowd, how giddy, lewd, and vain!
Didst thou come in but to go out again?

An accident of this nature might happen once in an age among the Greeks or Romans; but they were too wise and good to let the constant nightly entertainment be of such a nature, that people of the most sense and virtue could not be at it. Whatever vices are represented upon the stage, they ought to be so marked and branded by the poet, as not to appear either laudable or amiable in the person who is tainted with them. But if we look into the English comedies abovementioned, we would think they were formed upon a quite contrary maxim, and that this rule, though it held good upon the heathen stage, was not to be regarded in Christian theatres. There is another rule likewise, which was observed by authors of antiquity, and which these modern geniuses have no regard to and that was never to choose an improper subject for ridicule. Now a subject is improper for ridicule, if it is apt to stir up horror and commiseration rather than laughter. For this reason, we do not find any comedy in so polite an author as Terence, raised upon the violations of the marriage-bed. The falsehood of the wife or husband has given occasion to noble tragedies, but a Scipio or a Lelius would have looked upon incest or murder to have been as proper subjects for comedy. On the contrary, cuckoldom is the basis of most of our modern plays. If an alderman appears upon the stage, you may be sure it is in order to be cuckolded. An husband that is a little grave or elderly, generally meets with the same fate. Knights and baronets, country squires, and justices of the quorum, come up to town for no other purpose. I have seen poor Dogget cuckolded in all these capacities. In short, our English writers are as frequently severe upon this innocent unhappy creature, commonly known by the name of a cuckold, as the ancient comic writers were upon an eating parasite, or a vainglorious soldier.

At the same time the poet so contrives matters, that two criminals are the favourites of the audience. We sit still, and wish well to them through the whole play, are pleased when they meet with proper opportunities, and out of humour when they are disappointed. The truth of it is, the accomplished gentleman upon the English stage, is the person that is familiar with other men's wives, and indifferent to his own; as the fine woman is generally a composition of sprightliness and falsehood. I do not know whether it proceeds from barrenness of invention, depravation of manners, or ignorance of mankind; but I have often wondered that our ordinary poets cannot frame to themselves the idea of a fine man who is not a whoremaster, or of a fine woman that is not a jilt.

I have sometimes thought of compiling a system of ethics out of the writings of these corrupt poets, under the title of Stage Morality. But I have been diverted from this thought, by a project which has been executed by an igenious gentleman of my acquaintance. He has composed, it seems, the history of a young fellow, who has taken all his notions of the world from the stage, and who has directed himself in every circumstance of his life and conversation, by the maxims and examples of the fine gentlemen in English comedies. If I can prevail upon him to give me a copy of this new-fashioned novel, I will bestow on it a place in my works, and question not but it may have as good an effect upon the drama, as Don Quixote had upon romance.

MODESTY AND ASSURANCE DISCRIMINATED.

Fallit enim vitium specie virtutis et umbra. JUV.

Vice oft is hid in virtue's fair disguise,
And in her borrow'd form escapes inquiring eyes.

Mr. Locke, in his Treatise of Human Understanding, has spent two chapters upon the abuse of words. The first and most palpable abuse of words, he says, is, when they are used without clear and distinct ideas: the second, when we are so inconsistent and unsteady in the application of them, that we sometimes use them to signify one idea, sometimes another. He adds, that the result of our contemplations and reasonings, while we have no precise ideas fixed to our words, must needs be very confused and absurd. To avoid this inconvenience, more especially in moral discourses where the same word should constantly be used in the same sense, he earnestly recommends the use of definitions. A definition, says he, is the only way whereby the precise meaning of moral words can be known. He therefore accuses those of great negligence who discourse of moral things with the least obscurity in the terms they make use of, since, upon the fore-mentioned ground, he does not scruple to say, that he thinks morality is capable of demonstration, as well as the mathematics.

I know no two words that have been more abused by the different and wrong interpretations which are put upon them, than those two, modesty and assurance. To say such-a-one is a modest man, sometimes indeed passes for a good character; but at present is very often used to signify a sheepish awkward fellow, who has neither good breeding, politeness, nor any knowledge of the world.

Again, a man of assurance, though at first it only denoted a person of a free and open carriage, is now very usually applied to a profligate wretch, who can break through all the rules of decency and morality without a blush.

I shall endeavour therefore in this essay to restore these words to their true meaning, to prevent the idea of modesty from being confounded with that of sheepishness, and to hinder impudence from passing for assurance.

If I was put to define modesty, I would call it, The reflection of an ingenuous mind, either when a man has committed an action for which he censures himself, or fancies that he is exposed to the censure of others.

For this reason a man truly modest is as much so when he is alone as in company, and as subject to a blush in his closet, as when the eyes of multitudes are upon him.

I do not remember to have met with any instance of modesty with which I am so well pleased, as that celebrated one of the young prince, whose father being a tributary king to the Romans, had several complaints laid against him before the senate, as a tyrant and oppressor of his subjects. The prince went to Rome to defend his father; but coming into the senate, and hearing a multitude of crimes proved upon him, was so oppressed when it came to his turn to speak, that he was unable to utter a word. The story tells us, that the fathers were more moved at this instance of modesty and ingenuity, than they could have been by the most pathetic oration; and, in short, pardoned the guilty father for this early promise of virtue in the son.

I take assurance to be the faculty of possessing a man's self, or of saying and doing indifferent things without any uneasiness or emotion in the mind. That which generally gives a man assurance is a moderate knowledge of the world, but, above all, a mind fixed and determined in itself to do nothing against the rules of honour and decency. An open and assured behaviour is the natural consequence of such a resolution. A man thus armed, if his words or actions are at any time misinterpreted, retires within himself and, from a consciousness of his own integrity, assumes force enough to despise the little censures of ignorance or malice.

Every one ought to cherish and encourage in himself the modesty and assurance I have here mentioned.

A man without assurance is liable to be made uneasy by the folly or ill-nature of every one he converses with. A man without modesty is lost to all sense of honour and virtue.

It is more than probable, that the prince abovementioned possessed both these qualifications in a very eminent degree. Without assurance he would never have undertaken to speak before the most august assembly in the world; without modesty, he would have pleaded the cause he had taken upon him, though it had appeared ever so scandalous.

From what has been said, it is plain, that modesty and assurance are both amiable, and may very well meet in the same person. When they are thus mixed and blended together, they compose what we endeavour to express when we say a modest assurance; by which we understand the just mean between bashfulness and impudence.

I shall conclude with observing, that as the same man may be both modest and assured, so it is also possible for the same person to be both impudent and bashful.

We have frequent instances of this odd kind of mixture in people of depraved minds and mean education; who, though they are not able to meet a man's eyes, or pronounce a sentence without confusion, can voluntarily commit the greatest villanies, or most indecent actions.

Such a person seems to have made a resolution to do ill even in spite of himself, and in defiance of all those checks and restraints his temper and complexion seem to have laid in his way.

Upon the whole, I would endeavour to establish this maxim, That the practice of virtue is the most proper method to give a man a becoming assurance in his words and actions. Guilt always seeks to shelter itself in one of the extremes, and is sometimes attended with both.

L.

VANITY OF MOST MEN'S PRAYERS.

——Non tu prece poscis emaci,
Quæ nisi seductis nequeas committere divis
At bona pars procerum tacita libabit accerra.
Haud cuivis promptum est, murmurque humilesque susurros
Tollere de templis; et aperto vivere voto.
Mens bona, fama, fides, hæc clare et ut aut audiat hospes.
Illa sibi introrsum, et sub lingua immurmurat: O si
Ebullit patrui præclarum funus! Et O si
Sub rastro crepet argenti mihi seria dextro,
Hercule! pupillumve utinam quem proximus hæres
Impello expungam!—— PERS.

Thy pray'rs the test of heaven will bear:
Nor need'st thou take the gods aside to hear
While others, even the mighty men of Rome
Big swell'd with mischief, to the temples come;
And in low murmurs and with costly smoke,
Heav'ns help to prosper their black vows, invoke.
So boldly to the gods mankind reveal
What from each other they, for shame, conceal.
Give me good fame, ye pow'rs, and make me just:
Thus much the rogue to public ears will trust.
In private then,—when wilt thou, mighty Jove,
My wealthy uncle from this world remove?
Or,—O thou thunderer's son, great Hercules,
That once thy bounteous deity would please
To guide my rake upon the chincking sound
Of some vast treasure hidden under ground!
O were my pupil fairly knock'd o' the head!
I should possess th' estate if he were dead.

DRYDEN.

Where Homer represents Phœnix, the tutor of Achilles, as persuading his pupil to lay aside his resentments, and give himself up to the entreaties of his countrymen, the poet, in order to make him speak in character, ascribes to him a speech full of those fables and allegories, which old men take delight in relating, and which are very proper for instruction. "The gods," says he, "suffer themselves to be prevailed upon by entreaties. When mortals have offended them by their transgressions, they appease them by vows and sacrifices. You must know, Achilles, that Prayers are the daughters of Jupiter. They are crippled by frequent kneeling, have their faces full of cares and wrinkles, and their eyes always cast toward heaven. They are constant attendants on the goddess Ate, and march behind her This goddess walks forward with a bold and haughty air, and being very light of foot, runs through the whole earth, grieving and afflicting the sons of men. She gets the start of Prayers, who always follow her, in order to heal those persons whom she wounds. He who honours these daughters of Jupiter when they draw near to him, receives great benefit from them; but as for him who rejects them, they entreat their father to give his orders to the goddess Ate to punish him for his hardness of heart." This noble allegory needs but little explanation: for whether the goddess Ate signifies injury, as some have explained it; or guilt in general, as others; or divine justice, as I am the more apt to think, the interpretation is obvious enough.

I shall produce another heathen fable relating to prayers, which is of a more diverting kind. One would think, by some passages in it, that it was composed by Lucian, or at least by some author who has endeavoured to imitate his way of writing; but as dissertations of this nature are more curious than useful, I shall give my reader the fable, without any further inquiries after the author.

"Menippus the philosopher was a second time taken up into heaven by Jupiter, when for his entertainment he lifted up a trap-door that was placed by his footstool. At its rising, there issued through it such a din of cries as astonished the philosopher. Upon his asking what they meant, Jupiter told him they were the prayers that were sent up to him from the earth. Menippus, amidst the confusion of voices, which was so great that nothing less than the ear of Jove could distinguish them, heard the words 'riches, honour, and long life,' repeated to several different tones and languages. When the first hubbub of sounds was over, the trap-door being left open, the voices came up more separate and distinct. The first prayer was a very odd one; it came from Athens, and desired Jupiter to increase the wisdom and the beard of his humble supplicant. Menippus knew it by the voice to be the prayer of his friend Licander the philosopher. This was succeeded by the petition of one who had just laden a ship, and promised Jupiter, if he took care of it, and returned it home again full of riches, he would make him an offering of a silver cup. Jupiter thanked him for nothing; and bending down his ear more attentively than ordinary, heard a voice complaining to him of the cruelty of an Ephesian widow, and begging him to breed compassion in her heart: this, says Jupiter, is a very honest fellow: I have received a great deal of incense from him; I will not be so cruel to him as not to hear his prayers. He was then interrupted with a whole volley of vows, which were made for the health of a tyrannical prince by his subjects who prayed for him in his presence. Menippus was surprised, after having listened to prayers offered up with so much ardour and devotion, to hear low whispers from the same assembly, expostulating with Jove for suffering such a tyrant to live, and asking him how his thunder could lie idle? Jupiter was so offended at these prevaricating rascals, that he took down the first vows, and puffed away the last. The philosopher seeing a great cloud mounting upwards, and making its way directly to the trapdoor, inquired of Jupiter what it meant. This, says Jupiter, is the smoke of an whole hecatomb that is offered me by the general of an army, who is very importunate with me to let him cut off an hundred thousand men that are drawn up in array against him: what does the impudent wretch think I see in him, to believe that I will make a sacrifice of so many mortals as good as himself, and all this to his glory, forsooth! But hark, says Jupiter, there is a voice I never heard but in time of danger; it is a rogue that was shipwrecked in the Ionian sea. I saved him on a plank but three days ago, upon his promise to mend his manners; the scoundrel is not worth a groat, and yet has the impudence to offer me a temple, if I will keep him from sinking. But yonder, says he, is a special youth for you, he desires me to take his father, who keeps a great estate from him, out of the miseries of human life. The old fellow shall live till he makes his heart ache, I can tell him that for his pains. This was followed by the soft voice of a pious lady, desiring Jupiter that she might appear amiable and charming in the sight of her emperor. As the philosopher was reflecting on this extraordinary petition, there blew a gentle wind through the trap-door, which he at first mistook for a gale of zephyrs, but afterward found it to be a breeze of sighs; they smelt strong of flowers and incense, and were succeeded by most passionate complaints of wounds and torments, fires and arrows, cruelty, despair, and death. Menippus fancied that such lamentable cries arose from some general execution, or from wretches lying under the torture; but Jupiter told him that they came up to him from the isle of Paphos, and that he every day received complaints of the same nature from that whimsical tribe of mortals who are called lovers. I am so trifled with, says he, by this generation of both sexes, and find it so impossible to please them, whether I grant or refuse their petitions, that I shall order a western wind for the future to intercept them in their passage, and blow them at random upon the earth. The last petition I heard was from a very aged man of near an hundred years old, begging but for one year more of life, and then promising to die contented. This is the rarest old fellow, says Jupiter. He has made this prayer to me for above twenty years together. When he was but fifty years old, he desired only that he might live to see his son settled in the world: I granted it. He then begged the same favour for his daughter, and afterward that he might see the education of a grandson: when all this was brought about, he puts up a petition that he might live to finish a house he was building. In short, he is an unreasonable old cur, and never wants an excuse: I will hear no more of him. Upon which he flung down the trap-door in a passion, and was resolved to give no more audience that day."

Notwithstanding the levity of this fable, the moral of it very well deserves our attention, and is the same with that which has been inculcated by Socrates and Plato, not to mention Juvenal and Perseus, who have each of them made the finest satire in their whole works upon this subject. The vanity of men's wishes, which are the natural prayers of the mind, as well as many of those secret devotions which they offer to the Supreme Being, are sufficiently exposed by it. Among other reasons for set forms of prayer, I have often thought it a very good one, that by this means the folly and extravagance of men's desires may be kept within due bounds, and not break out in absurd and rediculous petitions, on so great and solemn an occasion. *I.*

MODERN CRITICS.

——*Studium sine divite vena.* HOR.

Art without a vein. ROSCOMMON.

I LOOK upon the play-house as a world within itself. They have lately furnished the middle region of it with a new set of meteors, in order to give the sublime to many modern tragedies. I was there last winter at the first rehearsal of the new thunder, which is much more deep and sonorous than any hitherto made use of. They have a Salmoneus behind the scenes who plays it off with great success. Their lightnings are made to flash more briskly than heretofore; their clouds are also better furbelowed, and more voluminous; not to mention a violent storm locked up in a great chest, that is designed for the Tem pest. They are also provided with above a dozen showers of snow, which, as I am informed, are the plays of many unsuccessful poets artificially cut and shredded for that use.

I do not indeed wonder that the actors should be such professed enemies to those among our nation who are commonly known by the name of critics, since it is a rule among these gentlemen to fall upon a play, not because it is written, but because it takes. Several of them lay it down as a maxim, that whatever dramatic performance has a long run, must of necessity be good for nothing: as though the first precept in poetry were "not to please." Whether this rule holds good or not, I shall leave to the determination of those who are better judges than myself; if it does, I am sure it tends very much to the honour of those gentlemen who have established it; few of their pieces having been disgraced by a run of three days, and most of them being so exquisitely written, that the town would never give them more than one night's hearing.

I have a great esteem for a true critic, such as Aristotle and Longinus among the Greeks, Horace and Quintillian among the Romans, Boileau and Dacier among the French. But it is our misfortune, that some who set up for professed critics among us are so stupid, that they do not know how to put ten words together with elegance or common propriety, and withal so illiterate, that they have no taste of the learned languages, and therefore criticise upon old authors only at second hand. They judge of them by what others have written, and not by any notions they have of the authors themselves. The words unity, action, sentiment, and diction, pronounced with an air of authority, give them a figure among unlearned readers, who are apt to believe they are very deep, because they are unintelligible. The ancient critics are full of the praises of their contemporaries; they discover beauties which escaped the observation of the vulgar, and very often find out reasons for palliating and excusing such little slips and oversights as were committed in the writings of eminent authors. On the contrary, most of the smatterers in criticism who appear among us, make it their business to vilify and depreciate every new production that gains applause, to descry imaginary blemishes, and to prove by far fetched arguments that what pass for beauties in any celebrated piece, are faults and errors. In short, the writings of these critics, compared with those of the ancients, are like the works of the sophists compared with those of the old philosophers.

Envy and cavil are the natural fruits of laziness and ignorance; which was probably the reason, that in the heathen mythology Momus is said to be the son of Nox and Somnus, of darkness and sleep. Idle men, who have not been at the pains to accomplish or distinguish themselves, are very apt to detract from others; as ignorant men are very subject to decry those beauties in a celebrated work which they have not eyes to discover. Many of our sons of Momus, who dignify themselves by the name of critics, are the genuine descendants of these two illustrious ancestors. They are often led into those numerous absurdities, in which they daily instruct the people, by not considering that, First, There is sometimes a greater judgment shown in deviating from the rules of art, than in adhering to them; and, Secondly, That there is more beauty in the works of a great genius, who is ignorant of all the rules of art, than in the works of a little genius, who not only knows, but scrupulously observes them.

First, We may often take notice of men who are perfectly acquainted with all the rules of good writing, and notwithstanding choose to depart from them on extraordinary occasions. I could give instances out of all the tragic writers of antiquity who have shown their judgment in this particular; and purposely receded from an established rule of the drama, when it has made way for a much higher beauty than the observation of such a rule would have been. Those who have surveyed the noblest pieces of architecture and statuary, both ancient and modern, know very well that there are frequent deviations from art in the works of the greatest masters, which have produced a much nobler effect than a more accurate and exact way of proceeding could have done. This often arises from what the Italians call the *Gusto grande* in these arts, which is what we call the sublime in writing.

In the next place, our critics do not seem sensible that there is more beauty in the works of a great genius who is ignorant of the rules of art, than in those of a little genius who knows and observes them. It is of these men of genius that Terence speaks, in opposition to the little artificial cavillers of his time;

Quorum æmulari expotat negligentiam
Potius quam istorum obscuram diligentiam.

"Whose negligence he would rather imitate than these men's obscure diligence."

A critic may have the same consolation in the ill-success of his play, as Dr. South tells us a physician has at the death of a patient, that he was killed *secundum artem.* Our inimitable Shakspeare is a stumbling-block to the whole tribe of these rigid critics. Who would not rather read one of his plays, where there is not a single rule of the stage observed, than any production of a modern critic, where there is not one of them violated? Shakspeare was indeed born with all the seeds of poetry, and may be compared to the stone in Pyrrhus's ring, which, as Pliny tells us, had the figure of Apollo and the nine Muses in the veins of it, produced by the spontaneous hand of nature, without any help from art.

SCANDAL-BEARERS BAD HEARTED.

Quantum a rerum turpitudine abes, tantnm te a verborum libertate sejungas. TULL.

We should be as careful of our words as our actions and as far from speaking, as from doing ill.

IT is a certain sign of an ill heart to be inclined to defamation. They who are harmless and innocent, can have no gratification that way; but it ever arises from a neglect of what is laudable in a man's self, and an impatience of seeing it in another. Else why should Virtue provoke? Why should Beauty displease in such a degree, that a man given to scandal never lets the mention of either pass by him without offering some thing to the diminution of it? A lady the other day at a visit being attacked somewhat rudely by one, whose own character has been very roughly treated, answered a great deal of heat and intemperance very calmly, "Good madam, spare me, who am none of your match; I speak ill of nobody, and it is a new thing to me to be spoken ill of." Little minds think fame consists in the number of votes they have on their side among the multitude, whereas it is really the inseparable follower of good and worthy actions. Fame is as natural a follower of merit, as shadow is of a body. It is true, when crowds press upon you, this shadow cannot be seen, but when they separate from around you, it will again appear. The lazy, the idle, and the froward, are the persons who are most pleased with the little tales which pass about the town to the disadvantage of the rest of the world. Were it not for the pleasure of speaking ill, there are numbers of people who are too lazy to go out of their own houses, and too ill-natured to open their lips in conversation. It was not a little diverting the other day to observe a lady reading a post-letter, and at these words, "After all her airs, he has heard some story or other, and the match is broke off," give orders in the midst of her reading, *Put to the horses.* That a young woman of merit has missed an advantageous settlement, was news not to be delayed, lest somebody else should have given her malicious acquaintauce that satisfaction before her. The unwillingness to receive good tidings is a quality as inseparable from a scandal-bearer, as the readiness to divulge bad. But, alas, how wretchedly low and contemptible is that state of mind, that cannot be pleased but by what is the subject of lamentation. This temper has ever been in the highest degree odious to gallant spirits. The Persian soldier, who was heard reviling Alexander the Great, was well admonished by his officer: "Sir, you are paid to fight against Alexander, and not to rail at him."

Cicero in one of his pleadings, defending his client from general scandal, says very handsomely, and with much reason, "There are many who have particular engagements to the prosecutor: there are many who are known to have ill-will to him for whom I appear; there are many who are naturally addicted to defamation, and envious of any good to any man, who may have contributed to spread reports of this kind: for nothing is so swift as scandal, nothing is more easily sent abroad, nothing received with more welcome, nothing diffuses itself so universally. I shall not desire, that if any report to our disadvantage has any ground for it, you would overlook or extenuate it. but if there be any thing advanced without a person who can say whence he had it, or which is attested by one who forgot who told him it, or who had it from one of so little consideration that he did not then think it worth his notice, all such testimonies as these, I know, you will think too slight to have any credit against the innocence and honour of your fellow-citizen." When an ill report is traced, it very often vanishes among such as the orator has here recited. And how despicable a creature must that be, who is in pain for what passes among so frivolous a people? There is a town in Warwickshire of good note, and formerly pretty famous for much animosity and dissention, the chief families of which have now turned all their whispers, backbitings, envies, and private malices, into mirth and entertainment, by means of a peevish old gentlewoman, known by the title of the Lady Bluemantle. This heroine had for many years together outdone the whole sisterhood of gossips, in invention, quick utterance, and unprovoked malice This good body is of a lasting constitution, though extremely decayed in her eyes, and decrepit in her feet. The two circumstances of being always at home from her lameness, and very attentive from her blindness, make her lodgings the receptacle of all that passes in town, good or bad; but for the latter, she seems to have the better memory. There is another thing to be noted of her, which is, that as it is usual with old people, she has a livelier memory of things which passed when she was very young, than of late years. Add to all this, that she does not only not love any body, but she hates every body. The statue in Rome does not serve to vent malice half so well, as this old lady does to disappoint it. She does not know the author of any thing that is told her, but can readily repeat the matter itself; therefore, though she exposes all the whole town, she offends no one body in it. She is so exquisitely restless and peevish, that she quarrels with all about her, and sometimes in a freak will instantly change her habitation. To indulge this humour, she is led about the grounds belonging to the same house she is in, and the persons to whom she is to remove, being in the plot, and ready to receive her at her own chamber again. At stated times, the gentlewoman at whose house she supposes she is at the time, is sent for to quarrel with, according to her common custom: when they have a mind to drive the jest, she is immediately urged to that degree, that she will board in a family with which she has never yet been; and away she will go this instant, and tell them all that the rest have been saying of them. By this means she has been an inhabitant of every house in the place without stirring from the same habitation; and the many stories which every body furnishes her with to favour that deceit, make her the general intelligencer of the town of all that can be said by one woman against another. Thus groundless stories die away, and sometimes truths are smothered under the general word; when they have a mind to discountenance a thing, Oh! that is in my Lady Bluemantle's memoirs.

Whoever receives impressions to the disadvantage of others without examination, is to be had in no other credit for intelligence than this good Lady Bluemantle, who is subjected to have her ears imposed upon for want of other helps to better information. Add to this, that other scandal-bearers suspend the use of these faculties which she has lost, rather than apply them to do justice to their neighbours: and I think, for the service of my fair readers, to acquaint them, that there is a voluntary Lady Bluemantle at every visit in town. T.

MESSIAH.

A SACRED ECLOGUE, COMPOSED OF SEVERAL PASSAGES OF ISAIAH THE PROPHET.

Aggredere. O magnos, aderit jam tempus, honores.
VIRG. Ecl. iv. ver. 48.

Mature in years, to ready honours move.
DRYDEN.

Written in imitation of Virgil's Pollio.

Ye nymphs of Solyma! begin the song:
To heav'nly themes sublimer strains belong.
The mossy fountains, and the sylvan shades,
The dreams of Pindus, and th' Aonian maids,
Delight no more——O thou my voice inspire,
Who touch'd Isaiah's hallow'd lips with fire!
Rapt into future times, the bard begun;
A virgin shall conceive, a virgin bear a son!
From Jesse's root behold a branch arise,
Whose sacred flow'r with fragrance fills the skies.*
Th' ethereal spirit o'er its leaves shall move,
And on its top descends the mystic dove.
Ye heav'ns! from high the dewy nectar pour,†
And in soft silence shed the kindly show'r!
The sick and weak, the healing plant shall aid,‡
From storms a shelter, and from heat a shade.
All crimes shall cease, and ancient fraud shall fail;
Returning justice lift aloft her scale;§
Peace o'er the world her olive wand extend,
And white-rob'd innocence from heav'n descend.
Swift fly the years, and rise th' expected morn!
Oh, spring to light, auspicious Babe, be born!
See, nature hastes her earliest wreaths to bring,
With all the incense of the breathing spring:‖
See lofty Lebanon his head advance,

* Isa. Cap. 11. v. 1.
† Cap. 45. v. 8.
‡ Cap. 25. v. 4.
§ Cap. 9, v. 7.
‖ Cap. 35. v. 3

See nodding forests on the mountains dance;
See spicy clouds from lowly Sharon rise,
And Carmel's flow'ry top perfumes the skies!
Hark! a glad voice the lonely desert cheers;*
Prepare the way! a God, a God appears!
A God! a God! the vocal hills reply;
The rocks proclaim th' approaching Deity.
Lo, earth receives him from the bending skies!
Sink down, ye mountains, and ye vallies, rise!
With heads declin'd, ye cedars, homage pay!
Be smooth, ye rocks; ye rapid floods, give way!
The Saviour comes! by ancient bards foretold:
Hear him, ye deaf, and all ye blind, behold!†
He from thick films shall purge the visual ray,
And on the sightless eye-ball pour the day.
'Tis he th' obstructed paths of sound shall clear,
And bid new music charm th' unfolding ear;
The dumb shall sing, the lame his crutch forego,
And leap exulting, like the bounding roe.
No sigh, no murmur, the wide world shall hear,
From ev'ry face he wipes off ev'ry tear.
In adamantine chains shall death be bound,‡
And hell's grim tyrant feel th' eternal wound,
As the good shepherd tends his fleecy care,§
Seeks freshest pastures and the purest air,
Explores the lost, the wand'ring sheep directs,
By day o'ersees them, and by night protects;
The tender lambs he raises in his arms,
Feeds from his hand, and in his bosom warms
Thus shall mankind his guardian care engage,
The promis'd father of the future age.‖
No more shall nation against nation rise,¶
Nor ardent warriors meet with hateful eyes,
Nor fields with gleaming steel be cover'd o'er,
The brazen trumpets kindle rage no more;
But useless lances into scythes shall bend,
And the broad falchion in a ploughshare end.

* Cap. 40. v. 3, 4. † Cap. 42. v. 18. cap. xxxv. v. 5, 6.
‡ Cap. 25. v. 8 § Cap. 40. v. 11.
‖ Cap. 9. v. 6. ¶ Cap. 2. v. 1.

Then palaces shall rise; the joyful son*
Shall finish what his short-liv'd sire begun;
Their vines a shadow to their race shall yield,
And the same hand that sow'd shall reap the field;
The swain in barren deserts with surprise†
Sees lilies spring, and sudden verdure rise,
And starts amidst the thirsty wilds to hear
New falls of water murm'ring in his ear.
On rifted rocks, the dragon's late abodes,
The green reed trembles, and the bulrush nods.
Waste sandy vallies, once perplex'd with thorn,‡
The spiry fir and shapely box adorn;
The leafless shrubs the flow'ring palm succeed,
And od'rous myrtle to the noisome weed.
The lambs with wolves shall graze the verdant mead,§
And boys in flow'ry bands the tiger lead;
The steer and lion at one crib shall meet,
And harmless serpents lick the pilgrim's feet.
The smiling infant in his hand shall take
The crested basilisk and speckled snake;
Pleas'd the green lustre of his scales survey,
And with their forky tongue and pointless sting shall play.
Rise, crown'd with light, imperial Salem, rise!‖
Exalt thy tow'ry head, and lift thy eyes!
See, a long race thy spacious courts adorn;¶
See future sons and daughters yet unborn,
In crowding ranks on every side arise,
Demanding life, impatient for the skies!
See barbarous nations at thy gates attend,**
Walk in thy light, and in thy temple bend;
See thy bright altars throng'd with prostrate kings,
And heap'd with products of Sabæan springs!††
For thee Idumea's spicy forests blow,
And seeds of gold in Ophir's mountains glow.
See heav'n its sparkling portals wide display,

* Cap. 65. v. 21, 22.
† Cap. 35, v. 1, 7.
‡ Cap. 41. v. 19. & cap. 55. v. 13.
§ Cap. 11. v. 6, 7, 8
‖ Cap. 60. v. 1.
¶ Cap. 60. v. 4.
** Cap. 60. v. 3.
†† Ib. v. 6.

And break upon thee in a flood of day?
No more the rising sun shall gild the morn!*
Nor ev'ning Cynthia fill her silver horn;
But lost, dissolv'd in thy superior rays,
One tide of glory, one unclouded blaze,
O'erflow thy courts: the Light himself shall shine
Reveal'd, and God's eternal day be thine!
The seas shall waste, the skies in smoke decay,†
Rocks fall to dust, and mountains melt away;
But fix'd His word, His saving power remains;
Thy realm for ever lasts, thy own Messiah reigns!

T.

DECLAMATION.

——— *abest facundis gratia dictis.*

OVID.

Eloquent words a graceful manner want.

MOST foreign writers who have given any character of the English nation, whatever vices they ascribe to it, allow, in general, that the people are naturally modest. It proceeds perhaps from this our national virtue, that our orators are observed to make use of less gesture or action than those of other countries. Our preachers stand stock-still in the pulpit, and will not so much as move a finger to set off the best sermons in the world. We meet with the same speaking statues at our bars, and in all public places of debate. Our words flow from us in a smooth continued stream without those strainings of the voice, motions of the body, and majesty of the hand, which are so much celebrated in the orators of Greece and Rome. We can talk of life and death in cold blood, and keep our temper in a discourse which turns upon every thing that is dear to us. Though our zeal breaks out in the finest tropes and figures, it is not able to stir a limb

* Cap. 60. v. 19, 20.
† Cap. 51. v. 6. & cap. 54. v. 10.

about us. I have heard it observed more than once by those who have seen Italy, that an untravelled Englishman cannot relish all the beauties of Italian pictures, because the postures which are expressed in them are often such as are peculiar to that country. One who has not seen an Italian in the pulpit, will not know what to make of that noble gesture in Raphael's picture of St. Paul preaching at Athens, where the Apostle is represented as lifting up both his arms, and pouring out the thunder of his rhetoric amidst an audience of pagan philosophers.

It is certain that proper gestures and vehement exertions of the voice cannot be too much studied by a public orator. They are a kind of comment to what he utters, and enforce every thing he says, with weak hearers, better than the strongest argument he can make use of. They keep the audience awake, and fix their attention to what is delivered to them, at the same time that they show the speaker is in earnest, and affected himself with what he so passionately recommends to others. Violent gesture and vociferation naturally shake the hearts of the ignorant, and fill them with a kind of religious horror. Nothing is more frequent than to see women weep and tremble at the sight of a moving preacher, though he is placed quite out of their hearing; as in England we very frequently see people lulled asleep with solid and elaborate discourses of piety, who would be warmed and transported out of themselves by the bellowings and distortions of enthusiasm.

If nonsense, when accompanied with such an emotion of voice and body, has such an influence on men's minds, what might we not expect from many of those admirable discourses which are printed in our tongue, were they delivered with a becoming fervour and with the most agreeable graces of voice and gesture?

We are told, that the great Latin orator very much impaired his health by this *laterum contentio*, this vehemence of action, with which he used to deliver himself. The Greek orator was likewise so very famous for this particular in rhetoric, that one of his antagonists, whom he had banished from Athens, reading over the oration which had procured his banishment, and seeing his friends admire it, could not forbear asking them, if they were so much affected by the bare reading of it, how much more they would have been alarmed, had they heard him actually throwing out such a storm of eloquence?

How cold and dead a figure, in comparison of these two great men, does an orator often make at the British bar, holding up his head with the most insipid serenity, and stroking the sides of a long wig that reaches down to his middle? The truth of it is, there is often nothing more ridiculous than the gestures of an English speaker; you see some of them running their hands into their pockets as far as ever they can thrust them, and others looking with great attention on a piece of paper that has nothing written in it; you may see many a smart rhetorician turning his hat in his hands, moulding it into several different cocks; examining sometimes the lining of it, and sometimes the button, during the whole course of his harangue. A deaf man would think he was cheapening a beaver, when perhaps he is talking of the fate of the British nation. I remember, when I was a young man, and used to frequent Westminster-Hall, there was a counsellor who never pleaded without a piece of packthread in his hand, which he used to twist about a thumb, or a finger, all the while he was speaking; the wags of those days used to call it the thread of his discourse, for he was not able to utter a word without it. One of his clients, who was more merry than wise, stole it from him one day in the midst of his pleading; but he had better have let it alone, for he lost his cause by his jest.

I believe every one will agree, that we ought either to lay aside all kinds of gesture, (which seems to be very suitable to the genius of our nation) or at least to make use of such only as are graceful and expressive. O.

RELIGIOUS HOPE.

Ἐν ἐλπισι χρη τυς σοφυς εχειν βιον.

EURIPID.

The wise with hope support the pains of life.

THE time present seldom affords sufficient employment to the mind of man. Objects of pain or pleasure, love or admiration, do not lie thick enough together in life to keep the soul in constant action, and supply an immediate exercise to its faculties. In order, therefore, to remedy this defect, that the mind may not want business, but always have materials for thinking, she is endowed with certain powers, that can recal what is passed, and anticipate what is to come.

That wonderful faculty, which we call the memory, is perpetually looking back, when we have nothing present to entertain us. It is like those repositories in several animals, that are filled with stores of their former food, on which they may ruminate when their present pasture fails.

As the memory relieves the mind in her vacant moments, and prevents any chasms of thought by ideas of what is past, we have other faculties that agitate and employ her upon what is to come. These are the passions of hope and fear.

By these two passions we reach forward into futurity, and bring up to our present thoughts objects that lie hid in the remotest depths of time. We suffer misery and enjoy happiness before they are in being; we can set the sun and stars forward, or lose sight of them by wandering into those retired parts of eternity, when the heavens and earth shall be no more.

By the way, who can imagine that the existence of a creature is to be circumscribed by time, whose thoughts are not? But I shall here confine myself to that particular passion which goes by the name of hope.

Our actual enjoyments are so few and transient, that man would be a very miserable being, were he not endowed with this passion, which gives him a taste of those good things that may possibly come into his possession. "We should hope for every thing that is good," says the old poet Linus, "because there is nothing which may not be hoped for, and nothing but what the gods are able to give us." Hope quickens all the still parts of life, and keeps the mind awake in her most remiss and indolent hours. It gives habitual serenity and good-humour. It is a kind of vital heat in the soul, that cheers and gladdens her, when she does not attend to it. It makes pain easy, and labour pleasant.

Besides these several advantages which rise from hope, there is another which is none of the least, and that is, its great efficacy in preserving us from setting too high a value on present enjoyments. The saying of Cæsar is very well known. When he had given away all his estate in gratuities among his friends, one of them asked what he had left for himself, to which that great man replied, *Hope.* His natural magnanimity hindered him from prizing what he was certainly possessed of, and turned all his thoughts upon something more valuable that he had in view. I question not but every reader will draw a moral from this story, and apply it to himself without my direction.

The old story of Pandora's box (which many of the learned believe was formed among the heathens upon the tradition of the fall of man) shows us how deplorable a state they thought the present life without hope. To set forth the utmost condition of misery, they tell us, that our forefather, according to the pagan theology, had a great vessel presented him by Pandora: upon his lifting up the lid of it, says the fable, there flew out all the calamities and distempers incident to men, from which, till that time, they had been altogether exempt. Hope, who had been inclosed in the cup with so much bad company, instead of flying off with the rest, stuck so close to the lid of it, that it was shut down upon her.

I shall make but two reflections upon what I have hitherto said. First, that no kind of life is so happy as that which is full of hope, especially when the hope, is well grounded, and when the object of it is of an exalted kind, and in its nature proper to make the person happy who enjoys it. This proposition must be very evident to those who consider how few are the present enjoyments of the most happy man, and how insufficient to give him an entire satisfaction and acquiescence in them.

My next observation is this, that a religious life is that which most abounds in a well-grounded hope, and such an one as is fixed on objects that are capable of making us entirely happy. This hope in a religious man, is much more sure and certain than the hope of any temporal blessing, as it is strengthened not only by reason, but by faith. It has at the same time its eye perpetually fixed on that state, which implies in the very notion of it the most full and the most complete happiness.

I have before shown how the influence of hope in general sweetens life, and makes our present condition supportable, if not pleasing; but a religious hope has still greater advantages. It does not only bear up the mind under her sufferings, but makes her rejoice in them, as they may be the instruments of procuring her the great and ultimate end of all her hope.

Religious hope has likewise this advantage above any other kind of hope, that it is able to revive the dying man, and to fill his mind not only with secret comfort and refreshment, but sometimes with rapture and transport. He triumphs in his agonies, while the soul springs forward with delight to the great object which she has always had in view, and leaves the body with an expectation of being reunited to her in a glorious and joyful resurrection.

I shall conclude this essay with those emphatical expressions of a lively hope, which the Psalmist made use of in the midst of those dangers and adversities which surrounded him; for the following passage had its present and personal, as well as its future and prophetic sense. "I have set the Lord always before me because he is at my right hand I shall not be moved. Therefore my heart is glad, and my glory rejoiceth my flesh also shall rest in hope. For thou wilt not leave my soul in hell, neither wilt thou suffer thine Holy One to see corruption. Thou wilt show me the path of life: in thy presence is fulness of joy, at thy right hand there are pleasures for evermore."

C.

MEN BLIND TO THEIR HAPPINESS.

Qui fit, Mæcenas, ut nemo, quam sibi sortem
Seu ratio dederit, seu fors objecerit, illa
Contentas vivat: laudet diversa sequentes?
O fortunati mercatores, gravis annis
Miles ait, multo jam fractus membra labore!
Contra mercator, navim jactantibus austris.
Militia est potior. Quid enim? concurritur: hora
Momento cita mors venit, aut victoria læta,
Agricolam laudat juris legumque peritus,
Sub galli cantum consultor ubi osita pulsat.
Ille datis vadibus, qui rure extractus in urbem est.
Solos felices viventes clamat in urbe.
Cætera de genere hoc (adeo sunt multa) loquacem
Delassare valent Fabium. Ne te morer audi
Quo rem deducam. Si quis Deus, en ego, dicat,
Jam faciam quod vultis: eris tu, qui modo, miles,
Mercator: tu consultus modo, rusticus. Hinc vos,
Vos hinc mutatis discedite partibus. Eja,
Quid flatis? Nolint. Atqui licet esse beatis. HOR

Whence is't Mæcenas, that so few approve
The state they're plac'd in, and incline to rove;
Whether against their will by fate impos'd,
Or by consent and prudent choice espous'd?
Happy the merchant! the old soldier cries,
Broke with fatigues and warlike enterprise.
The merchant, when the dreaded hurricane
Tosses his wealthy cargo on the main,
Applauds the wars and toils of a campaign:
There an engagement soon decides your doom,
Bravely to die, or come victorious home.
The lawyer vows the farmer's life is best,
When, at the dawn, his clients break his rest.
The farmer, having put in bail t' appear,
And forc'd to town, cries, they are happiest there:
With thousands more of this inconstant race,

Would tire e'en Fabius to relate each case.
Not to detain you longer, pray attend
The issue of all this; should Jove descend,
And grant to every man his rash demand,
To run his lengths with a neglectful hand:
First, grant the harrass'd warrior a release,
Bid him go trade, and try the faithless seas,
To purchase treasure and declining ease:
Next call the pleader from his learned strife,
To the calm blessings of a country life:
And, with these separate demands dismiss
Each suppliant to enjoy the promised bliss:
Don't you believe they'd run? Not one will move,
Though proffer'd to be happy from above.

HORNECK.

It is a celebrated thought of Socrates, that if all the misfortunes of mankind were cast into a public stock, in order to be equally distributed among the whole species, those who now think themselves the most unhappy, would prefer the share they are already possessed of, before that which would fall to them by such a division. Horace has carried this thought a great deal further in the motto of my paper, which implies that the hardships or misfortunes we lie under, are more easy to us than those of any other person would be, in case we could change conditions with him.

As I was ruminating on these two remarks, and seated in my elbow-chair, I insensibly fell asleep; when, on a sudden, methought there was a proclamation made by Jupiter, that every mortal should bring in his griefs and calamities, and throw them together in a heap. There was a large plain appointed for this purpose. I took my stand in the centre of it, and saw with a great deal of pleasure the whole human species marching one after another, and throwing down their several loads, which immediately grew up into a prodigious mountain, that seemed to rise above the clouds.

There was a certain lady of a thin airy shape, who was very active in this solemnity. She carried a magnifying glass in one of her hands, and was clothed in a loose flowing robe, embroidered with several figures of fiends and spectres, that discovered themselves in a thousand chimerical shapes, as her garment hovered in the wind. There was something wild and distracted in her looks. Her name was Fancy. She led up every mortal to the appointed place, after having very officiously assisted him in making up his pack, and laying it upon his shoulders. My heart melted within me to see my fellow-creatures groaning under their respective burdens, and to consider that prodigious bulk of human calamities which lay before me.

There were however several persons who gave me great diversion upon this occasion. I observed one bringing in a fardel very carefully concealed under an old embroidered cloak, which, upon his throwing it into the heap, I discovered to be poverty. Another, after a great deal of puffing, threw down his luggage, which, upon examining, I found to be his wife.

There were multitudes of lovers saddled with very whimsical burdens composed of darts and flames: but what was very odd, though they sighed as if their hearts would break under these bundles of calamities, they could not persuade themselves to cast them into the heap, when they came up to it; but, after a few faint efforts, shook their heads and marched away, as heavy laden as they came. I saw multitudes of old women throw down their wrinkles, and several young ones who stripped themselves of a tawny skin. There were very great heaps of red noses, large lips, and rusty teeth. The truth of it is, I was surprised to see the greatest part of the mountain made up of bodily deformities. Observing one advancing toward the heap, with a larger cargo than ordinary upon his back, I found upon his near approach that it was only a natural hump, which he disposed of, with great joy of heart, among this collection of human miseries. There were likewise distempers of all sorts, though I could not but observe, that there were many more imaginary than real. One little packet I could not but take notice of, which was a complication of all the diseases incident to human nature, and was in the hand of a great many fine people: this was called the Spleen. But what most of all surprised me was a remark I made, that there was not a single vice or folly thrown into the whole heap: at which I was very much astonished, having concluded within myself, that every one would take this opportunity of getting rid of his passions, prejudices, and frailties.

I took notice in particular of a very profligate fellow, who I did not question came loaded with his crimes; but upon searching into his bundle, I found that instead of throwing his guilt from him, he had only laid down his memory. He was followed by another worthless rogue, who flung away his modesty instead of his ignorance.

When the whole race of mankind, had thus cast their burdens, the phantom which had been so busy on this occasion, seeing me an idle spectator of what had passed, approached toward me. I grew uneasy at her presence, when of a sudden she held her magnifying glass full before my eyes. I no sooner saw my face in it, but was startled at the shortness of it, which now appeared to me in its utmost aggravation. The immoderate breadth of the features made me very much out of humour with my own countenance, upon which I threw it from me like a mask. It happened very luckily, that one who stood by me had just before thrown down his visage, which, it seems, was too long for him. It was indeed extended to a most shameful length; I believe the very chin was, modestly speaking, as long as my whole face. We had both of us an opportunity of mending ourselves; and all the contributions being now brought in, every man was at liberty to exchange his misfortunes for those of another person.

As we stood round the heap, and surveyed the several materials of which it was composed, there was scarce a mortal in this vast multitude, who did not discover what he thought pleasures and blessings of life; and wondered how the owners of them ever came to look upon them as burbens and grievances.

As we were regarding very attentively this confusion of miseries, this chaos of calamity, Jupiter issued out a second proclamation, that every one was now at liberty to exchange his affliction, and to return to his habitation with any such other bundle as should be delivered to him.

Upon this, Fancy began again to bestir herself, and parcelling out the whole heap with incredible activity, recommending to every one his particular packet. The hurry and confusion at this time was not to be expressed. Some observations, which I made upon the occasion, I shall communicate to the public. A venerable grey-headed man, who had laid down the cholic, and who, I found, wanted an heir to his estate, snatched up an undutiful son, that had been thrown into the heap by his angry father. The graceless youth, in less than a quarter of an hour, pulled the old gentleman by the beard, and had like to have knocked his brains out; so that the true father, who came toward him with a fit of the gripes, he begged him to take his son again, and give him back his cholic; but they were incapable either of them to recede from the choice he had made. A poor galley-slave, who had thrown down his chains, took up the gout in their stead, but made such wry faces, that one might easily perceive he was no great gainer by the bargain. It was pleasant enough to see the several exchanges that were made, for sickness against poverty, hunger against want of appetite, and care against pain.

The female world were very busy among themselves in bartering for features: one was trucking a lock of grey hairs for a carbuncle, another was making over a short waist for a pair of round shoulders, and a third cheapening a bad face for a lost reputation: but on all these occasions there was not one of them who did not think the new blemish, as soon as she had got it into her possession, much more disagreeable than the old one. I made the same observation on every other misfortune or calamity, which every one in the assembly brought upon himself in lieu of what he had parted with; whether it be that all the evils which befall us are in some measure suited and proportioned to our strength, or that every evil becomes more supportable by our being accustomed to it, I shall not determine.

I could not from my heart forbear pitying the poor hump-backed gentleman, who went off a very well-shaped person with a stone in his bladder: nor the fine gentleman who had struck up this bargain with him, that limped through a whole assembly of ladies, who used to admire him, with a pair of shoulders peeping over his head.

I must not omit my own particular adventure. My friend with a long visage had no sooner taken upon him my short face, but he made such a grotesque figure in it, that as I looked upon him I could not forbear laughing at myself, insomuch that I put my own face out of countenance. The poor gentleman was so sensible of the ridicule, that I found he was ashamed of what he had done: on the other side, I found that I myself had no great reason to triumph, for as I went to touch my forehead I missed the place, and clapped my finger upon my upper lip. Besides, as my nose was exceedingly prominent, I gave it two or three unlucky knocks as I was playing my hand about my face, and aiming at some other part of it. I saw two other gentlemen by me, who were in the same ridiculous circumstances. These had made a foolish swop between a couple of thick bandy legs, and two long trapsticks that had no calves to them. One of these looked like a man walking upon stilts, and was so lifted up in the air, above his ordinary height, that his head turned round with it, while the other made such awkward circles, as he attempted to walk, that he scarce knew how to move forward upon his new supporters. Observing him to be a pleasant kind of fellow, I stuck my cane in the ground, and told him I would lay him a bottle of wine that he did not march up to it on a line, that I drew for him, in a quarter of an hour.

The heap was at last distributed among the two sexes, who made a most piteous sight, as they wandeıed up and down under the pressure of their several burdens. The whole plain was filled with murmurs and complaints, groans and lamentations Jupiter at length taking compassion on the poor mortals, ordered them a second time to lay down their loads, with a design to give every one his own again. They discharged themselves with a great deal of pleasure; after which, the phantom, who had led them into such gross delusions, was commanded to disappear. There was sent in her stead a goddess of quite different figure: her motions were steady and composed, and her aspect serious but cheerful. She every now and then cast her eyes toward heaven, and fixed them upon Jupiter: her name was Patience. She had no sooner placed herself by the Mount of Sorrows, but, what I thought very remarkable, the whole heap sunk to such a degree, that it did not appear a third part so big as it was before. She afterwards returned every man his own proper calamity, and teaching him how to bear it in the most commodious manner, he marched off with it contentedly, being very well pleassd that he had not been left to his own choice, as to the kind of evils which fell to his lot.

Besides the several pieces of morality to be drawn out of this vision, I learnt from it, never to repine at my own misfortunes, or to envy the happiness of another, since it is impossible for any man to form a right judgment of his neighbour's sufferings; for which reason also I am determined never to think too lightly of another's complaints, but to regard the sorrows of my fellow-creatures with sentiments of humanity and compassion

CONTENTMENT.

Non possidentem multa vocaveris
Recte beatum: rectius occupat
Nomen beati, qui deorum
Muneribus sapientur uti,
Duramque callet pauperiem pati. HOR.

Believe not those that lands possess,
And shining heaps of useless ore,
The only lords of happiness;
But rather those that know,
For what kind fates bestow,
And have the art to use the store:
And have the generous skill to bear
The hated weight of poverty. CREECH.

I WAS once engaged in discourse with a Rosicrucian about "the great secret." As this kind of men (I mean those of them who are not professed cheats) are over-run with enthusiasm and philosophy, it was very amusing to hear this religious adept descanting on his pretended discovery. He talked of the secret as of a spirit which lived within an emerald, and converted every thing that was near it to the highest perfection it is capable of, "It gives a lustre," says he, "to the sun, and water to the diamond. It irradiates every metal, and enriches lead with all the properties of gold. It heightens smoke into flame, flame into light, and light into glory." He further added, "that a single ray of it dissipates pain, and care, and melancholy, from the person on whom it falls. In short," says he, "its presence naturally changes every place into a kind of heaven." After he had gone on for some time in this unintelligible cant, I found that he jumbled natural and moral ideas together in the same discourse, and that his great secret was nothing else but content.

This virtue does indeed produce, in some measure, all those effects which the alchymist usually ascribes to what he calls the philosopher's stone; and if it does not bring riches, it does the same thing, by banishing the desire of them. If it cannot remove the disquietudes arising out of a man's mind, body, or fortune, it makes him easy under them. It has indeed a kindly influence on the soul of man, in respect of every being to whom he stands related. It extinguishes all murmur, repining, and ingratitude toward that Being who has allotted him his part to act in this world. It destroys all inordinate ambition, and every tendency to corruption, with regard to the community wherein he is placed. It gives sweetness to his conversation, and a perpetual serenity to all his thoughts.

Among the many methods which might be made use of for the acquiring of this virtue, I shall only mention the two following. First of all, a man should always consider how much he has more than he wants; and, secondly, How much more unhappy he might be than he really is.

First of all, a man should always consider how much he has more than he wants. I am wonderfully pleased with the reply which Aristippus made to one who condoled him upon the loss of a farm: "Why," said he, "I have three farms still, and you have but one; so that I ought rather to be afflicted for you, than you for me." On the contrary, foolish men are more apt to consider what they have lost than what they possess; and to fix their eyes upon those who are richer than themselves, rather than on those who are under greater difficulties. All the real pleasures and conveniences of life lie in a narrow compass; but it is the humour of mankind to be always looking forward, and straining after one who has got the start of them in wealth and honour. For this reason, as there are none that can properly be called rich, who have not more than they want: there are few rich men in any of the politer nations but among the middle sort of people, who keep their wishes within their fortunes, and have more wealth than they know how to enjoy. Persons of a higher rank live in a kind of splendid poverty, and are perpetually wanting, because, instead of acquiescing in the solid pleasures of life, they endeavour to outvie one another in shadows and appearances. Men of sense have at all times beheld with a great deal of mirth this silly game that is playing over their heads and by contracting their desires, enjoy all that secret satisfaction, which others are always in quest of. The truth is, this ridiculous chase after imaginary pleasures cannot be sufficiently exposed, as it is the great source of those evils which generally undo a nation. Let a man's estate be what it will, he is a poor man if he does not live within it, and naturally sets himself to sale to any one that can give him his price. When Pittacus, after the death of his brother, who had left a good estate, was offered a great sum of money by the King of Lydia, he thanked him for his kindness, but told him he had more by half than he knew what to do with. In short, content is equivalent to wealth, and luxury to poverty; or, to give the thought a more agreeable turn, "Content is natural wealth," says Socrates: to which I shall add, "Luxury is artificial poverty." I shall therefore recommend to the consideration of those who are always aiming after superfluous and imaginary enjoyments, and will not be at the trouble of contracting their desires, an excellent saying of Bion the philosopher; namely, "That no man has so much care, as he who endeavours after the most happiness."

In the second place, every one ought to reflect how much more unhappy he might be than he really is. The former consideration took in all those who are sufficiently provided with the means to make themselves easy. This regards such as actually lie under some pressure or misfortune. These may receive great alleviation from such a comparison as the unhappy person may make between himself and others, or between the misfortunes which he suffers, and greater misfortunes which might have befallen him.

I like the story of the honest Dutchman, who, upon breaking his leg by a fall from the mainmast, told the standers-by, it was a great mercy that it was not his neck. To which, since I am got into quotations, give me leave to add the saying of an old philosopher, who after having invited some of his friends to dine with him, was ruffled by his wife that came into the room in a passion, and threw down the table that stood before them; "Every one," says he, "has his calamity, and he is a happy man that has no greater than this." We find an instance to the same purpose in the Life of Dr. Hammond, written by Bishop Fell. As this good man was troubled with a complication of distempers, when he had the gout upon him, he used to thank God that it was not the stone; and when he had the stone, that he had not both these distempers on him at the same time.

I cannot conclude this essay without observing that there was never any system besides that of Christianity, which could effectually produce in the mind of man the virtue I have been hitherto speaking of. In order to make us content with our present condition, many of the ancient philosophers tell us that our discontent only hurts ourselves, without ever being able to make any alteration in our circumstances; others, that whatever evil befalls us is derived to us by a fatal necessity, to which the gods themselves are subject; while others very gravely tell the man who is miserable, that it is necessary he should be so to keep up the harmony of the universe, and that the scheme of Providence would be troubled and perverted were he otherwise. These, and the like considerations, rather silence than satisfy a man. They may show him that his discontent is unreasonable, but are by no means sufficient to relieve it. They rather give despair than consolation. In a word, a man might reply to one of these comforters, as Augustus did to his friend, who advised him not to grieve for the death of a person whom he loved, because his grief could not fetch him again: "It is for that very reason," said the Emperor, "that I grieve."

On the contrary, religion bears a more tender regard to human nature. It prescribes to every miserable man the means of bettering his condition; nay, it shows him that the bearing of his afflictions as he ought to do will naturally end in the removal of them; it makes him easy here, because it can make him happy hereafter.

Upon the whole, a contented mind is the greatest blessing a man can enjoy in this world; and if in the present life his happiness arises from the subduing of his desires, it will arise in the next from the gratification of them.

THE POINT OF HONOUR AMONG MEN AND WOMEN.

Turpi secernis honestum. HOR.

You know to fix the bounds of right and wrong.

I SHALL methodize here several reflections upon what passes for the chief point of honour among men and women.

The great point of honour in men is courage, and in women chastity. If a man loses his honour in one rencounter, it is not impossible for him to regain it in another; a slip in a woman's honour is irrecoverable. I can give no reason for fixing the point of honour to these two qualities, unless it be that each sex sets the greatest value on the qualification which renders them the most amiable in the eyes of the contrary sex. Had men chosen for themselves, without regard to the opinions of the fair sex, I should believe the choice would have fallen on wisdom or virtue; or had women determined their own point of honour, it is probable that wit or good-nature would have carried it against chastity.

Nothing recommends a man more to the female sex than courage;* whether it be that they are pleased to see one who is a terror to others fall like a slave at their feet, or that this quality supplies their own principal defect, in guarding them from insults, and avenging their quarrels; or that courage is a natural indica-

* Fielding has happily and admirably illustrated this observation, in that chapter of his Tom Jones in which the hero breaks his arm in saving Sophia Western.

son of a strong and sprightly constitution. On the other side, nothing makes woman more esteemed by the opposite sex than chastity; whether it be that we always prize those most who are hardest to come at, or that nothing besides chastity, with its collateral attendants, truth, fidélity, and constancy, gives the man a property in the person he loves, and consequently endears her to him above all things.

I am very much pleased with a passage in the inscription on a monument erected in Westminster Abbey to the late Duke and Dutchess of Newcastle. "Her name was Margaret Lucas, youngest sister to the Lord Lucas of Colchester; a noble family, for all the brothers were valiant, and all the sisters virtuous."

In books of chivalry, where the point of honour is strained to madness, the whole story runs on chastity and courage. The damsel is mounted on a white palfrey, as an emblem of her innocence; and, to avoid scandal, must have a dwarf for her page. She is not to think of a man, until some misfortune has brought a knight errant to her relief. The knight falls in love, and did not gratitude restrain her from murdering her deliverer, would die at her feet by her disdain. However, he must wait many years in the desert, before her virgin-heart can think of a surrender. The knight goes off, attacks every thing he meets that is bigger and stronger than himself, seeks all opportunities of being knocked on the head, and after seven years rambling, returns to his mistress, whose chastity has been attacked in the mean time by giants and tyrants, and undergone as many trials as her lover's valour.

In Spain, where there are still great remains of this romantic humour, it is a transporting favour for a lady to cast an accidental glance on her lover from a window, though it be two or three stories high: as it is usual for the lover to assert his passion for his mistress, in single combat with a mad bull.

The great violation of the point of honour from man to man, is giving the lie. One may tell another he whores, drinks, blasphemes, and it may pass unresented; but to say he lies, though but in jest, is an affront that nothing but blood can expiate. The reason perhaps may be, because no other vice implies a want of courage, so much as the making of a lie; and therefore telling a man he lies, is touching him in the most sensible part of honour, and indirectly calling him a coward. I cannot omit under this head what Herodotus tells us of the ancient Persians, that from the age of five years to twenty they instruct their sons only in three things: to manage the horse, to make use of the bow, and to speak truth.

The placing the point of honour in this false kind of courage, has given occasion to the very refuse of mankind, who have neither virtue nor common sense, to set up for men of honour. An English peer, who has not been long dead, used to tell a pleasant story of a French gentleman that visited him early one morning at Paris, and after great professions of respect, let him know that he had it in his power to oblige him; which, in short, amounted to this, that he believed he could tell his lordship the person's name who jostled him as he came out from the opera; but before he would proceed, he begged his lordship, that he would not deny him the honour of making him his second. The English lord, to avoid being drawn into a very foolish affair, told him that he laid under engagements for his two next duels to a couple of particular friends. Upon which the gentleman immediately withdrew, hoping his lordship would not take it ill if he meddled no further in an affair from which he himself was to receive no advantage.

The beating down this false notion of honour, in so vain and lively people as those of France, is deservedly looked upon as one of the most glorious parts of their present king's reign. It is a pity but the punishment of these mischievous notions should have in it some particular circumstances of shame and infamy, that those who are slaves to them may see, that instead of advancing their reputation, they lead them to ignominy and dishonour.

Death is not sufficient to deter men who make it their glory to despise it; but if every one that fought a duel were to stand in the pillory, it would quickly lessen the number of these imaginary men of honour, and put an end to so absurd a practice.

When honour is a support to virtuous principles, and runs parallel with the laws of God and of our country, it cannot be too much cherished and encouraged; but when the dictates of honour are contrary to those of religion and equity, they are the greatest depravations of human nature, and should be exploded, and driven out as the bane and plague of human society. *L.*

MEN GREAT IN THEIR DYING MOMENTS.

——————Quos ille timorum
Maximus haud urget lethi metus: inde ruendi
In ferrum mens prona viris, animæque capaces
Mortis—— LUCAN.

Thrice happy they beneath their northern skies,
Who that worst fear, the fear of death despise!
Hence they no cares for this frail being feel,
But rush undaunted on the pointed steel,
Provoke approaching fate, and bravely scorn
To spare that life which must so soon return.
ROWE.

I AM very much pleased with a consolatory letter of Phalaris, to one who had lost a son that was a young man of great merit. The thought with which he comforts the afflicted father is, to the best of my memory, as follows: That he should consider death had set a kind of seal upon his son's character, and placed him out of the reach of vice and infamy: that while he lived he was still within the possibility of falling away from virtue, and losing the fame of which he was possessed. Death only closes a man's reputation, and determines it as good or bad.

This, among other motives, may be one reason why we are naturally averse to the launching out into a man's praise till his head is laid in the dust. Whilst he is capable of changing, we may be forced to retract our opinions. He may forfeit the esteem we have conceived of him, and some time or other appear to us under a different light from what he does at present. In short, as the life of any man cannot be called happy or unhappy, so neither can it be pronounced vicious or virtuous, before the conclusion of it.

It was upon this consideration that Epaminondas, being asked whether Chabrias, Iphicrates, or he himself, deserved most to be esteemed? you must first see us die, said he, before that question can be answered.

As there is not a more melancholy consideration to a good man than his being obnoxious to such a change, so there is nothing more glorious than to keep up an uniformity in his actions, and preserve the beauty of his character to the last

The end of a man's life is often compared to the winding up of a well-written play, where the principal persons still act in character, whatever the fate is which they undergo. There is scarce a great person in the Grecian or Roman history, whose death has not been remarked upon by some writer or other, and censured or applauded according to the genius or principles of the person who has descanted on it. Monsieur de St. Evremont is very particular in setting forth the constancy and courage of Petronius Arbiter during his last moments, and thinks he discovers in them a greater firmness of mind and resolution than in the death of Seneca, Cato, or Socrates. There is no question but this polite author's affectation of appearing singular in his remarks, and making discoveries which had escaped the observation of others, threw him into this course of reflection. It was Petronius's merit, that he died in the same gayety of temper in which he lived; but as his life was altogether loose and dissolute, the indifference which he showed at the close of it is to be looked upon as a natural carelessness and levity, rather than fortitude. The resolution of Socrates proceeded from very different motives, the consciousness of a well-spent life, and the prospect of a happy eternity. If the ingenious author above-mentioned was so pleased with gayety of humour in a dying man, he might have found a much nobler instance of it in our contryman, Sir Thomas More

This great and learned man was famous for enlivening his ordinary discourses with wit and pleasantry: and, as Erasmus tells him in an epistle dedicatory, acted in all parts of life like a second Democritus.

He died upon a point of religion, and is respected as a martyr by that side for which he suffered. That innocent mirth which had been so conspicuous in his life did not forsake him to the last; he maintained the same cheerfulness of heart upon the scaffold which he used to show at his table; and, upon laying his head on the block, gave instances of that good humour with which he had always entertained his friends in the most ordinary occurrences. His death was of a piece with his life: there was nothing in it new, forced, or affected. He did not look upon the severing his head from his body as a circumstance that ought to produce any change in the disposition of his mind; and as he died under a fixed and settled hope of immortality, he thought any unusual degree of sorrow and concern improper on such an occasion, as had nothing in it which could deject or terrify him.

There is no great danger of imitation from this example: men's natural fears will be a sufficient guard against it. I shall only observe, that what was philosophy in this extraordinary man would be a phrenzy in one who does not resemble him as well in the cheerfulness of his temper, as in the sanctity of his life and manners.

I shall conclude this paper with the instance of a person who seems to me to have shown more intrepidity and greatness of soul in his dying moments, than what we meet with among any of the most celebrated Greeks and Romans. I met with this instance in the History of the Revolutions in Portugal, written by the Abbot de Vertot

When Don Sebastian, King of Portugal, had invaded the territories of Muley Moluc, Emperor of Morocco, in order to dethrone him, and set his crown upon the head of his nephew, Moluc was wearing away with a distemper which he himself knew was incurable. However, he prepared for the reception of so formidable an enemy. He was indeed so far spent with his sickness, that he did not expect to live out the whole day, when the last decisive battle was given; but knowing the fatal consequences that would happen to his children and people, in case he should die before he put an end to that war, he commanded his principal officers, that, if he died during the engagement, they should conceal his death from the army, and that they should ride up to the litter, in which his corpse was carried, under pretence of receiving orders from him as usual. Before the battle begun, he was carried through all the ranks of his army in an open litter, as they stood drawn up in array, encouraging them to fight valiantly in defence of their religion and country. Finding afterwards the battle to go against him, though he was very near his last agonies, he threw himself out of his litter, rallied his army, and led them on to the charge; which afterwards ended in a complete victory on the side of the Moors. He had no sooner brought his men to the engagement, but, finding himself utterly spent, he was again replaced in his litter; where, laying his finger on his mouth, to enjoin secrecy to his officers, who stood about him, he died a few moments after in that posture.

L.

A QUAKER IN A STAGE-COACH.

—*Qui, aut tempus quid postulet non videt, aut piura loquitur, aut se ostentat, aut eorum quibuscum est rationem non habet, is ineptus esse dicitur.* TULL.

That man is guilty of impertinence, who considers not the circumstances of time, or engrosses the conversation, or makes himself the subject of his discourse, or pays no regard to the company he is in.

HAVING notified to my good friend Sir —— that I should set out for London the next day, his horses were ready at the appointed hour in the evening; and, attended by one of his grooms, I arrived at the county town at twilight, in order to be ready for the stage-coach the day following. As soon as we arrived at the inn, the servant, who waited upon me, inquired of the chamberlain in my hearing what company he had for the coach? The fellow answered, Mrs. Betty Arable, the great fortune, and the widow her mother; a recruiting officer, who took a place because they were to go; young Squire Qickset her cousin, that her mother wished her to be married to; and Ephraim, the Quaker, her guardian. I observed by what he had said, that according to his office he dealt much in intelligence; and doubted not but there was some foundation for his reports of the company. The next morning at day-break we were all called; and I, who know my own natural shyness, and endeavour to be as little liable to be disputed with as possible, dressed immediately, that I might make no one wait. The first preparation for our setting-out was, that the captain's half-pike was placed near the coach-man, and a drum behind the coach. In the mean time the drummer, the captain's equipage, was very loud, that none of the captain's things should be placed so as to be spoiled; upon which the cloak-bag was fixed in the seat of the coach: and the captain himself, according to a frequent, though invidious behaviour of military men, ordered his man to look sharp, that none but one of the ladies would have the place he had taken fronting the coach-box.

We were in some little time fixed in our seats, and sat with that dislike which people not too good-natured usually conceive of each other at first sight. The coach jumbled us insensibly into some sort of familiarity: and we had not moved above two miles, when the widow asked the captain what success he had in his recruiting? The officer, with a frankness he believed very graceful, told her, "that indeed he had but very little luck, and had suffered much by desertion, therefore should be glad to end his warfare in the service of her or her fair daughter. In a word," continued he, "I am a soldier, and to be plain is my character; you see me, madam, young, sound, and impudent: take me yourself, widow, or give me to her; I will be wholly at your disposal. I am a soldier of fortune, ha!" This was followed by a vain laugh of his own, and a deep silence of all the rest of the company. "Come," said he, "resolve upon it, we will make a wedding at next town: we will awake this pleasant companion who is fallen asleep to be the brideman, and," giving the quaker a clap on the knee, he concluded, "this sly saint, who, I will warrant, understands what is what as well as you or I, widow, shall give the bride as father." The quaker, who happened to be a man of smartness, answered, "Friend, I take it in good part that thou hast given me the authority of a father over this comely and virtuous child; and I must assure thee, that if I have the giving her, I shall not bestow her on thee. Thy mirth, friend, savoureth of folly: thou art a person of a light mind; thy drum is a type of thee, it soundeth because it is empty. Verily, it is not from thy fulness, but thy emptiness that thou hast spoken this day. Friend, friend, we have hired this coach in partnership with thee, to carry us to the great city: we cannot go any other way. This worthy mother must hear thee if thou wilt needs utter thy follies; we cannot help it, friend, I say: if thou wilt, we must hear thee; but if thou wert a man of understanding, thou wouldst not take advantage of thy courageous countenance to abash us children of peace. Thou art thou sayest, a soldier; give quarter to us, who cannot resist thee. Why didst thou fleer at our friend, who feigned himself asleep, and said nothing; but how dost thou know what he containeth? If thou speakest improper things in the hearing of this virtuous young virgin, consider it is an outrage against a distressed person that cannot get from thee: to speak indiscreetly what we are obliged to hear, by being hasped up with thee in this public vehicle, is in some degree assaulting on the high road."

Here Ephraim paused, and the captain, with an unhappy and uncommon impudence, which can be convicted and support itself at the same time, cries, "Faith, friend, I thank thee; I should have been a little impertinent if thou hadst not reprimanded me. Come, thou art, I see, a smoky old fellow, and I will be very orderly the ensuing part of my journey. I was going to give myself airs, but, ladies, I beg pardon."

The captain was so little out of humour, and our company was so far from being soured by this little ruffle, that Ephraim and he took a particular delight in being agreeable to each other for the future; and assumed their different provinces in the conduct of the company. Our reckonings, apartments, and accommodation, fell under Ephraim; and the captain looked to all disputes on the road, as the good behaviour of our coachman, and the right we had of taking place as going to London of all vehicles coming from thence. The occurrences we met with were ordinary, and very little happened which could entertain by the relation of them; but when I considered the company we were in, I took it for no small good fortune that the whole journey was not spent in impertinences, which to the one part of us might be an entertainment, to the other a suffering. What therefore Ephraim said when we were almost arrived at London, had to me an air not only of good understanding but good breeding. Upon the young lady's expressing her satisfaction in the journey, and declaring how delightful it had been to her, Ephraim delivered himself as follows: There is no ordinary part of human life which expresseth so much a good mind, and a right inward man, as his behaviour upon meeting with strangers, especially such as may seem the most unsuitable companions to him: such a man, when he falleth in the way with persons of simplicity and innocence, however knowing he may be in the ways of men, will not vaunt himself thereof but will the rather hide his superiority to them, that he may not be painful unto them. My good friend," continued he, turning to the officer, "thee and I are to part by and by, and peradventure we may never meet again: but be advised by a plain man; modes and apparel are but trifles to the real man, therefore do not think such a man as thyself terrible for thy garb, nor such a one as me contemptible for mine. When two such as thee and I meet, with affections as we ought to have toward each other, thou shouldst rejoice to see my peaceful demeanour, and I should be glad to see thy strength and ability to protect me in it." *T.*

QUALITIES OF A MAN IN PLACE.

Detrahere aliquid alteri, et hominem hominis incommodo suum augere commodum, magis est contra naturam, quam mors, quam paupertas, quam dolor, quam cætera quæ possunt aut corpori accidere, aut rebus externis. TULL.

To detract from other men, and turn their disadvantages to our own profit, is more contrary to nature than death, poverty, or grief, or any thing which can affect our bodies or external circumstances,

I AM persuaded there are few men, of generous principles who would seek after great places, were it not rather to have an opportunity in their hands of obliging their particular friends, or those whom they look upon as men of worth, than to procure wealth and honour for themselves. To an honest mind the best perquisites of a place are the advantages it gives a man of doing good.

Those who are under the great officers of state, and are the instruments by which they act, have more frequent opportunities for the exercise of compassion and benevolence than their superiors themselves. These men know every little case that is to come before the great man, and if they are possessed with honest minds, will consider poverty as a recommendation in the person who applies himself to them, and make the justice of his cause the most powerful solicitor in his behalf. A man of this temper, when he is in a post of business, becomes a blessing to the public: he patronizes the orphan and the widow, assists the friendless, and guides the ignorant · he does not reject the person's pretensions, who does not know how to explain them, or refuse doing a good office for a man because he cannot pay the fee of it. In short, though he regulates himself in all proceedings by justice and equity, he finds a thousand occasions for all the good-natured offices of generosity and compassion.

A man is unfit for such a place of trust, who is of a sour untractable nature, or has any other passion that makes him uneasy to those who approach him. Roughness of temper is apt to discountenance the timorous or modest. The proud man discourages those from approaching him, who are of a mean condition, and who most want his assistance. The impatient man will not give himself time to be informed of the matter that lies before him. An officer with one or more of these unbecoming qualities, is sometimes looked upon as a proper person to keep off impertinence and solicitation from his superior; but this is a kind of merit that can never atone for the injustice which may very often arise from it.

There are two other vicious qualities which render a man very unfit for such a place of trust. The first of these is a dilatory temper, which commits innumerable cruelties without design. The maxim which several have laid down for a man's conduct in ordinary life, should be inviolable with a man in office, never to think of doing that to-morrow which may be done to-day. A man who defers doing what ought to be done, is guilty of injustice so long as he defers it. The despatch of a good office is very often as beneficial to the solicitor as the good office itself. In short, if a man compared the inconveniencies which another suffers by his delays, with the trifling motives and advantages which he himself may reap by such a delay, he would never be guilty of a fault which very often does an irreparable prejudice to the person who depends upon him, and which might be remedied with little trouble to himself.

But in the last place, there is no man so improper to be employed in business, as he who is in any degree capable of corruption; and such an one is the man, who upon any pretence whatsoever, receives more than what is the stated and unquestioned fee of his office. Gratifications, tokens of thankfulness, despatch money, and the like specious terms, are the pretences under which corruption very frequently shelters itself. An honest man will however look on all these methods as unjustifiable, and will enjoy himself better in a moderate fortune that is gained with honour and reputation, than in an overgrown estate that is cankered with the acquisitions of rapine and exaction. Were all our offices discharged with such an inflexible integrity, we should not see men in all ages, who grow up to exorbitant wealth with the abilities which are to be met with in an ordinary mechanic. I cannot but think that such a corruption proceeds chiefly from men's employing the first that offer themselves, or those who have the character of shrewd worldly men, instead of searching out such as have had a liberal education, and have been trained up in the studies of knowledge and virtue.

It has been observed, that men of learning who take to business, discharge it generally with greater honesty than men of the world. The chief reason for it I take to be as follows: A man that has spent his youth in reading, has been used to find virtue extolled, and vice stigmatized. A man that has passed his time in the world, has often seen vice triumphant, and virtue discountenanced. Extortion, rapine, and injustice, which are branded with infamy in books, often give a man a figure in the world; while several qualities which are celebrated in authors, as generosity, ingenuity, and good nature, impoverish and ruin him. This cannot but have a proportionable effect on men, whose tempers and principles are equally good and vicious.

There would be at least this advantage in employing men of learning and parts in business, that their prosperity would set more gracefully on them, and that we should not see many worthless persons shot up into the greatest figures of life.

C.

FIDELIA;

OR,

THE DUTIFUL DAUGHTER.

——*Tibi scriptus, matrona, libellus.*
MART.

A book the chasest matron may peruse.

SHE who shall lead the small illustrious number of my female heroines shall be the amiable Fidelia.

Before I enter upon the particular parts of her character, it is necessary to preface, that she is the only child of a decrepit father, whose life is bound up in her's. This gentleman has used Fidelia from her cradle with all the tenderness imaginable, and has viewed her growing perfections with the partiality of a parent, that soon thought her accomplished above the children of all other men, but never thought she was come to the utmost improvement of which she herself was capable. This fondness has had very happy effects upon his own happiness, for she reads, she dances, she sings, uses her spinnet and lute to the utmost perfection: and the lady's use of all these excellencies is, to divert the old man in his easy chair when he is out of the pangs of a chronical distemper. Fidelia is now in the twenty-third year of her age; but the application of many lovers, her vigorous time of life, her quick sense of all that is truly gallant and elegant in the enjoyment of a plentiful fortune, are not able to draw her from the side of her good old father. Certain it is, that there is no kind of affection so pure and angelic as that of a father to a daughter. He beholds her both with and without regard to her sex. In love to our wives there is desire, to our sons there is ambition; but in that to our daughters, there is something which there are no words to express. Her life is designed wholly domestic, and she is so ready a friend and companion, that every thing that passes about a man, is accompanied with the idea of her presence. Her sex also is naturally so much exposed to hazard, both as to fortune and innocence, that there is, perhaps, a new cause of fondness arising from that consideration also. None but fathers can have a true sense of these sort of pleasures and sensations; but my familiarity with the father of Fidelia, makes me let drop the words which I have heard him speak, and observe upon his tenderness toward her.

Fidelia, on her part, as I was going to say, as accomplished as she is, with all her beauty, wit, air, and mien, employs her whole time in care and attendance upon her father. How have I been charmed to see one of the most beauteous women the age has produced on her knees helping on an old man's slipper! Her filial regard for him is what she makes her diversion, her business, and her glory. When she was asked by a friend of her deceased mother to admit of the courtship of her son, she answered, That she had a great respect and gratitude to her for the overture in behalf of one so near to her, but that during her father's life, she should admit into her heart no value for any thing that should interfere with her endeavour to make his remains of life as happy and easy as could be expected in his circumstances. The lady admonished her of the prime of life with a smile; which Fidelia answered with a frankness that always attends unfeigned virtue. "It is true, madam, there is to be sure very great satisfaction to be expected in the commerce of a man of honour, whom one tenderly loves; but I find so much satisfaction in the reflection, how much I mitigate a good man's pains, whose welfare depends upon my assiduity about him, that I willingly exclude the loose gratifications of passion for the solid reflections of duty. I know not whether any man's wife would be allowed, and (what I still more fear) I know not whether I, a wife, should be willing to be as officious as I am at present about my parent." The happy father has her declaration that she will not marry during his life, and the pleasure of seeing that resolution not uneasy to her. Were one to paint filial affection in its utmost beauty, he could not have a more lively idea of it than in beholding Fidelia serving her father at his hours of rising, meals, and rest.

When the general crowd of female youth are consulting their glasses, preparing for balls, assemblies, or plays; for a young lady, who could be regarded among the foremost in those places, either for her person, wit, fortune, or conversation, and yet contemn all these entertainments, to sweeten the heavy hours of a decrepit parent, is a resignation truly heroic. Fidelia performs the duty of a nurse with all the beauty of a bride; nor does she neglect her person, because of her attendance on him, when he is too ill to receive company, to whom she may make an appearance.

Fidelia, who gives him up her youth, does not think it any great sacrifice to add to it the spoiling of her dress. Her care and exactness in her habit, convince her father of the alacrity of her mind; and she has of all women the best foundation for affecting the praise of a seeming negligence. What adds to the entertainment of the good old man is, that Fidelia, where merit and fortune cannot be overlooked by epistolary lovers reads over the accounts of her conquests, plays on her spinet the gayest airs, (and while she is doing so you would think her formed only for gallantry) to intimate to him the pleasures she despises for his sake.

Those who think themselves the patterns of good breeding and gallantry, would be astonished to hear, that in those intervals when the old gentleman is at ease, and can bear company, there are at his house, in the most regular order, assemblies of people of the highest merit; where there is conversation without mention of the faults of the absent, benevolence between men and women without passion, and the highest subjects of morality treated of as a natural and accidental discourse; all which is owing to the genius of Fidelia, who at once makes her father's way to another world easy, and herself capable of being an honour to his name in this.

T.

FRIENDSHIP.

Nos duo turba sumus——

OVID. Met. i. 355.

"We two are a multitude."

One would think that the larger the company is in which we are engaged, the greater variety of thoughts and subjects would be started in discourse; but instead of this, we find that conversation is never so much straitened and confined as in numerous assemblies. When a multitude meet together on any subject of discourse, their debates are taken up chiefly with forms and general positions; nay, if we come into a more contracted assembly of men and women, the talk generally runs upon the weather, fashions, news, and the like public topics. In proportion as conversation gets into clubs and knots of friends, it descends into particulars, and grows more free and communicative; but the most open, instructive, and unreserved discourse, is that which passes between two persons who are familiar and intimate friends. On these occasions, a man gives a loose to every passion and every thought that is uppermost, discovers his most retired opinions of persons and things, tries the beauty and strength of his sentiments, and exposes his whole soul to the examination of his friend.

Tully was the first who observed, that friendship improves happiness and abates misery, by the doubling of our joy, and dividing of our grief; a thought in which he hath been followed by all the essayers upon Friendship, that have written since his time. Sir Francis Bacon has finely described other advantages, or, as he calls them, fruits of friendship; and, indeed, there is no subject of morality which has been better handled and more exhausted than this. Among the several fine things which have been spoken of it, I shall beg leave to quote some out of a very ancient author whose book would be regarded by our modern wits as one of the most shining tracts of morality that is extant, if it appeared under the name of a Confucius, or of any celebrated Grecian philosopher: I mean the little apocryphal treatise, entitled, "The Wisdom of the son of Sirach." How finely has he described the "art of making friends," by an obliging and affable behaviour! And laid down that precept, which a late excellent author has delivered as his own, "That we should have many well-wishers, but few friends." —"Sweet language will multiply friends; and a fair-speaking tongue will increase kind greetings. Be in peace with many, nevertheless have but one counsellor of a thousand."* With what prudence does he caution us in the choice of our friends! And with what strokes of nature (I could almost say of humour) has he described the behaviour of a treacherous and self-interested friend! "If thou wouldst get a friend, prove him first, and be not hasty to credit him: for some man is a friend for his own occasion, and will

* Ecclus. vii. 5, 6.

not abide in the day of thy trouble. And there is a friend, who, being turned to enmity and strife, will discover thy reproach." Again: "Some friend is a companion at the table, and will not continue in the day of thy affliction: But in thy prosperity he will be as thyself, and will be bold over thy servants. If thou be brought low he will be against thee, and hide himself from thy face."* What can be more strong and pointed than the following verse? "Separate thyself from thine enemies, and take heed of thy friends." In the next words he particularizes one of those fruits of friendship which are described at length by the two famous authors above-mentioned, and falls into a general eulogium of friendship, which is very just as well as very sublime. "A faithful friend is a strong defence; and he that hath found such an one, hath found a treasure. Nothing doth countervail a faithful friend, and his excellency is invaluable. A faithful friend is the medicine of life; and they that fear the Lord shall find him. Whoso feareth the Lord shall direct his friendship aright; for as he is, so shall his neighbour (that is, his friend) be also."† I do not remember to have met with any saying that has pleased me more than that of a friend's being the medicine of life, to express the efficacy of friendship in healing the pains and anguish which naturally cleave to our existence in this world; and am wonderfully pleased with the turn in the last sentence, that a virtuous man shall as a blessing meet with a friend who is as virtuous as himself. There is another saying in the same author, which would have been very much admired in an heathen writer: "Forsake not an old friend, for the new is not comparable to him: a new friend is as new wine; when it is old thou shalt drink it with pleasure."‡ With what strength of allusion, and force of thought, has he described the breaches and violations of friendship! "Whoso casteth a stone at the birds, frayeth them away; and he that upbraideth his friend, breaketh friendship. Though thou drawest

* Ecclus. vi. 7, & seq. † Ibid. vi. 15—18. ‡ Ibid. ix. 10

a sword at a friend, yet despair not, for there may be a returning to favour. If thou hast opened thy mouth against thy friend, fear not, for there may be a reconciliation; except for upbraiding, or pride, or disclosing of secrets, or a treacherous wound; for, for these things every friend will depart."* We may observe in this and several other precepts in this author, those little familiar instances and illustrations which are so much admired in the moral writings of Horace and Epictetus. There are very beautiful instances of this nature in the following passages, which are likewise written upon the same subject: "Whoso discovereth secrets, loseth his credit, and shall never find a friend to his mind. Love thy friend, and be faithful unto him; but if thou bewrayest his secrets, follow no more after him; for as a man hath destroyed his enemy, so hast thou lost the love of thy friend; as one that letteth a bird go out of his hand, so hast thou let thy friend go, and shalt not get him again: follow after him no more, for he is too far off; he is as a roe escaped out of the snare. As for a wound it may be bound up, and after reviling there may be a reconciliation: but he that betrayeth secrets, is without hope."†

Among the several qualifications of a good friend, this wise man has very justly singled out constancy and faithfulness as the principal; to these, others have added virtue, knowledge, discretion, equality in age and fortune, and, as Cicero calls it, *morum comitas*, a pleasantness of temper. If I were to give my opinion upon such an exhausted subject, I should join to these other qualifications a certain equability or evenness of behaviour. A man often contracts a friendship with one whom perhaps he does not find out till after a year's conversation; when on a sudden some latent ill-humour breaks out upon him, which he never discovered or suspected at his first entering into an intimacy with him. There are several persons who in some certain periods of there lives are inexpressibly agreeable, and in others as odious and detes-

* Ecclus. ix. 20, 21, 22. † Ibid. xxvii. 16, & seq

table. Martial has given us a very pretty picture of one of this species, in the following epigram.

> *Difficilis, facilis, jucundus, acerbus es idem,*
> *Nec tecum possum vivere, nec sine te.*
> EPIG. xlvii. 12.

> "In all thy humours, whether grave or mellow,
> Thou'rt such a touchy, testy, pleasant fellow;
> Hast so much wit, and mirth, and spleen about thee,
> There is no living with thee, nor without thee."

It is very unlucky for a man to be entangled in a friendship with one, who by these changes and vicissitudes of humour, is sometimes amiable, and sometimes odious; and as most men are at some times in an admirable frame and disposition of mind, it should be one of the greatest tasks of wisdom to keep ourselves well when we are so, and never to go out of that which is the agreeable part of our character.

Friendship is a strong and habitual inclination in two persons to promote the good and happiness of one another. Though the pleasures and advantages of friendship have been largely celebrated by the best moral writers, and are considered by all as great ingredients of human happiness, we very rarely meet with the practice of this virtue in the world.

Every man is ready to give in a long catalogue of those virtues and good qualities he expects to find in the person of a friend, but very few of us are careful to cultivate them in ourselves.

Love and esteem are the first principles of friendship, which always is imperfect where either of these two is wanting.

As on the one hand, we are soon ashamed of loving a man whom we cannot esteem; so, on the other, though we are truly sensible of a man's abilities, we can never raise ourselves to the warmth of friendship, without an affectionate good-will toward his person.

Friendship immediately banishes envy under all its disguises. A man who can once doubt whether he should rejoice in his friend's being happier than him self, may depend upon it that he is an utter stranger to this virtue.

There is something in friendship so very great and noble, that in those fictitious stories which are invented to the honour of any particular person, the authors have thought it as necessary to make the hero a friend as a lover. Achilles has his Patroclus, and Æneas his Achates. In the first of these instances we may observe, for the reputation of the subject I am treating of, that Greece was almost ruined by the hero's love, but was preserved by his friendship.

The character of Achates suggests to us an observation we may often make on the intimacies of great men, who frequently choose their companions rather for the qualities of the heart than those of the head, and prefer fidelity in an easy inoffensive complying temper to those endowments which make a much greater figure among mankind. I do not remember that Achates, who is represented as the first favourite, either gives his advice, or strikes a blow, through the whole Æneid.

A friendship which makes the least noise, is very often most useful; for which reason I should prefer a prudent friend to a zealous one.

Atticus, one of the best men of ancient Rome, was a very remarkable instance of what I am here speaking. This extraordinary person, amidst the civil wars of his country, when he saw the designs of all parties equally tended to the subversion of liberty, by constantly preserving the esteem and affection of both the competitors, found means to serve his friends on either side: and while he sent money to young Marius, whose father was declared an enemy of the commonwealth, he was himself one of Sylla's chief favourites, and always near that general.

During the war between Cæsar and Pompey, he still maintained the same conduct. After the death of Cæsar he sent money to Brutus in his troubles, and did a thousand good offices to Antony's wife and friends when that party seemed ruined. Lastly, even in that bloody war between Antony and Augustus

Atticus still kept his place in both their friendships insomuch, that the first, says Cornelius Nepos, whenever he was absent from Rome in any part of the empire, writ punctually to him what he was doing, what he read, and whither he intended to go; and the latter gave him constantly an exact account of all his affairs.

A likeness of inclinations in every particular is so far from being requisite to form a benevolence in two minds toward each other, as it is generally imagined, that I believe we shall find some of the firmest friendships to have been contracted between persons of different humours: the mind being often pleased with those perfections which are new to it, and which it does not find among its own accomplishments. Besides that a man in some measure supplies his own defects, and fancies himself at second hand possessed of those good qualities and endowments, which are in the possession of him, who, in the eye of the world, is looked on as his other self.

The most difficult province in friendship is the letting a man see his faults and errors, which should, if possible, be so contrived that he may perceive our advice is given him, not so much to please ourselves, as for his own advantage. The reproaches therefore of a friend should always be strictly just, and not too frequent.

The violent desire of pleasing in the person reproved, may otherwise change into a despair of doing it, while he finds himself censured for faults he is not conscious of. A mind that is softened and humanized by friendship, cannot bear frequent reproaches; either it must quite sink under the oppression, or abate considerably of the value and esteem it had for him who bestows them.

The proper business of friendship is to inspire life and courage; and a soul thus supported, outdoes itself; whereas, if it be unexpectedly deprived of these succours, droops and languishes.

We are in some measure more inexcusable if we violate our duties to a friend, than to a relation; since the former arise from a voluntary choice, the latter from a necessity to which we could not give our own consent.

As it has been said on one side, that a man ought not to break with a faulty friend, that he may not expose the weakness of his choice; it will doubtless hold much stronger with respect to a worthy one, that he may never be upbraided for having lost so valuable a treasure which was once in his possession.

DECENCY.

——*Qualis equos Threissa fatigat*
Herpalice—— VIRG.

With such array Herpalice bestrode
Her Thracian courser. DRYDEN.

It would be a noble improvement, or rather a recovery of what we call good breeding, if nothing were to pass amongst us for agreeable which was the least transgression against that rule of life called Decorum or a regard to decency. This would command the respect of mankind, because it carries in it deference to their good opinion; as humility lodged in a worthy mind is always attended with a certain homage, which no haughty soul, with all the art imaginable, will ever be able to purchase. Tully says, "Virtue and decency are so nearly related, that it is difficult to separate them from each other, but in our imagination: as the beauty of the body always accompanies the health of it, so certainly is decency concomitant to virtue; as, beauty of body, with an agreeable carriage, pleases the eye, and that pleasure consists in that we observe, all the parts with a certain elegance are proportioned to each other, so does decency of behaviour, which appears in our lives, obtain the approbation of all. This flows from the reverence we bear toward every good man, and to the world in general; for to be negligent of what any one thinks of you not only shows you arrogant, but abandoned." In all these considerations we are to distinguish how one virtue differs from another. As it is the part of justice never to do violence, it is of modesty never to commit offence. In this last particular lies the whole force of what is called Decency; to this purpose that excellent moralist above-mentioned talks of Decency; but this quality is more easily comprehended by an ordinary capacity, than expressed with all his eloquence. This decency of behaviour is generally transgressed among all orders of men; nay, the very women, though themselves created it as it were for ornament, are often very much mistaken in this ornamental part of life. It would, methinks, be a short rule for behaviour, if every young lady in her dress, words, and actions, were only to recommend herself as a sister, daughter, or wife, and make herself the more esteemed in one of those characters. The care of themselves, with regard to the families in which women are born, is the best motive for their being courted to come into the alliance of other houses. Nothing can promote this end more than a strict preservation of Decency. I should be glad if a certain equestrian order of ladies, some of whom one meets in an evening at every outlet of the town, would take this subject into their serious consideration.

Going lately to take the air in one of the most beautiful evenings this season has produced; as I was admiring the serenity of the sky, the lively colours of the fields, and the variety of the landscape every way around me, my eyes were suddenly called off from these inanimate objects by a little party of horsemen I saw pasing the road. The greater part of them escaped my particular observation, by reason that my whole attention was fixed on a very fair youth who rode in the midst of them, and seemed to have been dressed by some description in a romance. His features complexion, and habit, had a remarkable effeminacy, and a certain languishing vanity appeared in his air. His hair well curled and powdered, hung to a considerable length on his shoulders, and was wantonly tied as if by the hands of his mistress, in a scarlet riband, which played like a streamer behind him; he had a coat and waistcoat of blue camlet, trimmed and embroidered with silver; a cravat of the finest lace; and wore in a smart cock, a little beaver hat edged with silver, and made more sprightly by a feather. His horse too, which was a pacer, was adorned after the same airy manner, and seemed to share in the vanity of the rider. As I was pitying the luxury of this young person, who appeared to me to have been educated only as an object of sight, I perceived on my nearer approach, and as I turned my eyes downward a part of the equipage I had not observed before, which was a petticoat of the same with the coat and waistcoat. After this discovery, I looked again on the face of the fair Amazon who had thus deceived me, and thought those features which had before offended me by their softness, where now strengthened into as improper a boldness: and though her eyes, nose, and mouth seemed to be formed with perfect symmetry, I am not certain whether she, who in appearance was a very handsome youth, may not be in reality a very indifferent woman.

There is an objection which naturally presents itself against these occasional perplexities and mixtures of dress, which is, that they seem to break in upon that propriety and distinction of appearance in which the beauty of different characters is preserved and if they should be more frequent than they are at present, would look like turning our public assemblies into a general masquerade. The model of this Amazonian hunting-habit for ladies was, as I take it, first imported from France, and well enough expresses the gayety of a people, who are taught to do any thing so it be with an assurance; but I cannot help thinking it sits awkwardly yet on our English modesty. The petticoat is a kind of encumbrance upon it, and if the Amazons should think fit to go on in this plunder of our sex's ornaments, they ought to add to their spoils, and complete their triumph over us, by wearing the breeches.

If it be natural to contract insensibly the manners of those we imitate, the ladies who are pleased with assuming our dresses will do us more honour than we deserve, but they will do it at their own expense. Why should the lovely Camilla deceive us in more shapes than her own, and affect to be represented in her picture with a gun and a spaniel: while her elder brother, the heir of a worthy family, is drawn in silks like his sister? The dress and air of a man are not well to be divided; and those who would not be content with the latter, ought never to think of assuming the former. There is so large a portion of natural agreeableness among the fair sex of our island, that they seem betrayed into these romantic habits without having the same occasion for them with their inventors: all that needs to be desired of them is that they would be themselves, that is, what Nature designed them. And to see their mistake when they depart from this, let them look upon a man who affects the softness and effeminacy of a woman, to learn how their sex must appear to us when approaching to the resemblance of a man. *T.*

THE JOURNEY OF LIFE.

A VISION.

Nos pupolo damus. SEN.

As the world leads, we follow.

METHOUGHT I was just awoke out of a sleep, that I could never remember the beginning of; the place where I found myself to be, was a wide and spacious plain full of people that wandered up and down through several beaten paths, whereof some few were straight, and in direct lines, but most of them winding and turning like a labyrinth; but yet it appeared to me afterward, that these last all met in one issue, so that many that seemed to steer quite contrary courses, did at length meet and face one another, to the no small amazement of many of them.

In the midst of the plain there was a great fountain; they called it the Spring of Self-Love; out of it issued two rivulets to the eastward and westward; the name of the first was Heavenly-Wisdom, its water was wonderfully clear, but of a yet more wonderful effect: the other's name was Worldly-Wisdom, its water was thick, and yet far from being dormant or stagnating, for it was in a continual violent agitation; which kept the traveller, whom I shall mention by and by, from being sensible of the foulness and thickness of the water, which had this effect, that it intoxicated those who drank it, and made them mistake every object which lay before them: both rivulets were parted near their springs into so many others, as there were straight and crooked paths, which they attended all along to their respective issues.

I observed from the several paths many now and then diverting, to refresh and otherwise qualify themselves for their journey, to the respective rivulets that ran near them; they contracted a very observable courage and steadiness in what they were about, by drinking these waters. At the end of the perspective of every straight path, all which did end in one issue and point, appeared a high pillar, all of diamond, casting rays as bright as those of the sun into the paths; which rays had also certain sympathizing and alluring virtues in them, so that whosoever had made some considerable progress in his journey onwards toward the pillar, by the repeated impression of these rays upon him, was wrought into an habitual inclination and conversion of his sight toward it, so that it grew at last in a manner natural to him to look and gaze upon it, whereby he was kept steady in the straight paths, which alone led to that radiant body, the beholding of which was now a grown gratification to his nature.

At the issue of the crooked paths there was a great black tower, out of the centre of which streamed a long succession of flames, which did rise even above the clouds; it gave a very great light to the whole plain which did sometimes outshine the light, and oppressed the beams of the adamantine pillar; though by the observation I made afterward, it appeared that it was not for any diminution of light, but that this lay in the travellers, who would sometimes step out of the straight paths, where they lost the full prospect of the radiant pillar, and saw it but sideways: but the great light from the black tower, which was somewhat particularly scorching to them, would generally light and hasten them to their proper climate again.

Round about the black tower, there were, methought, many thousands of huge misshapen ugly monsters: these had great nets, which they were perpetually plying and casting toward the crooked paths, and they would now and then catch up those that were nearest to them: these they took up straight, and whirled over the walls into the flaming tower, and they were no more seen or heard of.

They would sometimes cast their nets toward the right paths to catch the stragglers, whose eyes, for want of frequent drinking at the brook that ran by them, grew dim, whereby they lost their way; these would sometimes very narrowly miss being catched away, but I could not hear whether any of those had ever been so unfortunate, that had been before very hearty in the straight paths.

I considered all these strange sights with great attention, till at last I was interrupted by a cluster of the travellers in the crooked paths, who came up to me, bid me go along with them, and presently fell to singing and dancing; they took me by the hand, and so carried me away along with them. After I had followed them a considerable while, I perceived I had lost the black tower of light, at which I greatly wondered; but as I looked and gazed round about me, and saw nothing, I began to fancy my first vision had been but a dream, and there was no such thing in reality ·

but then I considered, that if I could fancy to see what was not, I might as well have an illusion wrought on me at present, and not see what was really before me. I was very much confirmed in this thought by the effect I then just observed the water of Worldly-Wisdom had upon me; for as I had drunk a little of it again, I felt a very sensible effect in my head; methought it distracted and disordered all there: this made me stop of a sudden, suspecting some charm or enchantment. As I was casting about within myself what I should do, and whom to apply to in this case, I spied at some distance off me a man beckoning, and making signs to me to come over to him. I cried to him, I did not know the way. He then called to me audibly, to step at least out of the path I was in, for if I staid there any longer, I was in danger to be catched in a great net that was just hanging over me, and ready to catch me up; that he wondered I was so blind, or so distracted, as not to see so imminent and visible a danger, assuring me, that as soon as I was out of that way, he would come to me to lead me into a more secure path. This he did, and he brought me his palm full of the water of Heavenly-Wisdom, which was of very great use to me, for my eyes were straight cleared, and I saw the great black tower just before me; but the great net which I spied so near me, cast me in such a terror, that I ran back as far as I could in one breath, without looking behind me: then my benefactor thus bespoke me: "You have made the wonderfulest escape in the world, the water you used to drink is of a bewitching nature, you would else have been mightily shocked at the deformities and meanness of the place; for beside the set of blind fools in whose company you was, you may now behold many others who are only bewitched after another no less dangerous manner. Look a little that way, there goes a crowd of passengers, they have indeed so good a head as not to suffer themselves to be blinded by this bewitching water; the black tower is not vanished out of their sight, they see it whenever they look up to it; but see how they go sideways, and with their eyes downward, as if they were mad, that they may thus rush into the net, without being beforehand troubled at the thought of so miserable a destruction. Their wills are so perverse, and their hearts so fond of the pleasures of the place, that rather than forego them they will run all hazards, and venture upon all the miseries and woes before them.

"See there that other company, though they should drink none of the bewitching water, yet they take a course bewitching and deluding; see how they choose the crookedest paths, whereby they have often the black tower behind them, and sometimes see the radiant column sideways, which gives them some weak glimpse of it. These fools content themselves with that, not knowing whether any other have any more of its influence and light than themselves; this road is called that of Superstition or Human Invention: they grossly overlook that which the rules and laws of the place prescribe to them, and contrive some other scheme and set of directions and prescriptions for themselves, which they hope will serve their turn." He showed me many other kind of fools, which put me quite out of humour with the place. At last he carried me to the right paths, where I found true and solid pleasure, which entertained me all the way, till we came in closer sight of the pillar, where the satisfaction increased to that measure that my faculties were not able to contain it; in the straining of them I was violently waked, not a little grieved at the vanishing of so pleasing a dream.

EMILIA;

OR,

THE IRRESISTIBLE CHARM OF WISDOM AND BEAUTY.

——Lachrymæque decoræ,
Gratior et pulchro veniens e corpore virtus.
VIRG. Æn. 5.

Becoming sorrows in a virtuous mind,
More lovely in a beauteous form enshrin'd.

THERE is nothing which gives one so pleasing a prospect of human nature, as the contemplation of wisdom and beauty: the latter is the peculiar portion of that sex which is therefore called fair; but the happy concurrence of both these excellencies in the same person, is a character too celestial to be frequently met with. Beauty is an overweening, self-sufficient thing, careless of providing itself any more substantial ornaments; nay, so little does it consult its own interests, that it too often defeats itself by betraying that innocence which renders it lovely and desirable. As therefore virtue makes a beautiful woman appear more beautiful, so beauty makes a virtuous woman really more virtuous. Whilst I am considering these two perfections gloriously united in one person, I cannot help representing to my mind the image of Emilia.

Who ever beheld the charming Emilia, without feeling in his breast at once the glow of love and the tenderness of virtuous friendship? The unstudied graces of her behaviour, and the pleasing accents of her tongue, insensibly draw you on to wish for a nearer enjoyment of them; but even her smiles carry in them a silent reproof to the impulses of licentious love. Thus, though the attractives of her beauty play almost irresistibly upon you and create desire, you immediately stand corrected, not by the severity but the decency of her virtue. That sweetness and good-humour which is so visible in her face, naturally diffuses itself into every word and action: a man must be a savage, who at the sight of Emilia is not more inclined to do her good than gratify himself. Her person, as it is thus studiously embellished by nature, thus adorned with unpremeditated graces, is a fit lodging for a mind so fair and lovely; there dwell rational piety, modest hope, and cheerful resignation.

Many of the prevailing passions of mankind do undeservedly pass under the name of religion; which is thus made to express itself in action, according to the nature of the constitution in which it resides: so that were we to make a judgment from appearances, one would imagine religion in some is little better than sullenness and reserve, in many fear, in others the despondings of a melancholy complexion, in others the formality of insignificant unaffecting observances, in others severity, in others ostentation. In Emilia it is a principle founded in reason and enlivened with hope; it does not break forth into irregular fits and sallies of devotion, but is a uniform and consistent tenor of action; it is strict without severity, compassionate without weakness; it is the perfection of that good-humour which proceeds from the understanding, not the effect of an easy constitution.

By a generous sympathy in nature, we feel ourselves disposed to mourn when any of our fellow-creatures are afflicted; but injured innocence and beauty in distress, is an object that carries in it something inexpressibly moving: it softens the most manly heart with the tenderest sensations of love and compassion, till at length it confesses its humanity, and flows out into tears.

Were I to relate that part of Emilia's life which has given her an opportunity of exerting the heroism of Christianity, it would make too sad, too tender a story: but when I consider her alone in the midst of her distresses, looking beyond this gloomy vale of affliction and sorrow into the joys of heaven and immortality, and when I see her in conversation thoughtless and easy as if she were the most happy creature in the world, I am transported with admiration. Surely never did such a philosophic soul inhabit such a beauteous form! for beauty is often made a privilege against thought and reflection; it laughs at wisdom, and will not abide the gravity of its instructions.

Were I able to represent Emilia's virtues in their proper colours and their due proportions, love or flattery might perhaps be thought to have drawn the picture larger than life; but as this is but an imperfect draught of so excellent a character, and as I cannot, will not hope to have any interest in her person, all that I can say of her is but impartial praise, extorted from me by the prevailing brightness of her virtues. So rare a pattern of female excellence ought not to be concealed, but should be set out to the view and imitation of the world; for how amiable does virtue appear thus as it were made visible to us by so fair an example!

Honoria's disposition is of a very different turn: her thoughts are wholly bent upon conquest and arbitrary power. That she has some wit and beauty nobody denies, and therefore has the esteem of all her acquaintance as a woman of an agreeable person and conversation; but (whatever her husband may think of it) that is not sufficient for Honoria: she waives that title to respect as a mean acquisition, and demands veneration in the right of an idol: for this reason her natural desire of life is continually checked with an inconsistent fear of wrinkles and old age.

Emilia cannot be supposed ignorant of her personal charms, though she seems to be so; but she will not hold her happiness upon so precarious a tenure, whilst her mind is adorned with beauties of a more exalted and lasting nature. When in the full bloom of youth and beauty, we saw her surrounded with a crowd of adorers, she took no pleasure in slaughter and destruction, gave no false deluding hopes which might increase the torments of her disappointed lovers; but having for some time given to the decency of a virgin coyness, and examined the merit of their several pretensions, she at length gratified her own, by resigning herself to the ardent passion of Bromius. Bromius was then master of many good qualities and a moderate fortune, which was soon after unexpectedly increased to a plentiful estate. This for a good while proved his misfortune, as it furnished his unexperienced age with the opportunities of evil company and a sensual life. He might have longer wandered in the labyrinths of vice and folly, had not Emilia's prudent conduct won him over to the government of his reason. Her ingenuity has been constantly employed in humanizing his passions and refining his pleasures. She has showed him by her own example, that virtue is consistent with decent freedoms and good humour, or rather, that it cannot subsist without them. Her good sense readily instructed her, that a silent example and an easy unrepining behaviour will always be more persuasive than the severity of lectures and admonitions; and that there is so much pride interwoven in the make of human nature, that an obstinate man must only take the hint from another, and then be left to advise and correct himself. Thus by an artful train of management and unseen persuasions, having at first brought him not to dislike, and at length to be pleased with that which otherwise he would not have bore to hear of, she then knew how to press and secure this advantage, by approving it as his thought, and seconding it as his proposal. By this means she has gained an interest in some of his leading passions, and made them accessary to his reformation.

There is another particular of Emilia's conduct which I cannot forbear mentioning: to some perhaps it may at first sight appear but a trifling inconsiderable circumstance; but for my part, I think it highly worthy of observation, and to be recommended to the consideration of the fair sex. I have often thought wrapping gowns and dirty linen, with all that huddled economy of dress which passes under the general name of a mob, the bane of conjugal love, and one of the readiest means imaginable to alienate the affection of an husband, especially a fond one. I have heard some ladies, who have been surprised by company in such a dishabille, apologize for it after this manner: "Truly I am ashamed to be caught in this pickle; but my husband and I were sitting all alone by ourselves, and I did not expect to see such good company." This by the way is a fine compliment to the good man, which it is ten to one but he returns in dogged answers and a churlish behaviour without knowing what it is that puts him out of humour.

Emilia's observation teaches her, that as little inadvertencies and neglects cast a blemish upon a great character; so the neglect of apparel, even among the most intimate friends, does insensibly lessen their regards to each other, by creating a familiarity too low and contemptible. She understands the importance of those things which the generality account trifles; and considers every thing as a matter of consequence, that has the least tendency towards keeping up or abating the affection of her husband; him she esteems as a fit object to employ her ingenuity in pleasing, because he is to be pleased for life.

By the help of these, and a thousand other nameless arts, which it is easier for her to practise than for another to express, by the obstinacy of her goodness and unprovoked submission, in spite of all her afflictions and ill usage, Bromius is become a man of sense and a kind husband, and Emilia a happy wife.

Ye guardian angels to whose care Heaven has intrusted its dear Emilia, guide her still forward in the paths of virtue, defend her from the insolence and wrongs of this undiscerning world; at length when we must no more converse with such purity on earth, lead her gently hence innocent and unreproveable to a better place, where by an easy transition from what she now is she may shine forth an angel of light.

T.

NATURE OF RELIGION.

——*quicquid dignum sapiente bonoque est.*
HOR.

—— what befits the wise and good.
CREECH

Religion may be considered under two general heads. The first comprehends what we are to believe, the other what we are to practise. By those things which we are to believe, I mean whatever is revealed to us in the Holy Writings, and which we could not have obtained the knowledge of by the light of nature; by the things which we are to practise, I mean all those duties to which we are directed by reason or natural religion. The first of these I shall distinguish by the name of faith, the second by that of morality.

If we look into the more serious part of mankind, we find many who lay so great a stress upon faith, that they neglect morality; and many who build so much upon morality, that they do not pay a due regard to faith. The perfect man should be defective in neither of these particulars, as will be very evident to those who consider the benefits which arise from each of them, and which I shall make the subject of this day's paper.

Notwithstanding this general division of Christian duty into morality and faith, and that they have both their peculiar excellencies, the first has the pre-eminence in several respects.

First, Because the greatest part of morality (as I have stated the notion of it) is of a fixed eternal nature, and will endure when faith shall fail, and be lost in conviction.

Secondly, Because a person may be qualified to do greater good to mankind, and become more beneficial to the world, by morality, without faith, than by faith without morality.

Thirdly, Because morality gives a greater perfection to human nature, by quieting the mind, moderating the passions, and advancing the happiness of every man in his private capacity.

Fourthly, Because the rule of morality is much more certain than that of faith, all the civilized nations of the world agreeing in the great points of morality, as much as they differ in those of faith.

Fifthly, Because infidelity is not of so malignant a nature as immorality; or, to put the same reason in another light, because it is generally owned, there may be salvation for a virtuous infidel, (particularly in the case of invincible ignorance) but none for a vicious believer.

Sixthly, Because faith seems to draw its principal, if not all its excellency, from the influence it has upon morality; as we shall see more at large, if we consider wherein consists the excellency of faith, or the belief of revealed religion; and this I think is,

First, In explaining and carrying to greater heights several points of morality.

Secondly, In furnishing new and stronger motives to enforce the practice of morality.

Thirdly, In giving us more amiable ideas of the Supreme Being, more endearing notions of one another, and a truer state of ourselves, both in regard to the grandeur and vileness of our natures.

Fourthly, By showing us the blackness and deformity of vice, which in the Christian system is so very great, that he who is possessed of all perfection and the sovereign judge of it, is represented by several of our divines as hating sin to the same degree that he loves the sacred person who was made the propitiation of it.

Fifthly, In being the ordinary and prescribed method of making morality effectual to salvation.

I have only touched on these several heads, which every one who is conversant in discourses of this nature will easily enlarge upon in his own thoughts, and draw conclusions from them which may be useful to him in the conduct of his life. One I am sure is so obvious, that he cannot miss it, namely, that a man cannot be perfect in his scheme of morality, who does not strengthen and support it with that of the Christian faith.

Besides this, I shall lay down two or three other maxims which I think we may deduce from what has been said.

First, That we should be particularly cautious of making any thing an article of faith, which does not contribute to the confirmation or improvement of morality.

Secondly, That no article of faith can be true and authentic, which weakens or subverts the practical part of religion, or what I have hitherto called morality.

Thirdly, That the greatest friend of morality, or natural religion, cannot possibly apprehend any danger from embracing Christianity, as it is preserved pure and uncorrupt in the doctrines of our national church.

There is likewise another maxim which I think may be drawn from the foregoing considerations, which is this, that we should in all dubious points consider any ill consequences that may arise from them, supposing they should be erroneous, before we give up our assent to them.

For example, in that disputable point of persecuting men for conscience sake, besides the imbittering their minds with hatred, indignation, and all the vehemence of resentment, and ensnaring them to profess what they do not believe; we cut them off from the pleasures and advantages of society, afflict their bodies, distress their fortunes, hurt their reputations, ruin their families, make their lives painful, or put an end to them. Sure when I see such dreadful consequences rising from a principle, I would be as fully convinced of the truth of it, as of a mathematical demonstration, before I would venture to act upon it, or make it a part of my religion.

In this case the injury done our neighbour is plain and evident, the principle that puts us upon doing it, of a dubious and disputable nature. Morality seems highly violated by the one, and whether or no a zea-

for what a man thinks the true system of faith may justify it, is very uncertain. I cannot but think, if our religion produce charity as well as zeal, it will not be for showing itself by such cruel instances. But to conclude with the words of an excellent author, "We have just enough religion to make us hate, but not enough to make us love one another."

C.

PUBLIC AND PRIVATE EDUCATION CONTRASTED.

Exigite ut mores teneros ceu pollice ducat,
Ut si quis cera vultum facit—— JUV.

Bid him besides, his daily pains employ,
To form the tender manners of the boy;
And work him like a waxen babe, with art,
To perfect symmetry in every part.
DRYDEN.

I INTEND to discuss that famous question, Whether the education at a public school, or under a private tutor, is to be preferred?

As some of the greatest men in most ages have been of very different opinions in this matter, I shall give a short account of what I think may be best urged on both sides, and afterward leave every person to determine for himself.

It is certain from Suetonius, that the Romans thought the education of their children a business properly belonging to the parents themselves; and Plutarch, in the Life of Marcus Cato, tells us, that as soon as his son was capable of learning, Cato would suffer nobody to teach him but himself, though he had a servant named Chilo, who was an excellent grammarian, and who taught a great many other youths.

On the contrary, the Greeks seemed more inclined to public schools and seminaries.

A private education promises in the first place virtue and good-breeding; a public school manly assurance, and an early knowledge in the ways of the world.

Mr. Locke, in his celebrated Treatise of Education, confesses that there are inconveniences to be feared on both sides. "If," says he, "I keep my son at home, he is in danger of becoming my young master; if I send him abroad, it is scarce possible to keep him from the reigning contagion of rudeness and vice. He will perhaps be more innocent at home, but more ignorant of the world, and more sheepish when he comes abroad." However, as this learned author asserts, that virtue is much more difficult to be attained than knowledge of the world; and that vice is a more stubborn, as well as a more dangerous fault than sheepishness, he is altogether for a private education; and the more so, because he does not see why a youth, with right management, might not attain the same assurance in his father's house as at a public school. To this end he advises parents to accustom their sons to whatever strange faces come to the house; to take them with them when they visit their neighbours, and to engage them in conversation with men of parts and breeding.

It may be objected to this method, that conversation is not the only thing necessary, but that unless it be a conversation with such as are in some measure their equals in parts and years, there can be no room for emulation, contention, and several of the most lively passions of the mind; which, without being sometimes moved by these means, may possibly contract a dulness and insensibility.

One of the greatest writers our nation ever produced observes, that a boy who forms parties, and makes himself popular in a school or college, would act the same part with equal ease in a senate or a privy council; and Mr. Osburn, speaking like a man versed in the ways of the world, affirms, that the well laying and carrying on of a design to rob an orchard, trains up a youth insensibly to caution, secrecy, and circumspection, and fits him for matters of greater importance.

In short a private education seems the most natural method for the forming of a virtuous man; a public education for making a man of business. The first would furnish out a good subject for Plato's republic; the latter a member for a community overrun with artifice and corruption.

It must however be confessed, that a person at the head of a public school has sometimes so many boys under his direction, that it is impossible he should extend a due proportion of his care to each of them. This is, however, in reality the fault of the age, in which we often see twenty parents, who, though each expects his son should be made a scholar, are not contented all together to make it worth while for any man of a liberal education to take upon him the care of their instruction.

In our great schools indeed this fault has been of late years rectified, so that we have at present not only ingenious men for the chief masters, but such as have proper ushers and assistants under them; I must nevertheless own, that for want of the same encouragement in the country, we have many a promising genius spoiled and abused in those little seminaries.

I am the more inclined to this opinion, having myself experienced the usage of two rural masters, each of them very unfit for the trust they took upon them to discharge. The first imposed much more upon me than my parts, though none of the weakest, could endure, and used me barbarously for not performing impossibilities. The latter was of quite another temper; and a boy, who would run upon his errands, wash his coffee-pot, or ring the bell, might have as little conversation with any of the classics as he thought fit. I have known a lad of this place excused his exercise for assisting the cook-maid; and remember a neighbouring gentleman's son was among us five years, most of which time he employed in airing and watering our master's gray pad. I scorned to compound for my faults, by doing any of these elegant offices, and was accordingly the best scholar, and the worst used of any boy in the school.

I shall conclude with an advantage mentioned by Quintilian, as accompanying a public way of education, which I have not yet taken notice of; namely, that we very often contract such friendships at school, as are a service to us all the following parts of our lives.

I shall give, under this head, a story very well known to several persons, and which may be depended upon as real truth.

Every one who is acquainted with Westminster school, knows that there is a curtain which used to be drawn across the room, to separate the upper school from the lower. A youth happened by some mischance to tear the above-mentioned curtain: the severity of the master was too well known for the criminal to expect any pardon for such a fault; so that the boy, who was of a meek temper, was terrified to death at the thoughts of his appearance, when his friend, who sat next to him, bade him be of good cheer, for that he would take the fault on himself. He kept his word accordingly. As soon as they were grown up to be men, the civil war broke out, in which our two friends took the opposite sides; one of them followed the Parliament, the other the Royal party.

As their tempers were different, the youth who had torn the curtain endeavoured to raise himself on the civil list, and the other, who had borne the blame of it, on the military. The first succeeded so well, that he was in a short time made a judge under the Protector; the other was engaged in the unhappy enterprise of Penruddock and Groves in the West. I suppose, sir, I need not acquaint you with the event of that undertaking. Every one knows that the Royal party was routed, and all the heads of them, among whom was the curtain champion, imprisoned at Exeter. It happened to be his friend's lot at that time to go the Western circuit: the trial of the rebels, as they were then called, was very short, and nothing now remained but to pass sentence on them; when the judge, hearing the name of his old friend, and observing his face more attentively, which he had not seen for many years, asked him, if he was not formerly a Westminster scholar? by the answer he was soon convinced that it was his former generous friend; and, without saying any thing more at that time, made the best of his way to London, where employing all his power and interest with the Protector, he saved his friend from the fate of his unhappy associates.

The gentleman whose life was thus preserved by the gratitude of his school-fellow, was afterward the father of a son, whom he lived to see promoted in the church, and who still deservedly fills one of the highest stations in it.

* * *

I have endeavoured to give the best reasons that could be urged in favour of a private or public education. Upon the whole, I rather incline to the latter, though at the same time I confess that virtue, which ought to be our first and principal care, is more usually acquired in the former.

I intend, therefore, to offer methods by which I conceive boys might be made to improve in virtue as they advance in letters.

I know that in most of our public schools vice is punished and discouraged, whenever it is found out: but this is far from being sufficient, unless our youth are at the same time taught to form a right judgment of things, and to know what is properly virtue.

To this end, whenever they read the lives and actions of such men as have been famous in their generation, it should not be thought enough to make them barely understand so many Greek or Latin sentences, but they should be asked their opinion of such an action or saying, and obliged to give their reasons why they take it to be good or bad. By this means they would insensibly arrive at proper notions of courage, temperance, honour, and justice.

There must be great care taken how the example

of any particular person is recommended to them in gross: instead of which they ought to be taught wherein such a man, though great in some respects, was weak and faulty in others.

For want of this caution, a boy is often so dazzled with the lustre of a great character, that he confounds its beauties with its blemishes, and looks even upon the faulty parts of it with an eye of admiration.

I have often wondered how Alexander, who was naturally of a generous and merciful disposition, came to be guilty of so barbarous an action as that of dragging the governor of a town after his chariot. I know this is generally ascribed to his passion for Homer; but I lately met with a passage in Plutarch, which, if I am not very much mistaken, still gives us a clearer light into the motives of this action. Plutarch tells us, that Alexander in his youth had a master named Lysimachus, who, though he was a man destitute of all politeness, ingratiated himself both with Philip and his pupil, and became the second man at court, by calling the King Peleus, the Prince Achilles, and himself Phœnix. It is no wonder if Alexander, having been thus used not only to admire but to personate Achilles, should think it glorious to imitate him in this piece of cruelty and extravagance.

To carry this thought yet further, I shall submit it to the reader's consideration, whether instead of a theme or copy of verses, which are the usual exercises, as they are called in the school-phrase, it would not be more proper that a boy should be tasked once or twice a-week to write down his opinion of such persons and things as occur to him in his reading; that he should descant upon the actions of Turnus or Æneas, show wherein they excelled or were defective, censure or approve any particular action, observe how it might have been carried to a greater degree of perfection, and how it exceeded or fell short of another. He might at the same time mark what was moral in any speech, and how far it agreed with the character of the person speaking. This exercise would soon strengthen his judgment in what is blameable or praiseworthy, and give him an early seasoning of morality.

Next to those examples which may be met with in books, I very much approve Horace's way of setting before youth the infamous or honourable characters of their contemporaries; that poet tells us, this was the method his father made use of to incline him to any particular virtue, or give him an aversion to any particular vice. If, says Horace, my father advised me to live within bounds, and be contented with the fortune he should leave me, "Do you not see," says he, "the miserable condition of Burrus, and the son of Albus? Let the misfortunes of those two wretches teach you to avoid luxury and extravagance." If he would inspire me with an abhorrence to debauchery, "Do not," says he, "make yourself like Sectanus, when you may be happy in the enjoyment of lawful pleasures. How scandalous," says he, "is the character of Trebonius, who was lately caught in bed with another man's wife?" To illustrate the force of this method, the poet adds, that as a headstrong patient, who will not at first follow his physician's prescriptions, grows orderly when he hears that his neighbours die all about him, so youth is often frighted from vice by hearing the ill report it brings upon others.

Xenophon's schools of equity, in his life of Cyrus the Great, are sufficiently famous: he tells us, that the Persian children went to school, and employed their time as diligently in learning the principles of justice and sobriety, as the youth in other countries did to acquire the most difficult arts and sciences; their governors spent most part of the day in hearing their mutual accusations one against the other, whether for violence, cheating, slander, or ingratitude; and taught them how to give judgment against those who were found to be any ways guilty of these crimes. I omit the story of the long and short coat, for which Cyrus himself was punished, as a case equally known with any in Lyttleton.

The method which Apuleius tells us the Indian

gymnosophists took to educate their disciples, is still more curious and remarkable. His words are as follows : When their dinner is ready, before it is served up, the masters inquire of every particular scholar how he has employed his time since sun-rising ; some of them answer, that having been chosen as arbiters between two persons, they have composed their differences, and made them friends ; some, that they have been executing the orders of their parents ; and others, that they have either found out something new by their own application, or learned it from the instructions of their fellows. But if there happens to be any one among them who cannot make it appear that he has employed the morning to advantage, he is immediately excluded from the company, and obliged to work while the rest are at dinner.

" It is not impossible that, from these several ways of producing virtue in the minds of boys, some general method might be invented. What I would endeavour to inculcate is, that our youth cannot be too soon taught the principles of virtue, seeing the first impressions which are made on the mind are always the strongest. X

PLEASURES

OF

THE IMAGINATION.

ANALYSIS—PAPER I.

The perfection of our sight above our other senses.—The pleasures of the imagination arise originally from sight.—The pleasures of the imagination divided under two heads.—The pleasures of the imagination in some respects equal to those of the understanding.—The extent of the pleasures of the imagination.—The advantages a man receives from a relish of these pleasures.—In what respect they are preferable to those of the understanding.

Avia Pieridum peragro loca nullius ante
Trita solo: juvat integros accedere fontes,
Atque haurire.——— *Lucr.* lib. 1. v. 925

—— Inspir'd I trace the muses seats,
Untrodden yet; 'tis sweet to visit first
Untouch'd and virgin streams, and quench my thirst.
Creech.

Our sight is the most perfect and most delightful of all our senses: it fills the mind with the largest variety of ideas converses with its objects at the greatest distance, and continues the longest in action without being tired or satiated with its proper enjoyments. The sense of feeling can indeed give us a notion of extension, shape, and all other ideas that enter at the eye except colours: but at the same time, it is very much strained and confined in its operations, to the number, bulk, and distance of its particular objects. Our sight seems designed to supply all these defects, and may be considered as a more delicate and diffu sive kind of touch, that spreads itself over an infinite multitude of bodies, comprehends the largest figures, and brings into our reach some of the most remote parts of the universe.

It is this sense which furnishes the imagination with its ideas; so that, by the pleasures of the imagination or fancy, (which I shall use promiscuously,) I here mean such as arise from visible objects, either when we have them actually in our view or when we call up their ideas into our minds by paintings, statues, descriptions, or any the like occasion. We cannot indeed have a single image in the fancy that did not make its first entrance through the sight; but we have the power of retaining, altering, and compounding those images, which we have once received, into all the varieties of picture and vision that are most agreeable to the imagination; for by this faculty a man in a dungeon is capable of entertaining himself with scenes and landscapes more beautiful than any that can be found in the whole compass of nature.

There are few words in the English language which are employed in a more loose and uncircumscribed sense than those of the *fancy* and the *imagination.* I therefore thought it necessary to fix and determine the notion of these two words, as I intend to make use of them in the thread of my following speculations, that the reader may conceive rightly what is the subject which I proceed upon. I must therefore desire him to remember, that, by the pleasures of the imagination, I mean only such pleasures as arise originally from sight, and that I divide these pleasures into two kinds: my design being first of all to discourse of those primary pleasures of the imagination which entirely proceed from such objects as are before our eyes; and, in the next place, to speak of those secondary pleasures of the imagination which flow from the ideas of visible objects, when the objects are not actually before the eye, but are called up into our memories, or formed into agreeable visions of things that are either absent or fictitious.

The pleasures of the imagination, taken in the full

extent, are not so gross as those of sense, nor so refined as those of the understanding. The last are indeed more preferable, because they are founded on some new knowledge or improvement in the mind of man; yet it must be confessed that those of the imagination are as great and as transporting as the other A beautiful prospect delights the soul as much as a demonstration; and a description in Homer has charmed more readers than a chapter in Aristotle. Besides, the pleasures of the imagination have this advantage above those of the understanding, that they are more obvious, and more easy to be acquired: it is but opening the eye, and the scene enters: the colours paint themselves on the fancy, with very little attention of thought or application of mind in the beholder. We are struck, we know not how, with the symmetry of any thing we see, and immediately assent to the beauty of an object, without inquiring into the particular causes and occasions of it.

A man of a polite imagination is let into a great many pleasures that the vulgar are not capable of receiving. He can converse with a picture, and find an agreeable companion in a statue. He meets with a secret refreshment in a description, and often feels a greater satisfaction in the prospect of fields and meadows than another does in the possession. It gives him, indeed, a kind of property in every thing he sees, and makes the most rude uncultivated parts of nature administer to his pleasures: so that he looks upon the world, as it were, in another light, and discovers in it a multitude of charms that conceal themselves from the generality of mankind.

There are, indeed, but very few who know how to be idle and innocent, or have a relish of any pleasures that are not criminal; every diversion they take is at the expense of some one virtue or another, and their very first step out of business is into vice or folly. A man should endeavour, therefore, to make the sphere of his innocent pleasures as wide as possible, that he may retire into them with safety, and find in them such a satisfaction as a wise man would not blush to take. Of this nature are those of the imagination, which do not require such a bent of thought as is necessary to our more serious employments, nor at the same time suffer the mind to sink into that negligence and remissness which are apt to accompany our more sensual delights, but, like a gentle exercise to the faculties, awaken them from sloth and idleness, without putting them upon any labour or difficulty.

We might here add, that the pleasures of the fancy are more conducive to health than those of the understanding, which are worked out by dint of thinking, and attended with too violent a labour of the brain. Delightful scenes, whether in nature, painting, or poetry, have a kindly influence on the body as well as the mind, and not only serve to clear and brighten the imagination, but are able to disperse grief and melancholy, and to set the animal spirits in pleasing and agreeable motions. For this reason Sir Francis Bacon, in his essay upon health, has not thought it improper to prescribe to his reader a poem or a prospect, where he particularly dissuades him from knotty and subtle disquisitions, and advises him to pursue studies that fill the mind with splendid and illustrious objects, as histories, fables, and contemplations of nature.

I have in this paper, by way of introduction, settled the notion of those pleasures of the imagination which are the subject of my present undertaking, and endeavoured by several considerations to recommend to my reader the pursuit of those pleasures. I shall, in my next paper, examine the several sources from whence these pleasures are derived.

O.

PAPER II.

Three sources of all the pleasures of the imagination in our survey of outward objects. How what is great pleases the imagination. How what is new pleases the imagination. How what is beautiful in our own species pleases the imagination. How what is beautiful in general pleases the imagination. What other accidental causes may contribute to the heightening of those pleasures.

—— *Divisum sic breve, fiet opus.—Mart. Ep.* 83. l. 4.
The work, divided aptly, shorter grows.

I SHALL first consider those pleasures of the imagination which arise from the actual view and survey of outward objects; and these, I think, all proceed from the sight of what is *great, uncommon*, or *beautiful.* There may, indeed, be something so terrible or offensive, that the horror or loathsomeness of an object may overbear the pleasure which results from its *greatness, novelty*, or *beauty;* but still there will be such a mixture of delight in the very disgust it gives us, as any of these three qualifications are most conspicuous and prevailing.

By *greatness* I do not only mean the bulk of any single object, but the largeness of a whole view, considered as one entire piece. Such are the prospects of an open champaign country, a vast uncultivated desert of huge heaps of mountains, high rocks and precipices, or a wide expanse of water, where we are not struck with the novelty or beauty of the sight, but with that rude kind of magnificence which appears in many of these stupendous works of nature.

Our imagination loves to be filled with an object, or to grasp at any thing that is too big for its capacity. We are flung into a pleasing astonishment at such unbounded views, and feel a delightful stillness and amazement in the soul at the apprehensions of them. The mind of man naturally hates every thing that looks like a restraint upon it, and is apt to fancy itself under a sort of confinement, when the sight is pent up in a narrow compass, and shortened on every side by the neighbourhood of walls or mountains. On the contrary, a spacious horizon is an image of liberty, where the eye has room to range abroad, to expatiate at large on the immensity of its views, and to lose itself amidst the variety of objects that offer themselves to its observation. Such wide and undetermined prospects are as pleasing to the fancy, as the speculations of eternity or infinitude are to the understanding. But if there be a beauty or uncommonness joined with this grandeur, as in a troubled ocean, a heaven adorned with stars and meteors, or a spacious landscape cut out into rivers, woods, rocks, and meadows, the pleasure still grows upon us, as it arises from more than a single principle.

Every thing that is *new* or *uncommon* raises a pleasure in the imagination, because it fills the soul with an agreeable surprise, gratifies its curiosity, and gives it an idea of which it was not before possessed. We are indeed so often conversant with one set of objects, and tired out with so many repeated shows of the same things, that whatever is *new* or *uncommon* contributes a little to vary human life, and to divert our minds for a while with the strangeness of its appearance: it serves us for a kind of refreshment, and takes off from that satiety we are apt to complain of in our usual and ordinary entertainments. It is this that bestows charms on a monster, and makes even the imperfections of nature please us. It is this that recommends variety, where the mind is every instant called off to something new, and the attention not suffered to dwell too long, and waste itself on any particular object: it is this, likewise, that improves what is great or beautiful, and makes it afford the mind a double entertainment. Groves, fields, and meadows, are at any season of the year pleasant to look upon, but never so much as in the opening of the spring, when they are all new and fresh, with their first gloss upon them, and not yet too much accustomed and familiar to the eye. For this reason there is nothing that more enlivens a prospect than rivers, jetteaus, or falls of water, where the scene is perpetually shifting, and entertaining the sight every moment with something that is new. We are quickly tired with looking upon hills and valleys, where every thing continues fixt and settled in the same place and posture, but find our thoughts a little agitated and relieved at the sight of such objects as are ever in motion, and sliding away from beneath the eye of the beholder.

But there is nothing that makes its way more directly to the soul than *beauty*, which immediately diffuses a secret satisfaction and complacency through the imagination, and gives a finishing to any thing that is great or uncommon. The very first discovery of it strikes the mind with an inward joy, and spreads a cheerfulness and delight through all its faculties. There is not perhaps any real beauty or deformity more in one piece of matter than another, because we might have been so made, that whatsoever now appears loathsome to us might have shown itself agreeable; but we find by experience, that there are several modifications of matter, which the mind, without any previous consideration, pronounces at first sight beautiful or deformed. Thus we see that every different species of sensible creatures has its different notions of beauty, and that each of them is most affected with the beauties of its own kind. This is nowhere more remarkable than in birds of the same shape and proportion, where we often see the male determined in his courtship by the single grain or tincture of a feather, and never discovering any charms but in the colour of its species.

Scit thalamo servare fidem sanctasque veretur
Connubii leges, non illum in pectore candor
Sollicitat niveus; neque pravum accendit amorem
Splendida lanugo, vel honesta in virtice crista,
Purpureusve nitor pennarum; ast agmina late
Fœminea explorat cautus, maculasque, requirit
Cognatas, paribusque interlita corpora guttis:
Ni faceret, pictis sylvam circum undique monstris
Confusam aspiceres vulgo, partusque biformes,
Et genus ambiguum, et veneris monumenta nefanda.

Hinc merula in nigro se oblectat nigra marito,
Hinc socium lasciva petit philomela canorum,
Agnoscitque pares sonitus, hinc noctua tetram
Canitiem alarum, et glaucos miratur ocellos
Nempe sibi semper constat, crescitque quotannis
Lucida progenies, castos confessa parentes;
Dum virides inter saltus locosque sonoros
Vere novo exultat, plumasque decora juventus
Explicat ad solem, patriisque coloribus ardet.

The feather'd husband, to his partner true,
Preserves connubial rites inviolate.
With cold indifference ev'ry charm he sees,
The milky whiteness of the stately neck,
The shining down, proud crest, and purple wings;
But cautious with a searching eye explores
The female tribes, his proper mate to find,
With kindred colours mark'd: did he not so,
The grove with painted monsters would abound,
Th' ambiguous product of unnatural love.
The black-bird hence selects her sooty spouse;
The nightingale her musical compeer,
Lur'd by the well-known voice; the bird of night,
Smit with his dusky wings, and greenish eyes,
Woos his dun paramour. The beauteous race
Speak the chaste loves of their progenitors;
When, by the spring invited, they exult
In woods and fields, and to the sun unfold
Their plumes, that with paternal colours glow.

There is a second kind of *beauty* that we find in the several products of art and nature, which does not work in the imagination with that warmth and violence as the beauty that appears in our proper species, but is apt, however, to raise in us a secret delight, and a kind of fondness for the places or objects in which we discover it. This consists either in the gayety or variety of colours, in the symmetry and proportion of parts, in the arrangement and disposition of bodies, or in a just mixture and concurrence of all together. Among these several kinds of beauty the eye takes most delight in colours. We nowhere meet with a more glorious or pleasing show in nature, than what appears in the heavens at the rising and setting of the sun, which is wholly made up of those different stains of light that show themselves in clouds of a different situation. For this reason we find the poets, who are always addressing themselves to the imagination, borrowing more of their epithets from colours than from any other topic.

As the fancy delights in every thing that is great, strange, or beautiful, and is still more pleased the more it finds of these perfections in the same object, so it is capable of receiving a new satisfaction by the assistance of another sense. Thus any continued sound, as the music of birds, or a fall of water, awakens every moment the mind of the beholder, and makes him more attentive to the several beauties of the place that lie before him. Thus, if there arises a fragrancy of smells or perfumes, they heighten the pleasures of the imagination, and make even the colours and verdure of the landscape appear more agreeable; for the ideas of both senses recommend each other, and are pleasanter together, than when they enter the mind separately; as the different colours of a picture, when they are well disposed, set off one another, and receive an additional beauty from the advantage of their situation. O.

PAPER III.

Why the neccessary cause of our being pleased with what is great, new, or beautiful, unknown. Why the final cause more known and more useful. The final cause of our being pleased with what is great. The final cause of our being pleased with what is new. The final cause of our being pleased with what is beautiful in our own species. The final cause of our being pleased with what is beautiful in general.

—— *Causa latet, vis est notissima* ——
Ovid. Metam. l. 4. v. 207.

The cause is secret, but th' effect is known.—*Addison*

Though in yesterday's paper we considered how every thing that is *great*, *new*, or *beautiful*, is apt to affect the imagination with pleasure, we must own that it is impossible for us to assign the necessary cause of this pleasure, because we know neither the nature of an idea, nor the substance of a human soul, which might help us to discover the conformity or disagreeableness of the one to the other; and therefore, for want of such a light, all that we can do, in speculations of this kind, is to reflect on those operations of the soul that are most agreeable, and to range, under their proper heads, what is pleasing or displeasing to the mind, without being able to trace out several necessary and efficient causes from whence the pleasure or displeasure arises.

Final causes lie more bare and open to our observation as there are often a greater variety that belong to the same effect; and these, though they are not altogether so satisfactory, are generally more useful than the other, as they give us greater occasion of admiring the goodness and wisdom of the first contriver.

One of the final causes of our delight in any thing that is *great* may be this. The Supreme Author of our being has so formed the soul of man, that nothing but himself can be its last, adequate, and proper happiness. Because therefore a great part of our happiness must arise from the contemplation of his being, that he might give our souls a just relish of such a contemplation, he has made them naturally delight in the apprehension of what is great or unlimited. Our admiration, which is a very pleasing motion of the mind, immediately arises at the consideration of any object that takes up a great deal of room in the fancy, and, by consequence, will improve into the highest pitch of astonishment and devotion when we contemplate his nature, that is neither circumscribed by time nor place, nor to be comprehended by the largest capacity of a created being.

He has annexed a secret pleasure to the idea of any thing that is *new* or *uncommon*, that he might encourage us in the pursuit after knowledge, and engage us to search into the wonders of his creation; for every new idea brings such a pleasure along with it as rewards any pains we have taken in its acquisition, and consequently serves as a motive to put us upon fresh discoveries.

He has made every thing that is *beautiful in our own species* pleasant, that all creatures might be tempted to multiply their kind, and fill the world with inhabitants; for it is very remarkable, that wherever nature is crossed in the production of a monster (the result of any unnatural mixture,) the breed is incapable of propagating its likeness, and of founding a new order of creatures; so that, unless all animals were allured by the beauty of their own species, generation would be at an end, and the earth unpeopled.

In the last place, He has made every thing that is beautiful in all other objects pleasant, or rather has made so many objects appear beautiful, that he might render the whole creation more gay and delightful. He has given almost every thing about us the power of raising an agreeable idea in the imagination: so that it is impossible for us to behold his works with coldness or indifference, and to survey so many beauties without a secret satisfaction and camplacency.

Things would make but a poor appearance to the eye if we saw them only in their proper figures and motions: and what reason can we assign for their exciting in us many of those ideas which are different from any thing that exists in the objects themselves (for such are light and colours,) were it not to add supernumerary ornaments to the universe, and make it more agreeable to the imagination? We are every where entertained with pleasing shows and apparitions; we discover imaginary glories in the heavens, and in the earth, and see some of this visionary beauty poured out upon the whole creation, but what a rough unsightly sketch of nature should we be entertained with did all her colouring disappear, and the several distinctions of light and shade vanish? In short, our souls are at present delightfully lost and bewildered in a pleasing delusion, and we walk about like the enchanted hero in a romance, who sees beautiful castles, woods, and meadows; and at the same time hears the warbling of birds, and the purling of streams; but, upon the finishing of some secret spell, the fantastic scene breaks up, and the disconsolate knight finds himself on a barren heath, or in a solitary desert. It is not improbable that something like this may be the state of the soul after its first separation, in respect of the images it will receive from matter; though indeed the ideas of colours are so pleasing and beautiful in the imagination, that it is possible the soul will not be deprived of them, but perhaps find them excited by some other occasional cause, as they are at present by the different impressions of the subtle matter on the organ of sight.

I have here supposed that my reader is acquainted with that great modern discovery which is at present universally acknowledged by all the inquirers into natural philosophy; namely, that light and colours, as apprehended by the imagination, are only ideas in the mind, and not qualities that have any existence in matter. As this is a truth which has been proved incontestably by many modern philosophers, and is indeed one of the finest speculations in that science, if the English reader would see the notion explained at large, he may find it in the eighth chapter of the second book of Mr. Locke's Essay on Human Understanding. *O.*

PAPER IV.

The works of nature more pleasing to the imagination than those of art. The works of nature still more pleasant the more they resemble those of art. The works of art more pleasant the more they resemble those of nature. Our English plantations and gardens considered in the foregoing light.

—— Alterius sic
Altera poscit opem res, et conjurat amice.
Hor. Ars. Poet. v. 411.

But mutually they need each other's help.
Roscommon.

If we consider the works of *nature* and *art* as they are qualified to entertain the imagination, we shall find the last very defective in comparison of the former; for though they may sometimes appear as beautiful or strange, they can have nothing in them of that vastness and immensity which afford so great an entertainment to the mind of the beholder. The one may be as polite and delicate as the other, but can never show herself so august and magnificent in the design. There is something more bold and masterly in the rough careless strokes of nature, than in the nice touches and embellishments of art. The beauties of the most stately garden or palace lie in a narrow compass, the imagination immediately runs them over, and requires something else to gratify her; but, in the wide fields of nature, the sight wanders up and down without confinement, and is fed with an infinite variety of images, without any certain stint or number. For this reason we always find the poet in love with a country-life, where nature appears in the greatest perfection, and furnishes out all those scenes that are most apt to delight the imagination.

Scriptorum chorus omnis amat nemus, et fugit urbes.
Hor. Ep. 2. l. 2. v. 77.

—— To grottos and to groves we run,
To ease and silence ev'ry muse's son.—*Pope.*

Hic secura quies, et nescia fallere vita,
Dives opum variarum; hic latis otia fundis,
Speluncæ, vivique lacus; hic frigida tempe,
Mugitusque boum, mollesque sub arbore somni.
Virg. Georg. l. 2. v. 467.

Here easy quiet, a secure retreat,
A harmless life that knows not how to cheat,
With home-bred plenty the rich owner bless,
And rural pleasures crown his happiness.
Unvex'd with quarrels, undisturb'd with noise,
The country king his peaceful realm enjoys:
Cool grots, and living lakes, the flow'ry pride
Of meads and streams that through the valley glide,
And shady groves that easy sleep invite,
And, after toilsome days, a sweet repose at night.
Dryden.

But though there are several of those wild scenes that are more delightful than any artificial shows, yet we find the works of nature still more pleasant the more they resemble those of art: for in this case our pleasure rises from a double principle; from the agreeableness of the objects to the eye, and from their similitude to other objects: we are pleased as well with comparing their beauties as with surveying them, and can represent them to our minds either as copies or originals. Hence it is that we take delight in a prospect which is well laid out, and diversified with fields and meadows, woods and rivers; in those accidental andscapes of trees, clouds, and cities, that are some times found in the veins of marble; in the curious fret-work of rocks and grottos; and, in a word, in any thing that hath such a variety or regularity as may seem the effect of design in what we call the works of chance.

If the products of nature rise in value according as they more or less resemble those of art, we may be sure that artificial works receive a greater advantage from their resemblance of such as are natural; because here the similitude is not only pleasant, but the pattern more perfect. The prettiest landscape I ever saw was one drawn on the walls of a dark room, which stood opposite on one side to a navigable river, and on the other to a park. The experiment is very common in optics. Here you might discover the waves and fluctuations of the water in strong and proper colours, with the picture of a ship entering at one end, and sailing by degrees through the whole piece. On another there appeared the green shadows of trees waving to and fro with the wind, and herds of deer among them in miniature, leaping about upon the wall. I must confess the novelty of such a sight may be one occasion of its pleasantness to the imagination; but certainly the chief reason is its near resemblance to nature, as it does not only, like other pictures, give the colour and figure, but the motion of the thing it represents.

We have before observed, that there is generally in nature something more grand and august than what we meet with in the curiosities of art. When therefore we see this imitated in any measure, it gives us a nobler and more exalted kind of pleasure than what we receive from the nicer and more accurate productions of art. On this account our English gardens are not so entertaining to the fancy as those in France and Italy, where we see a large extent of ground covered over with an agreeable mixture of garden and forest, which represent every where an artificial rudeness, much more charming than that neatness and elegance which we meet with in those of our own country. It might indeed be of ill consequence to the public, as well as unprofitable to private persons, to alienate so much ground from pasturage and the plough in many parts of a country that is so well peopled and cultivated to a far greater advantage. But why may not a whole estate be thrown into a kind of a garden by frequent plantations, that may turn as much to the profit as the pleasure of the owner? A marsh overgrown with willows, or a mountain shaded with oaks, are not only more beautiful, but more beneficial, than when they lie bare and unadorned. Fields of corn make a pleasant prospect; and if the walks were a little taken care of that lie between them, if the natural embroidery of the meadows were helped and improved by some small additions of art, and the several rows of hedges set off by trees and flowers that the soil was capable of receiving, a man might make a pretty landscspe of his own possessions.

Writers, who have given us an account of China, tell us the inhabitants of that country laugh at the plantations of our Europeans, which are laid out by the rule and line; because they say, any one may place trees in equal rows and uniform figures. They choose rather to show a genius in works of this nature; and therefore always conceal the art by which they direct themselves. They have a word it seems in their language, by which they express the particular beauty of a plantation that thus strikes the imagination at first sight, without discovering what it is that has so agreeable an effect. Our British gardeners, on the contrary, instead of humouring nature, love to deviate from it as much as possible. Our trees rise in cones, globes, and pyramids. We see the marks of the scissors upon every plant and bush. I do not know whether I am singular in my opinion; but for my own part, I would rather look upon a tree in all its luxuriancy and diffusion of boughs and branches, than when it is thus cut and trimmed into a mathematical figure; and cannot but fancy, that an orchard in flower looks infinitely more delightful than all the little labyrinths of the most finished parterre. But as our great modellers of gar dens have their magazines of plants to dispose of, it is very natural for them to tear up all the beautiful plantations of fruit trees, and contrive a plan that may most turn to their own profit, in taking off their evergreens, and the like moveable plants, with which their shops are plentifully stocked. *O.*

PAPER V.

Of architecture, as it affects the imagination. Greatness in achitecture relates either to the bulk or to the manner. Greatness of bulk in the ancient oriental buildings. The ancient accounts of these buildings confirmed, 1. From the advantages for raising such works, in the first ages of the world, in the eastern climates. 2. From several of them which are still extant. Instances how greatness of manner affects the imagination. A French author's observations on this subject. Why concave and convex figures give a greatness of manner to works of architecture. Every thing that pleases the imagination in architecture, is either great, beautiful, or new.

Adde tot egregias urbes, operumque laborem.
Vir. Geo. 2. v. 155.

Next add our cities of illustrious name,
Their costly labour, and stupendous frame.—*Dryden.*

Having already shown how the fancy is affected by the works of nature, and afterward considered in general both the works of nature and of art, how they mutually assist and complete each other, in forming such scenes and prospects as are most apt to delight the mind of the beholder: I shall in this paper throw together some reflections on that particular art, which has a more immediate tendency than any other to produce those primary pleasures of the imagination, which have hitherto been the subject of this discourse. The art I mean is that of architecture; which I shall consider only with regard to the light in which the foregoing speculations have placed it, without entering into those rules and maxims which the great masters of architecture have laid down and explained at large in numberless treatises upon that subject.

Greatness, in the works of architecture, may be considered as relating to the bulk and body of the structure, or to the *manner* in which it is built. As for the first, we find the ancients, especially among the eastern nations of the world, infinitely superior to the moderns.

Not to mention the tower of Babel, of which an old author says there were the foundations to be seen in his time, which looked like a spacious mountain; what could be more noble than the walls of Babylon, its hanging gardens, and its temple to Jupiter Belus, that rose a mile high by eight several stories, each story a furlong in height, and on the top of which was the Babylonian observatory? I might here likewise take notice of the huge rock that was cut into the figure of Semiramis, with the smaller rocks that lay by it in the shape of tributary kings; the prodigious basin, or artificial lake, which took in the whole Euphrates, till such time as a new canal was formed for its reception, with the several trenches through which that river was conveyed. I know there are persons who look upon some of these wonders of art as fabulous; but I cannot find any ground for such a suspicion, unless it be that we have no such works among us at present. There were indeed many greater advantages for building in those times, and in that part of the world, than have been met with ever since. The earth was extremely fruitful, men lived generally on pasturage, which requires a much smaller number of hands than agriculture: there were very few trades to employ the busy part of mankind, and fewer arts and sciences to give work to men of speculative tempers; and what is more than all the rest, the prince was absolute: so that, when he went to war, he put himself at the head of a whole people: as we find Semiramis leading her three millions to the field, and yet overpowered by the number of her enemies. 'Tis no wonder, therefore, when she was at peace, and turning her thoughts on building, that she could accomplish so great works with such a prodigious multitude of labourers: besides, that in her climate there was small interruption of frost and winters, which make the northern workmen lie half the year idle. I might mention too, among the benefits of the climate, what historians say of the earth, that it sweated out a bitumen or natural kind of mortar, which is doubtless the same with that mentioned in holy writ, as contributing to the structure of Babel. 'Slime they used instead of mortar.'

In Egypt we still see their pyramids, which answer to the descriptions that have been made of them; and I question not but a traveller might find out some remains of the labyrinth that covered a whole province, and had a hundred temples disposed among its several quarters and divisions.

The wall of China is one of these eastern pieces of magnificence, which makes a figure even in the map of the world, although an account of it would have been thought fabulous, were not the wall itself still extant.

We are obliged to devotion for the noblest buildings that have adorned the several countries of the world. It is this which has set men at work on temples and public places of worship, not only that they might, by the magnificence of the building, invite the Deity to reside within it, but that such stupendous works might at the same time open the mind to vast conceptions, and fit it to converse with the divinity of the place. For every thing that is majestic imprints an awfulness and reverence on the mind of the beholders, and strikes in with the natural greatness of the soul.

In the second place, we are to consider *greatness*

of manner in architecture, which has such force upon the imagination, that a small building, where *it* appears, shall give the mind nobler ideas than one of twenty times the bulk, where the manner is ordinary or little. Thus, perhaps, a man would have been more astonished with the majestic air that appeared in one of Lysippus's statues of Alexander, though no bigger than the life, than he might have been with mount Athos, had it been cut into the figure of the hero, according to the proposal of Phidias, with a river in one hand, and a city in the other.

Let any one reflect on the disposition of mind he finds in himself at his first entrance into the Pantheon at Rome, and how the imagination is filled with something great and amazing; and at the same time consider how little, in proportion, he is affected with the inside of a Gothic cathedral, though it be five times larger than the other; which can arise from nothing else but the greatness of the manner in the one, and the meanness in the other.

I have seen an observation upon this subject in a French author which very much pleased me. It is in Monsieur Freart's parallel of the ancient and modern architecture. I shall give it the reader with the same terms of art which he has made use of. 'I am observing (says he) a thing which, in my opinion, is very curious, whence it proceeds, that in the same quantity of superficies, the one manner seems great and magnificent, and the other poor and trifling; the reason is fine and uncommon. I say then, that to introduce into architecture this grandeur of manner, we ought so to proceed, that the division of the principal members of the order may consist but of few parts, that they be all great and of a bold and ample relievo, and swelling; and that the eye beholding nothing little and mean, the imagination may be more vigorously touched and affected with the work that stands before it. For example; in a cornice, if the gola or cymatium of the corona, the copping, the modillions, or dentelli, make a noble show by their graceful projections if we see none of that ordinary confusion which is the result of those little cavities, quarter rounds of the astragal, and I know not how many other intermingled particulars which produce no effect in great and massy works, and which very unprofitably take up place to the prejudice of the principal member,—it is most certain that this manner will appear solemn and great; as on the contrary, that it will have but a poor and mean effect, where there is a redundancy of those smaller ornaments which divide and scatter the angles of the sight into such a multitude of rays, so pressed together that the whole will but appear a confusion.'

Among all the figures in architecture, there are none that have a greater air than the concave and the convex; and we find in all the ancient and modern architecture, as well in the remote parts of China as in countries nearer home, that round pillars and vaulted roofs make a great part of those buildings which are designed for pomp and magnificence. The reason I take to be, because in these figures we generally see more of the body than in those of other kinds. There are indeed figures of bodies, where the eye may take in two thirds of the surface; but as in such bodies the sight must split upon several angles, it does not take in one uniform idea, but several ideas of the same kind. Look upon the outside of a dome, your eye half surrounds it: look up into the inside, and at one glance you have all the prospect of it; the entire concavity falls into your eye at once, the sight being as the centre that collects and gathers into it the lines of the whole circumference: in a square pillar, the sight often takes in but a fourth part of the surface; and in a square concave, must move up and down to the different sides, before it is master of all the inward surface. For this reason, the fancy is infinitely more struck with the view of the open air, and skies, that passes through an arch, than what comes through a square or any other figure. The figure of the rainbow does not contribute less to its magnificence than the colours to its beauty, as it is very poetically described by the son of Sirach: 'Look upon the rainbow and praise Him that made it. very beautiful it is in its brightness; it encompasses the heavens with a glorious circle, and the hands of the Most High have bended it.'

Having thus spoken of that greatness which affects the mind in architecture, I might next show the pleasure that rises in the imagination from what appears new and beautiful in this art; but as every beholder has naturally a greater taste of these two perfections in every building which offers itself to his view than of that which I have hitherto considered, I shall not trouble my readers with any reflections upon it. It is sufficient for my present purpose to observe, that there is nothing in this whole art which pleases the imagination, but as it is great, uncommon, or beautiful.

O.

PAPER VI.

The secondary pleasures of the imagination. The several sources of these pleasures (statuary, painting, description, and music) compared together. The final cause of our receiving pleasure from these several sources. Of descriptions in particular. The power of words over the imagination. Why one reader is more pleased with description than another.'

Quotenus hoc simile est oculis, quod mente videmus
Lucr. lib. 4. v. 754.

——Objects still appear the same,
To mind and eye, to colour and in frame.—*Creech.*

I AT first divided the pleasures of the imagination into such as arise from objects that are actually before our eyes, or that once entered in at our eyes, and are afterward called up into the mind, either barely by its own operations, or on occasion of something without us, as statues or descriptions. We have already considered the first division, and shall therefore enter on the other, which, for distinction's sake, I have called the secondary pleasures of the imagination. When I say the ideas we receive from statues, descriptions, or such like occasions, are the same that were once actually in our view, it must not be understood that we had once seen the very place, action, or person which are carved or described. It is sufficient that we have seen places, persons, or actions, in general, which bear a resemblance, or at least some remote analogy with what we find represented; since it is in the power of the imagination, when it is once stocked with particular ideas, to enlarge, compound, and vary them at her own pleasure.

Among the different kinds of representation, *statuary* is the most natural, and shows us something *likest* the object that is represented. To make use of a common instance, let one who is born blind take an image in his hands, and trace out with his fingers the different furrows and impressions of the chisel, and he will easily conceive how the shape of a man or beast may be represented by it; but should he draw his hand over a *picture*, where all is smooth and uniform, he would never be able to imagine how the several prominences and depressions of a human body could be shown on a plain piece of canvass, that has in it no unevenness or irregularity. *Description* runs yet farther from the things it represents than painting; for a picture bears a real resemblance to its original, which letters and syllables are wholly void of. Colours speak all languages, but words are understood only by such a people or nation. For this reason, though men's necessities quickly put them on finding out speech, writing is probably of a later invention than painting; particularly we are told, that in America, when the Spaniards first arrived there, expresses were sent to the Emperor of Mexico in paint, and the news of his country delineated by the strokes of a pencil, which was a more natural way than that of writing, though at the same time much more imperfect, because it is impossible to draw the little connexions of speech or to give the picture of a conjunction or an adverb. It would be yet more strange to represent visible objects by sounds that have no ideas annexed to them, and to make something like description in *music*. Yet it is certain, there may be confused, imperfect notions of this nature raised in the imagination by an artificial composition of notes; and we find that great masters in the art are able sometimes to set their hearers in the heat and hurry of a battle, to overcast their minds with melancholy scenes and apprehensions of deaths and funerals, or to lull them into pleasing dreams of groves and elysiums.

In all these instances, this secondary pleasure of the imagination proceeds from that action of the mind, which compares the ideas arising from the original objects with the ideas we receive from the statue, picture, description, or sound, that represents them. It is impossible for us to give the necessary reason, why this operation of the mind is attended with so much pleasure, as I have before observed on the same occasion; but we find a great variety of entertainments derived from this single principle: for it is this that not only gives us a relish of statuary, painting, and description, but makes us delight in all the actions and arts of mimicry. It is this that makes the several kinds of wit pleasant, which consists, as I have formerly shown, in the affinity of ideas: and we may add, it is this also that raises the little satisfaction we sometimes find in the different sorts of false wit, whether it consists in the affinity of letters, as an anagram, acrostic; or of syllables, as in doggerel rhymes, echoes; or of words, as in puns, quibbles; or of a whole sentence or poem, as wings and altars. The *final cause*, probably, of annexing pleasure to this operation of the mind was to quicken and encourage us in our searches after truth, since the distinguishing one thing from another, and the right discerning betwixt our ideas, depend wholly upon our comparing them together, and observing the congruity or disagreement that appears among the several works of nature.

But I shall here confine myself to those pleasures of the imagination which proceed from ideas raised by *words*, because most of the observations that agree with descriptions are equally applicable to painting and statuary.

Words, when well chosen, have so great a force in them, that a description often gives us more lively ideas than the sight of things themselves. The reader finds a scene drawn in stronger colours, and painted more to the life in his imagination, by the help of words, than by an actual survey of the scene which they describe. In this case the poet seems to get the better of nature; he takes, indeed, the landscape after her, but gives it more vigorous touches, heightens its beauty, and so enlivens the whole piece, that the images which flow from the objects themselves appear weak and faint, in comparison of those that come from the expressions. The reason probably may be, because in the survey of any object we have only so much of it painted on the imagination as comes in at the eye; but in its description the poet gives us as free a view of it as he pleases, and discovers to us several parts that either we did not attend to or that lay out of our sight when we first beheld it. As we look on any subject, our idea of it is, perhaps, made up of two or three simple ideas; but when the poet represents it, he may either give us a more complex idea of it, or only raise in us such ideas as are more apt to affect the imagination.

It may be here worth our while to examine how it comes to pass that several readers, who are all acquainted with the same language, and know the meaning of the words they read, should nevertheless have a different relish of the same descriptions. We find one transported with a passage, which another runs over with coldness and indifference; or finding the representation extremely natural, where another can perceive nothing of likeliness and conformity. This different taste must proceed either from the *perfection of imagination* in one more than in another, or from the *different ideas* that several readers affix to the same words. For to have a true relish and form a right judgment of a description, a man should be born with a good imagination, and must have well weighed the force and energy that lie in the several words of a language, so as to be able to distinguish which are most significant and expressive of their proper ideas, and what additional strength and beauty they are capable of receiving from conjunction with others. The fancy must be warm to retain the print of those images it hath received from outward objects; and the judgment discerning, to know what expressions are most proper to clothe and adorn them to the best advantage. A man who is deficient in either of these respects, though he may receive the general notion of a description, can never see distinctly all its particular beauties: as a person, with a weak sight, may have the confused prospect of a place that lies before him, without entering into its several parts, or discerning the variety of its colours in their full glory and perfection.

C.

PAPER VII.

How a whole set of ideas hang together, &c. A natural cause assigned for it. How to perfect the imagination of a writer. Who among the ancient poets had this faculty in its greatest perfection. Homer excelled in imagining what is great; Virgil in imagining what is beautiful; Ovid in imagining what is new. Our own countryman, Milton, very perfect in all these three respects.'

Quem tu, Melpomene, semel
Nascentum placida lumine videris
Mon illum labor Isthmius
Clarabit pugilem, non equus impiger, &c.
Sed quæ Tibur aquæ fertile perfluunt,
Et spissæ nemorum comæ
Fingent Æolio carmine nobilem.
Hor. Od. 3. l. 4. v. 1.

At whose blest birth propitious rays
The muses shed, on whom they smile,
No dusty Isthmian game
Shall stoutest of the ring proclaim,
Or, to reward his toil,
Wreath ivy crowns, and grace his head with bays.
But fruitful Tibur's shady groves,
Its pleasant springs and purling streams,
Shall raise a lasting name.
And set him high in sounding fame
For lyric verse.
Creech.

We may observe, that any single circumstance of what we have formerly seen, often raises up a whole scene of imagery, and awakens numberless ideas that before slept in the imagination; such a particular smell or colour is able to fill the mind on a sudden with a picture of the fields or gardens where we first met with it, and to bring up into view all the variety of images that once attended it. Our imagination takes the hint, and leads us unexpectedly into cities or theatres, plains or meadows. We may further observe, when the fancy thus reflects on the scenes that have past on it formerly, those which were at first pleasant to behold appear more so upon reflection, and that the memory heightens the delightfulness of the original. A Cartesian would account for both these instances in the following manner:

The set of ideas which we received from such a prospect or garden, having entered the mind at the same time, have a set of traces belonging to them in the brain, bordering very near one upon another; when, therefore, any one of these ideas arises in the imagination, and consequently despatches a flow of animal spirits to its proper trace, these spirits, in the violence of their motion, run not only into the trace to which they were more particularly directed, but into several of those that lie about it: by this means they awaken other ideas of the same set, which immediately determine a new despatch of spirits, that in the same manner open other neighbouring traces, till at last the whole set of them is blown up, and the whole prospect or garden flourishes in the imagination. But because the pleasure we receive from these places far surmounted and overcame the little disagreeableness we found in them, for this reason there was at first a wider passage worn in the pleasure traces; and, on the contrary, so narrow a one in those which belonged to the disagreeable ideas, that they were quickly stopt up, and rendered incapable of receiving any animal spirits, and consequently of exciting any unpleasant ideas in the memory.

It would be in vain to inquire, whether the power of imagining things strongly proceeds from any greater perfection in the soul, or from any nicer texture in the brain, of one man than of another. But this is certain, that a noble writer should be born with this faculty in its full strength and vigour, so as to be able to receive lively ideas from outward objects, to retain them long and to range together, upon occasion, in such figures and representations as are most likely to hit the fancy of the reader. A poet should take as much pains in forming his imagination as a philosopher in cultivating his understanding. He must gain a due relish of the works of nature, and be thoroughly conversant in the various scenery of a country life.

When he is stored with country images, if he would go beyond pastoral, and the lower kinds of poetry, he ought to acquaint himself with the pomp and magnificence of courts. He should be very well versed in every thing that is noble and stately in the productions of art, whether it appear in painting or statuary, in the great works of architecture which are in their present glory, or in the ruins of those which flourished in former ages.

Such advantages as these help to open a man's thoughts, and to enlarge his imagination, and will therefore have their influence on all kinds of writing, if the author knows how to make right use of them. And among those of the learned languages who excel in this talent, the most perfect in their several kinds are perhaps Homer, Virgil, and Ovid. The first strikes the imagination wonderfully with what is great, the second with what is beautiful, and the last with what is strange. Reading the Iliad is like travelling through a country uninhabited, where the fancy is entertained with a thousand savage prospects of vast deserts, wide uncultivated marshes, huge forests, misshappen rocks and precipices. On the contrary the Æneid is like a well-ordered garden, where it is impossible to find out any part unadorned, or to cast our eyes upon a single spot that does not produce some beautiful plant or flower. But when we are in the Metamorphosis, we are walking on enchanted ground, and see nothing but scenes of magic lying round us.

Homer is in his province when he is describing a battle or a multitude, a hero or a god. Virgil is never better pleased than when he is in his Elysium, or copying out an entertaining picture. Homer's epithets generally mark out what is great, Virgil's what is agreeable. Nothing can be more magnificent than the figure

Jupiter makes in the first Iliad, nor more charming than that of Venus in the first Æneid.

> Ἠ, και κυανεησιν επ οφρυσι νευσε Κρονιων
> Αμβροσιαι δ' αρα χαιται επερρωσαντι ανακτος,
> Κρατος απ' αγανατοιο μελαν δ' ελεγιξεν Ολυμπον.
> Il. x. v. 128.

> He spoke, and awful bends his sable brows,
> Shakes his ambrosial curls, and gives the nod,
> The stamp of fate, and sanction of the god:
> High heav'n with trembling the dread signal took,
> And all Olympus to the centre shook.

> *Dexit, et avertens, rosearcervice refulsit:*
> *Ambrosiæque comæ divinum vertice odorem*
> *Spiravere: pedes vestis defluxit ad imos,*
> *Et vera incossupatuit Dea*—— *Æn.* I. v. 406.

> Thus having said, she turn'd, and made appear
> Her neck refulgent and dishevell'd hair;
> Which, flowing from her shoulders, reach'd the ground,
> And widely spread ambrosial scents around:
> In length of train descends her sweeping gown,
> And by her graceful walk the queen of love is known.
> *Dryden.*

Homer's persons are most of them godlike and terrible; Virgil has scarce admitted any into his poem who are not beautiful, and has taken particular care to make his hero so.

> —— *Lumenque juventæ*
> *Purpureum, et lætos occulis afflævit honores.*
> *Æn.* 1. v. 594

> And gave his rolling eyes a sparkling grace,
> And breath'd a youthful vigour on his face.—*Dryden.*

In a word, Homer fills his readers with sublime ideas, and I believe, has raised the imagination of all the good poets that have come after him. I shall only instance Horace, who immediately takes fire at the first hint of any passage in the Iliad or Odyssey, and always rises above himself when he has Homer in his view. Virgil has drawn together into his Æneid all the pleasing scenes his subject is capable of admitting, and in his Georgics has given us a collection of the most delightful landscapes that can be made out of fields and woods, herds of cattle, and swarms of bees.

Ovid, in his Metamorphosis, has shown us how the imagination may be affected by what is strange. He describes a miracle in every story, and always gives us the sight of some new creature at the end of it. His art consists chiefly in well-timing his description, before the first shape is quite worn off and the new one perfectly finished; so that he every where entertains us with something we never saw before, and shows monster after monster to the end of the Metamorphosis.

If I were to name a poet that is perfect master in all these arts of working on the imagination, I think Milton may pass for one: and if his Paradise Lost falls short of the Æneid or Iliad in this respect, it proceeds rather from the fault of the language in which it is written, than from any defect of genius in the author. So divine a poem in English is like a stately palace, built of brick, where one may see architecture in as great perfection as in one of marble, though the materials are of a coarser nature. But to consider it only as it regards our present subject: what can be conceived greater than the battle of angels, the majesty of Messiah, the stature and behaviour of Satan and his peers? What more beautiful than Pandæmonium, Paradise, heaven, angels, Adam and Eve? What more strange than the creation of the world, the several metamorphoses of the fallen angels, and the surprising adventures their leader meets with in his search after Paradise? No other subject could have furnished a poet with scenes so proper to strike the imagination, as no other poet could have painted those scenes in more strong and lively colours.

O.

PAPER VIII.

Why any thing that is unpleasant to behold pleases the imagination when well described. Why the imagination receives a more exquisite pleasure from the description of what is great, new, or beautiful. The pleasure still heightened, if what is described raises passion in the mind. Disagreeable passions pleasing when raised by apt descriptions. Why terror and grief are pleasing to the mind when excited by description. A particular advantage the writers in poetry and fiction have to please the imagination. What liberties are allowed them.'

——*Ferte etrubus asper ammomu*
Virg. Ecl. 3. v. 89.

The rugged thorn shall bear the fragrant rose.

The pleasures of these secondary views of the imagination are of a wider and more universal nature than those it has when joined with sight; for not only what is great, strange, or beautiful, but any thing that is disagreeable when looked upon, pleases us in an apt description. Here, therefore, we must inquire after a new principle of pleasure, which is nothing else but the action of the mind, which *compares* the ideas that arise from words with the ideas that arise from the objects themselves; and why this operation of the mind is attended with so much pleasure, we have before considered. For this reason, therefore, the description of a dunghill is pleasing to the imagination, if the image be represented to our minds by suitable expressions; though, perhaps, this may be more properly called the pleasure of the understanding than of the fancy, because we are not so much delighted with the image that is contained in the description, as with the aptness of the description to excite the image.

But if the description of what is little, common, or deformed, be acceptable to the imagination, the description of what is great, surprising, or beautiful, is much more so: because here we are not only delighted with *comparing* the representation with the original, but are highly pleased with the original itself. Most readers, I believe, are more charmed with Milton's description of Paradise than of Hell: they are both, perhaps, equally perfect in their kind; but in the one the brimstone and sulphur are not so refreshing to the imagination as the beds of flowers and the wilderness of sweets in the other.

There is yet another circumstance which recommends a description more than all the rest, and that is, if it represents to us such objects as are apt to raise a secret ferment in the mind of the reader, and to work with violence upon his passions. For, in this case, we are at once warmed and enlightened, so that the pleasure becomes more universal, and is several ways qualified to entertain us. Thus, in painting, it is pleasant to look on the picture of any face where the resemblance is hit; but the pleasure increases if it be the picture of a face that is beautiful, and is still greater if the beauty be softened with an air of melancholy or sorrow. The two leading passions which the more serious parts of poetry endeavour to stir up in us are terror and pity. And here, by the way, one would wonder how it comes to pass, that such passions as are very unpleasant at all other times, and very agreeable when excited by proper descriptions. It is not strange, that we should take delight in such passages as are apt to produce hope, joy, admiration, love, or the like emotions, in us, because they never rise in the mind without an inward pleasure which attends them: But how comes it to pass, that we should take delight in being terrified or dejected by a description, when we find so much uneasiness in the fear or grief which we receive from any other occasion?

If we consider therefore the nature of this pleasure, we shall find that it does not arise so properly from the description of what is terrible, as from the reflection we make on ourselves at the time of reading it. When we look on such hideous objects, we are not a little pleased to think we are in no danger of them. We consider them, at the same time, as dreadful and harmless; so that the more frightful appearance they make, the greater is the pleasure we receive from the sense of our own safety. In short, we look upon the terrors of a description with the same curiosity and satisfaction that we survey a dead monster.

—— In forme cadaver
Protrahitur: nequeunt expleri corda tuendo
Terribilis occulos, vultum, villosaque setis
Pectora semiferi, atque extinctos faucibus ignes!
Virg. Æn. 8. v. 264.

—— They drag him from his den
The wond'ring neighbourhood, with glad surprise,
Beheld his shagged breast, his giant size,
His mouth that flames no more, and his extinguish'd eyes. *Dryden.*

It is for the same reason that we are delighted with the reflecting upon dangers that are past, or in looking on a precipice at a distance, which would fill us with a different kind of horror if we saw it hanging over our heads.

In the like manner, when we read of torments, wounds, deaths, and the like dismal accidents, our pleasure does not flow so properly from the grief which such melancholy descriptions give us, as from the secret comparison which we make between ourselves and the person who suffers:—Such representations teach us to set a just value upon our own condition, and make us prize our good fortune which exempts us from the like calamities. This is, however, such a kind of pleasure as we are not capable of receiving, when we see a person actually lying under the tortures that we meet with in a description: because, in this case, the object presses too close upon our senses, and bears so hard upon us, that it does not give us time or leisure to reflect on ourselves. Our thoughts are so intent on the miseries of the sufferer, that we cannot turn them upon our own happiness. Whereas, on the contrary, we consider the misfortunes we read in history or poetry, either as past, or as fictitious; so that the reflection upon ourselves rises in us insensibly, and overbears the sorrow we conceive for the sufferings of the afflicted.

But because the mind of man requires something more perfect in matter than what it finds there, and can never meet with any sight in nature which sufficiently answers its highest ideas of pleasantness; or, in other words, because the imagination can fancy to itself things more great, strange, or beautiful, than the eye ever saw, and is still sensible of some defect in what it has seen; on this account it is the part of a poet to humour the imagination in its own notions, by mending and perfecting nature where he describes reality, and by adding greater beauties than are put together in nature, where he describes a fiction.

He is not obliged to attend her in the slow advances which she makes from one season to another, or to observe her conduct in the successive production of plants and flowers: he may draw into his description all the beauties of the spring and autumn, and make the whole year contribute something to render it the more agreeable. His rose-trees, woodbines, and jessamines, may flower together, and his beds be covered at the same time with lilies, violets, and amaranths. His soil is not restrained to any particular set of plants, but is proper either for oaks or myrtles, and adapts itself to the products of every climate. Oranges may grow wild in it; myrrh may be met with in every hedge; and if he thinks it proper to have a grove of spices, he can quickly command sun enough to raise it. If all this will not furnish out an agreeable scene, he can make several new species of flowers, with richer scents and higher colours than any that grow in the gardens of nature. His concerts of birds may be as full and harmonious, and his woods as thick and gloomy, as he pleases. He is at no more expense in a long vista than a short one, and can as easily throw his cascades from a precipice of half a mile high as from one of twenty yards. He has his choice of the winds, and can turn the course of his rivers in all the variety of meanders that are most delightful to the reader's imagination. In a word, he has the modelling of nature in his own hands, and may give her what charms he pleases, provided he does not reform her too much, and run into absurdities, by endeavouring to excel.

PAPER IX.

'Of that kind of poetry which Mr. Dryden calls the fairy way of writing. How a poet should be qualified for it. The pleasures of the imagination that arise from it. In this respect why the moderns excel the ancients. Why the English excel the moderns. Who the best among the English. Of emblematical persons.

——*Mentis gratissimus error.*
Hor. Ep. 2. l. 2. v. 140.

In pleasing error lost, and charmingly deceiv'd.

There is a kind of writing wherein the poet quite loses sight of nature, and entertains his reader's imagination with the characters and actions of such persons as have many of them no existence but what he bestows on them; such as fairies, witches, magicians, dæmons, and departed spirits. This Mr. Dryden calls the *fairy way of writing*, which is, indeed, more difficult than any other that depends on the poet's fancy because he has no pattern to follow in it, and must work altogether out of his own invention.

There is a very odd turn of thought required for this sort of writing; and it is impossible for a poet to succeed in it, who has not a particular cast of fancy, and an imagination naturally fruitful and superstitious. Besides this, he ought to be very well versed in legends and fables, antiquated romances, and the traditions of nurses and old women, that he may fall in with our natural prejudices, and humour those notions which we have imbibed in our infancy. For otherwise he will be apt to make his fairies talk like people of his own species, and not like other sets of beings, who converse with different objects and think in a different manner from that of mankind;

Sylvis deducti caveant, me judice, fauni,
Ne velut innati triviis, ac pene forenses,
Aut nimium teneris juvenentur versibus.——
Hor. Ars Poet. v. 244.

A satyr that comes staring from the woods,
Must not at first speak like an orator.—*Roscommon.*

I do not say with Mr. Bays in the Rehearsal, that spirits must not be confined to speak sense; but it is certain their sense ought to be a little discoloured, that it may seem particular, and proper to the person and the condition of the speaker.

These descriptions raise a pleasing kind of horror in the mind of the reader, and amuse his imagination with the strangeness and novelty of the persons who are represented in them. They bring up into our memory the stories we have heard in our childhood, and favour those secret terrors and apprehensions to which the mind of man is naturally subject. We are pleased with surveying the different habits and behaviours of foreign countries; how much more must we be delighted and surprised when we are led, as it were, into a new creation, and see the persons and manners of another species? Men of cold fancies and philosophical dispositions object to this kind of poetry, that it has not probability enough to affect the imagination. But to this it may be answered, that we are sure, in general, there are many intellectual beings in the world besides ourselves, and several species of spirits, who are subject to different laws and economies from those of mankind: when we see, therefore, any of these represented naturally, we cannot look upon the representation as altogether impossible; nay, many are prepossessed with such false opinions, as dispose them to believe these particular delusions; at least we have all heard so many pleasing relations in favour of them, that we do not care for seeing through the falsehood, and willingly give ourselves up to so agreeable an imposture.

The ancients have not much of this poetry among them, for indeed almost the whole substance of it owes its original to the darkness and superstition of later ages, when pious frauds were made use of to amuse mankind, and frighten them into a sense of their duty. Our forefathers looked upon nature with more reverence and horror, before the world was enlightened by learning and philosophy, and loved to astonish themselves with the apprehensions of witchcraft, prodigies, charms, and enchantments. There was not a village in England, that had not a ghost in it, the church-yards were all haunted, every large common had a circle of fairies belonging to it, and there was scarce a shepherd to be met with who had not seen a spirit.

Among all the poets of this kind our English are much the best, by what I have yet seen; whether it be that we abound with more stories of this nature, or that the genius of our country is fitter for this sort of poetry. For the English are naturally fanciful, and very often disposed by that gloominess and melancholy of temper, which is so frequent in our nation, to many wild notions and visions to which others are not so liable.

Among the English, Shakspeare has incomparably excelled all others. That noble extravagance of fancy, which he had in so great perfection, thoroughly qualified him to touch this weak superstitious part of his readers' imagination: and made him capable of succeeding, where he had nothing to support him besides the strength of his own genius. There is something so wild and yet so solemn in the speeches of his ghosts, fairies, witches, and the like imaginary persons, that we cannot forbear thinking them natural, though we have no rule by which to judge of them; and must confess, if there are such beings in the world, it looks highly probable they should talk and act as he has represented them.

There is another sort of imaginary beings that we sometimes meet with among the poets, when the author represents any passion, appetite, virtue, or vice, under a visible shape, and makes it a person or an actor in his poem. Of this nature are the descriptions of hunger and envy in Ovid, of fame in Virgil, and of sin and death in Milton. We find a whole creation of the like shadowy persons in Spenser, who had an admirable talent in representations of this kind. I have discoursed of these emblematical persons in former papers, and shall therefore only mention them in this place. Thus we see how many ways poetry addresses itself to the imagination, as it has not only the whole circle of nature for its province, but makes new worlds of its own, shows us persons who are not to be found in being, and represents even the faculties of the soul, with the several virtues and vices, in a sensible shape and character.

I shall, in my two following papers, consider in general how other kinds of writing are qualified to please the imagination, with which I intend to conclude this essay.

PAPER X.

'What authors please the imagination who have nothing to do with fiction. How history pleases the imagination. How the authors of the new philosophy please the imagination. The bounds and defects of the imagination. Whether these defects are essential to the imagination.'

— *Quocunque volunt mentem auditoris agunto*
Hor. Ars Poet. v. 100.

And raise men's passions to what height they will.
Roscommon.

As the writers in poetry and fiction borrow their several materials from outward objects, and join them together at their own pleasure, there are others who are obliged to follow nature more closely, and to take entire scenes out of her.—Such are historians, natural philosophers, travellers, geographers, and, in a word, all who describe visible objects of a real existence.

It is the most agreeable talent of an historian, to be able to draw up his armies and fight his battles in proper expressions, to set before our eyes the divisions, cabals, and jealousies of great men, and to lead us step by step into the several actions and events of his history. We love to see the subject unfolding itself by just degrees, and breaking upon us insensibly, that so we may be kept in a pleasing suspense, and have time given us to raise our expectations, and to side with one of the parties concerned in the relation. I confess this shows more the art than the veracity of the historian: but I am only to speak of him as he is qualified to please the imagination. And, in this respect, Livy has perhaps excelled all who went before him, or have written since his time. He describes every thing in so lively a manner, that his whole history is an admirable picture, and touches on such proper circumstances in every story, that his reader becomes a kind of spectator, and feels in himself all the variety of passions which are correspondent to the several parts of the relations.

But among this set of writers there are none who more gratify and enlarge the imagination than the authors of the new philosophy, whether we consider their theories of the earth or heavens, the discoveries they have made by glasses, or any other of their contemplations on nature. We are not a little pleased to find every green leaf swarm with millions of animals, that at their largest growth are not visible to the naked eye. There is something very engaging to the fancy, as well as to our reason, in the treatises of metals, minerals, plants, and meteors. But when we survey the whole earth at once, and the several planets that lie within its neighbourhood, we are filled with a pleasing astonishment, to see so many worlds hanging one above another, and sliding round their axles in such an amazing pomp and solemnity. If, after this, we contemplate those wild fields of *æther*, that reach in height as far as from Saturn to the fixed stars, and run abroad almost to an infinitude, our imagination finds its capacity filled with so immense a prospect, and puts itself upon the stretch to comprehend it. But if we yet rise higher, and consider the fixed stars as so many vast oceans of flame, that are each of them attended with a different set of planets, and still discover new firmaments and new lights that are sunk farther in those unfathomable depths of *æther*, so as not to be seen by the strongest of our telescopes, we are lost in such a labyrinth of suns and worlds, and confounded with the immensity and magnificence of nature.

Nothing is more pleasing to the fancy than to enlarge itself by degrees in its contemplation of the various proportions which its several objects bear to each other, when it compares the body of man to the bulk of the whole earth, the earth to the circle it describes round the sun, that circle to the sphere of the fixed stars, the sphere of the fied stars to the circuit of the whole creation, the whole creation itself to the infinite space that is every where diffused about it; or, when the imagination works downward, and considers the bulk of a human body in respect of an animal a hundred times less than a mite, the particular limbs of such an animal, the different springs which actuate the limbs, the spirits which set these springs agoing, and the proportionable minuteness of these several parts, before they have arrived at their full growth and perfection. But if, after all this, we take the least particle of these animal spirits, and consider its capacity of being wrought into a world, that shall contain within those narrow demensions a heaven and earth, stars and planets, and every different species of living creatures, in the same analogy and proportion they bear to each other in our own universe: such a speculation, by reason of its nicety, appears ridiculous to those who have not turned their thoughts that way, though at the same time it is founded on no less than the evidence of a demonstration. Nay, we may yet carry it farther, and discover in the smallest particle of this little world a new inexhausted fund of matter, capable of being spun out into another universe.

I have dwelt the longer on this subject because I think it may show us the proper limits, as well as the defectiveness of our imagination: how it is confined to a very small quantity of space, and immediately stops in its operation, when it endeavours to take in any thing that is very great or very little. Let a man try to conceive the different bulk of an animal, which is twenty, from another which is a hundred times less than a mite, or to compare, in his thoughts, a length of a thousand diameters of the earth with that of a million, and he will quickly find that he has no different measures in his mind adjusted to such extraordinary degrees of grandeur or minuteness. The understanding, indeed, opens an infinite space on every side of us; but the imagination, after a few faint efforts, is immediately at a stand, and finds herself swallowed up in the immensity of the void that surrounds it; our reason can pursue a particle of matter through an infinite variety of divisions: but the fancy soon loses sight of it, and feels in itself a kind of chasm, that wants to be filled with matter of a more sensible bulk. We can neither widen nor contract the faculty to the dimension of either extreme: the object is too big for our capacity when we would comprehend the circumference of a world, and dwindles into nothing when we endeavour after the idea of an atom.

It is possible this defect of imagination may not be in the soul itself, but as it acts in conjunction with the body; perhaps there may not be room in the brain for such a variety of impressions, or the animal spirits may be incapable of figuring them in such a manner as is necessary to excite so very large or very minute ideas. However it be, we may well suppose that beings of a higher nature very much excel us in this respect, as it is probable the soul of man will be infinitely more perfect hereafter in this faculty, as in all the rest; insomuch that, perhaps, the imagination will be able to keep pace with the understanding, and to form in itself distinct ideas of all the different modes and quantities of space.

PAPER XI.

How those please the imagination who treat of subjects abstracted from matter, by allusions taken from it. What allusions most pleasing to the imagination. Great writers, how faulty in this respect. Of the art of imagining in general. The imagination capable of pain as well as pleasure. In what degree the imagination is capable either of pain or pleasure.

Ignotis errare locis, ignota videre
Flumina gaudebat; studio minuente laborem.
Ovid. Met. 4. v. 294.

He sought fresh fountains in a foreign soil;
The pleasure lessen'd the attending toil.—*Addison.*

The pleasures of the imagination are not wholly confined to such particular authors as are conversant in material objects, but are often to be met with among the polite masters of morality, criticism, and other speculations abstracted from matter, who, though they do not directly treat of the visible parts of nature, often draw from them their similitudes, metaphors, and allegories. By these allusions a truth in the understanding is as it were reflected by the imagination: we are able to see something like colour and shape in a notion, and to discover a scheme of thoughts traced out upon matter. And here the mind receives a great deal of satisfaction, and has two of its faculties gratified at the same time, while the fancy is busy in copying after the understanding, and transcribing ideas out of the intellectual world into the material.

The great art of a writer shows itself in the choice of pleasing allusions, which are generally to be taken from the *great* or *beautiful* works of art or nature; for, though whatever is new or uncommon is apt to delight the imagination, the chief design of an allusion being to illustrate and explain the passages of an author, it should be always borrowed from what is more known and common than the passages which are to be explained.

Allegories, when well chosen, are like so many tracts of light in a discourse, that make every thing about them clear and beautiful. A noble metaphor, when it is placed to an advantage, casts a kind of glory round it, and darts a lustre through a whole sentence. These different kinds of allusion are but so many different manners of similitude; and, that they may please the imagination, the likeness ought to be very exact, or very agreeable, as we love to see a picture where the resemblance is just, or the posture and air graceful. But we often find eminent writers very faulty in this respect: great scholars are apt to fetch their comparisons and allusions from the sciences in which they are most conversant, so that a man may see the compass of their learning in a treatise on the most indifferent subject. I have read a discourse upon love, which none but a profound chymist could understand, and have heard many a sermon that should only have been preached before a congregation of Cartesians. On the contrary, your men of business usually have recourse to such instances as are too mean and familiar; they are for drawing the reader into a game of chess or tennis, or for leading him from shop to shop, in the cant of particular trades and employments. It is certain, there may be found an infinite variety of very agreeable allusions in both these kinds; but, for the generality, the most entertaining ones lie in the works of nature, which are obvious to all capacities, and more delightful than what is to be found in arts and sciences.

It is this talent of affecting the imagination that gives an embellishment to good sense, and makes one man's compositions more agreeable than another's. It sets off all writings in general, but is the very life and highest perfection of poetry: where it shines in an eminent degree, it has preserved several poems for many ages, that have nothing else to recommend them; and where all the other beauties are present, the work appears dry and insipid if this single one be wanting. It has something in it like creation; it bestows a kind of existence, and draws up to the reader's view several objects which are not to be found in being. It makes additions to nature, and gives a greater variety to God's works. In a word, it is able to beautify and adorn the most illustrious scenes in the universe, or to fill the mind with more glorious shows and apparitions than can be found in any part of it.

We have now discovered the several originals of those pleasures that gratify the fancy; and here, perhaps, it would not be very difficult to cast under their proper heads those contrary objects which are apt to fill it with distaste and terror; for the imagination is as liable to pain as pleasure. When the brain is hurt by any accident, or the mind disordered by dreams or sickness, the fancy is over-run with wild dismal ideas, and terrified with a thousand hideous monsters of its own framing.

Eumenidum veluti demens videt agmina Pentheus,
Et solem geminum, et duplices se ostendere Thebas;
Aut Agamemnonius scenis agitatus Orestes,
Armatam facibus matrem et serpentibus atris
Cum fugit, ultricesque sedent in limine diræ.
Virg. Æn. 4. v. 469

Like Pentheus, when, distracted with his fear,
He saw two suns, and double Thebes appear:
Or mad Orestes, when his mother's ghost
Full in his face infernal torches tost,
And shook her snaky locks; he shuns the sight,
Flies o'er the stage, surpris'd with mortal fright;
The furies guard the door, and intercept his flight.
Dryden.

There is not a sight in nature so mortifying as that of a distracted person, when his imagination is troubled, and his whole soul disordered and confused: Babylon in ruins is not so melancholy a spectacle.

But, to quit so disagreeable a subject, I shall only consider, by way of conclusion, what an infinite advantage this faculty gives an Almighty Being over the soul of man, and how great a measure of happiness or misery we are capable of receiving from the imagination only.

We have already seen the influence that one man has over the fancy of another, and with what ease he conveys into it a variety of imagery; how great a power then may we suppose lodged in him, who knows all the ways of affecting the imagination, who can infuse what ideas he pleases, and fill those ideas with terror and delight to what degree he thinks fit? He can excite images in the mind without the help of words, and makes scenes rise up before us, and seem present to the eye, without the assistance of bodies or exterior objects. He can transport the imagination with such beautiful and glorious visions, as cannot possibly enter into our present conceptions, or haunt it with such ghastly spectres and apparitions, as would make us hope for annihilation, and think existence no better than a curse. In short, he can so exquisitely ravish or torture the soul through this single faculty, as might suffice to make the whole heaven or hell of any finite being. O.

THE END.

SPECTATOR

IN MINIATURE.

JEALOUSY.

In amore hæc omnia in sunt vitia: injuriæ,
Suspiciones, inimicitiæ, induciæ,
Bellum pax rursum. TER.

All these inconveniencies are incident to love re proaches, jealousies, quarrels, reconcilements, war, and then peace.

Jealousy is that pain which a man feels from the apprehension that he is not equally beloved by the person whom he entirely loves. Now because our inward passions and inclinations can never make themselves visible, it is impossible for a jealous man to be thoroughly cured of his suspicions. His thoughts hang at best in a state of doubtfulness and uncertainty; and are never capable of receiving any satisfaction on the advantageous side; so that his inquiries are most successful when they discover nothing. His pleasure arises from his disappointments, and his life is spent in pursuit of a secret that destroys his happiness if he chance to find it.

An ardent love is always a strong ingredient in this passion; for the same affection which stirs up the jealous man's desires, and gives the party beloved so beautiful a figure in his imagination, makes him believe she kindles the same passion in others, and appears as amiable to all beholders. And as jealousy thus arises from an extraordinary love, it is of so delicate a nature that it scorns to take up with any thing less than an equal return of love. Not the warmest expressions of affection, the softest and most tender hypocrisy, are able to give any satisfaction, where we are not persuaded that the affection is real, and the satisfaction mutual. For the jealous man wishes himself a kind of deity to the person he loves; he would be the only pleasure of her senses, the employment of her thoughts; and is angry at every thing she admires, or takes delight in, besides him-self.

Phœdria's request to his mistress upon his leaving her for three days, is inimitably beautiful and natural.

Cum milite isto præsens, absens ut sies:
Dies noctesque me ames: me desideres:
Me somnies: me expectes: de me cogites:
Me speres: me te oblectes: mecum tota sis:
Meus fac sis postremo, anemus, quando ego sum tuus
TER.

"When you are in company with that soldier, behave as if you were absent: but continue to love me by day and by night: want me; dream of me; expect me; think of me; wish for me; delight in me; be wholly with me: in short, be my very soul, as I am yours."

The jealous man's disease is of so malignant a nature, that it converts all he takes into its own nourishment. A cool behaviour sets him on the rack, and is interpreted as an instance of aversion or indifference; a fond one raises his suspicions, and looks too much like dissimulation and artifice. If the person he loves be cheerful, her thoughts must be employed on another; and if sad, she is certainly thinking on himself. In short, there is no word or gesture so insignificant, but it gives him new hints, feeds his suspicions, and furnishes him with fresh matters of discovery: So that if we consider the effects of this passion, one would rather think it proceeded from an inveterate hatred, than an excessive love; for certain ly none can meet with more disquietude and uneasiness than a suspected wife, if we except the jealous husband.

But the great unhappiness of this passion is, that it naturally tends to alienate the affection which it is so solicitous to engross; and that for these two reasons, because it lays too great a constraint on the words and actions of the suspected person, and at the same time shows you have no honourable opinion of her; both of which are strong motives to aversion.

Nor is this the worst effect of jealousy; for it often draws after it a more fatal train of consequences, and makes the person you suspect guilty of the very crimes you are so much afraid of. It is very natural for such who are treated ill and upbraided falsely, to find out an intimate friend that will hear their complaints, condole their sufferings, and endeavour to sooth and assuage their secret resentments. Besides, jealousy puts a woman often in mind of an ill thing that she would not otherwise perhaps have thought of, and fills her imagination with such an unlucky idea, as in time grows familiar, excites desire, and loses all the shame and horror which might at first attend it. Nor is it a wonder if she who suffers wrongfully in a man's opinion of her, and has therefore nothing to forfeit in his esteem, resolves to give him reason for his suspicions, and to enjoy the pleasure of the crimes, since she must undergo the ignominy. Such probably were the considerations that directed the wise man in his advice to husbands: "Be not jealous over the wife of thy bosom, and teach her not an evil lesson against thyself." *Eccles.*

And here, among other torments which this passion produces, we may usually observe that none are greater mourners than jealous men, when the person who provoked their jealousy is taken from them. Then it is that their love breaks out furiously, and throws off all the mixtures of suspicion which choked and smothered it before. The beautiful parts of the character rise uppermost in the jealous husband's memory, and upbraid him with the ill usage of so divine a creature as was once in his possession: whilst all the little imperfections that were before so uneasy to him, wear off from his remembrance, and show themselves no more.

We may see by what has been said, that jealousy takes the deepest root in men of amorous dispositions; and of these we may find three kinds who are most overrun with it.

The first are those who are conscious to themselves of any infirmity, whether it be weakness, old age, deformity, ignorance, or the like. These men are so well acquainted with the unamiable part of themselves, that they have not the confidence to think they are really beloved; and are so distrustful of their own merits, that all fondness toward them puts them out of countenance, and looks like a jest upon their persons. They grow suspicious on their first looking in a glass, and are stung with jealousy at the sight of a wrinkle. A handsome fellow immediately alarms them, and every thing that looks young or gay turns their thoughts upon their wives.

A second sort of men, who are most liable to this passion, are those of cunning, wary, and distrustful tempers. It is a fault very justly found in histories composed by politicians, that they leave nothing to chance or humour, but are still for deriving every action from some plot or contrivance. For drawing up a perpetual scheme of causes and events, and preserving a constant correspondence between the camp and the council table. And thus it happens in the affairs of love with men of too refined a thought. They put a construction on a look, and find out a design in a smile; they give new senses and significations to words and actions, and are ever tormenting themselves with fancies of their own raising. They generally act in a disguise themselves, and therefore mistake all outward shows and appearances for hypocrisy in others; so that I believe no men see less of the truth and reality of things, than these great refiners upon incidents, who are so wonderfully subtle and overwise in their conceptions.

Now what these men fancy they know of women by reflection, your lewd and vicious men believe they have learned by experience. They have seen the poor husband so misled by tricks and artifices, and in the midst of his inquiries so lost and bewildered in a crooked intrigue, that they still suspect an under plot in every female action; and especially when they see any resemblance in the behaviour of two persons, are apt to fancy it proceeds from the same design in both. These men therefore bear hard upon the suspected party, pursue her close through all her turnings and windings, and are too well acquainted with the chase, to be flung off by any false steps or doubles; besides, their acquaintance and conversation has lain wholly among the vicious part of womankind, and therefore it is no wonder they censure all alike, and look upon the whole sex as a species of impostors. But if, notwithstanding their private experience, they can get over these prejudices, and entertain a favourable opinion of some women; yet their own loose desires will stir up new suspicions from another side, and make them believe all men subject to the same inclinations with themselves.

Whether these or other motives are most predominant, we learn from the modern histories of America, as well as from our own experience in this part of the world, that jealousy is no northern passion, but rages most in those nations that lie nearest the influence of the sun. It is a misfortune for a woman to be born between the tropics; for there lie the hottest regions of jealousy, which, as you come northward, cools all along with the climate, until you scarce meet with any thing like it in the polar circle. Our own nation is very temperately situated in this respect; and if we meet with some few disordered with the violence of this passion, they are not the proper growth of our country, but are many degrees nearer the sun in their constitutions than in their climate.

After this frightful account of jealousy, and the persons who are most subject to it, it will be but fair to show by what means the passion may be best allayed, and those who are possessed with it set at ease. Other faults indeed are not under the wife's jurisdiction, and should, if possible, escape her observation; but jealousy calls upon her particularly for its cure, and deserves all her art and application in the attempt; besides, she has this for encouragement, that her endeavours will be always pleasing, and that she will still find the affection of her husband rising towards her in proportion as his doubts and suspicions vanish; for as we have seen all along, there is so great a mixture of love in jealousy, as is well worth the separating. But this shall be the subject of another paper.

* * * *

Having discovered the nature of jealousy, and pointed out the persons who are most subject to it, I must now apply myself to my fair readers, who desire to live well with a jealous husband, and to ease his mind of its unjust suspicions.

The first rule I shall propose to be observed is, that you never seem to dislike in another what the jealous man is most guilty of, or to admire any thing in which he himself does not excel. A jealous man is very quick in his applications, he knows how to find a double edge in an invective, and to draw a satire on himself out of a panegyric on another. He does not trouble himself to consider the person, but to direct the character; and is secretly pleased or confounded as he finds more or less of himself in it. The commendation of any thing in another stirs up his jealousy, as it shows you have a value for others besides himself; but the commendation of that, which he himself wants, inflames him more, as it shows that in some respects you prefer others before him. Jealousy is admirably described in this view by Horace in his ode to Lydia.

Quum tu, Lydia, Telephi
Cervicem roseam, et cerea Telephi
Laudas brachia, væ meum
Fervens difficili bile tumet jecur.

Tunc nec mens mihi, nec color
Certa sede manet; humor et in genas
Furtim labitur, arguens
Quam lentis penitus macerer ignibus.
Od. xiii.

When Telephus his youthful charms,
His rosy neck and winding arms,
With endless rapture you recite,
And in the pleasing name delight;
My heart, inflam'd by jealous heats,
With numberless resentments beats;
From my pale cheek the colour flies,
And all the man within me dies:
By turns my hidden grief appears
In rising sighs and falling tears,
That show too well the warm desires,
The silent, slow consuming fires,
Which on my inmost vitals prey,
And melt my very soul away.

The jealous man is not indeed angry if you dislike another; but if you find those faults which are to be found in his own character, you discover not only your dislike of another, but of himself. In short, he is so desirous of engrossing all your love, that he is grieved at the want of any charm, which he believes has power to raise it; and if he finds by your censures on others, that he is not so agreeable in your opinion as he might be, he naturally concludes you could love him better if he had other qualifications, and that by consequence your affection does not rise so high as he thinks it ought. If therefore his temper be grave or sullen, you must not be too much pleased with a jest, or transported with any thing that is gay or diverting. If his beauty be none of the best, you must be a professed admirer of prudence, or any other quality he is master of, or at least vain enough to think he is.

In the next place, you must be sure to be free and open in your conversation with him, and to let in light upon your actions, to unravel all your designs, and discover every secret, however trifling or indifferent.

A jealous husband has a particular aversion to winks and whispers, and if be does not see to the bottom of every thing, will be sure to go beyond it in his fears and suspicions. He will always expect to be your chief confidant, and where he finds himself kept out of a secret, will believe there is more in it than there should be. And here it is of great concern, that you preserve the character of your sincerity uniform and of a piece; for if he once finds a false gloss put upon any single action, he quickly suspects all the rest; his working imagination immediately takes a false hint, and runs off with it into several remote consequences, until he has proved very ingenious in working out his own misery.

If both these methods fail, the best way will be to let him see you are much cast down and afflicted for the ill opinion he entertains of you, and the disquietudes he himself suffers for your sake. There are many who take a kind of barbarous pleasure in the jealousy of those who love them, and insult over an aching heart, and triumph in the charms which are able to excite so much uneasiness.

Ardeat ipsa licet, tormentis gaudet amantis.
JUV.

Though equal pains her peace of mind destroy,
A lover's torments give her spiteful joy.

But these often carry the humour so far, until their affected coldness and indifference quite kills all the fondness of a lover, and are then sure to meet in their turn with all the contempt and scorn that is due to so insolent a behaviour. On the contrary, it is very probable, a melancholy, dejected carriage, the usual effects of injured innocence, may soften the jealous husband into pity, make him sensible of the wrong he does you, and work out of his mind all those fears and suspicions that make you both unhappy. At least it will have this good effect, that he will keep his jealousy to himself, and repine in private, either because he is sensible it is a weakness, and will therefore hide it from your knowledge, or because he will be apt to fear some ill effect it may produce, in cooling your love towards him, or diverting it to another.

There is still another secret that can never fail, if you can once get it believed, and which is often practised by women of greater cunning than virtue. This is to change sides for a while with the jealous man, and to turn his own passion upon himself; to take some occasion of growing jealous of him, and to follow the example he himself hath set you. This counterfeited jealousy will bring him a great deal of pleasure, if he thinks it real; for he knows experimentally how much love goes along with this passion, and will besides feel something like the satisfaction of revenge, in seeing you undergo all his own tortures. But this, indeed, is an artifice so difficult, and at the same time so disingenuous, that it ought never to be put in practice but by such as have skill enough to cover the deceit, and innocence to render it excusable.

I shall conclude this essay with the story of Herod and Mariamne, as I have collected it out of Josephus; which may serve almost as an example to whatever can be said on this subject.

Mariamne had all the charms that beauty, birth, wit, and youth, could give a woman, and Herod all the love that such charms are able to raise in a warm and amorous disposition. In the midst of this his fondness for Mariamne, he put her brother to death, as he did her father not many years after. The barbarity of the action was represented to Mark Antony, who immediately summoned Herod into Egypt, to answer for the crime that was laid to his charge. Herod attributed the summons to Antony's desire of Mariamne, whom therefore, before his departure, he gave into the custody of his uncle Joseph, with private orders to put her to death, if any such violence was offered to himself. This Joseph was much delighted with Mariamne's conversation, and endeavoured with all his art and rhetoric, to set out the excess of Herod's passion for her; but when he still found her cold and incredulous, he inconsiderately told her, as a certain instance of her lord's affection, the private orders he had left behind him, which plainly showed, according to Joseph's interpretation, that he could neither live nor die without her. This barbarous instance of a wild unreasonable passion quite put out, for a time, those little remains of affection she still had for her lord: her thoughts were so wholly taken up with the cruelty of his orders, that she could not consider the kindness that produced them, and therefore represented him, in her imagination, rather under the frightful idea of a murderer than a lover. Herod was at length acquitted and dismissed by Mark Antony, when his soul was all in flames for his Mariamne; but before their meeting, he was not a little alarmed at the report he had heard of his uncle's conversation and familiarity with her in his absence. This therefore was the first discourse he entertained her with, in which she found it no easy matter to quiet his suspicions. But at last he appeared so well satisfied of her innocence, that from reproaches and wranglings he fell to tears and embraces. Both of them wept very tenderly at their reconciliation, and Herod poured out his whole soul to her in the warmest protestations of love and constancy; when amidst all his sighs and languishings she asked him, whether the private orders he left with his uncle Joseph were an instance of such an inflamed affection The jealous king was immediately roused at so unexpected a question, and concluded his uncle must have been too familiar with her, before he would have discovered such a secret. In short, he put his uncle to death, and very difficultly prevailed upon himself to spare Mariamne.

After this he was forced on a second journey into Egypt, when he committed his lady to the care of Sohemus, with the same private orders he had before given his uncle, if any mischief befell him. In the meanwhile Mariamne so won upon Sohemus by her presents and obliging conversation, that she drew all the secret from him, with which Herod had intrusted him; so that after his return, when he flew to her with all the transports of joy and love, she received him coldly with sighs and tears, and all the marks of indifference and aversion. This reception so stirred up his indignation, that he had certainly slain her with his own hands, had not he feared he himself should have become the greater sufferer by it It was not long after this, when he had another violent return of love upon him; Mariamne was therefore sent for to him, whom he endeavoured to soften and reconcile with all possible conjugal caresses and endearments; but she declined his embraces, and answered all his fondness with bitter invectives for the death of her father and her brother. This behaviour so incensed Herod, that he very hardly refrained from striking her; when in the heat of their quarrel there came in a witness, suborned by some of Mariamne's enemies, who accused her to the king of a design to poison him. Herod was now prepared to hear any thing in her prejudice, and immediately ordered her servant to be stretched upon the rack; who in the extremity of his tortures confessed, that his mistress's aversion to the King arose from something Sohemus had told her; but as for any design of poisoning, he utterly disowned having the least knowledge of it. This confession quickly proved fatal to Sohemus, who now lay under the same suspicions and sentence that Joseph had before him on the like occasion. Nor would Herod rest here; but accused her with great vehemence of a design upon his life, and by his authority with the judges had her publicly condemned and executed. Herod soon after her death grew melancholy and dejected, retiring from the public administration of affairs into a solitary forest, and there abandoning himself to all the black considerations, which naturally arise from a passion made up of love, remorse, pity, and despair. He used to rave for his Mariamne, and to call upon her in his distracted fits; and in all probability would soon have followed her had not his thoughts been seasonably called off from so sad an object by public storms, which at that time very nearly threatened him.

1.

THEODOSIUS AND CONSTANTIA.

Illa, quis et me, inquit, et te perdidit, Orpheus?
Jamque vale: feror ingenti circumdata nocte,
Invalidasque tibi tendens, heu! non tua, palmas.
VIRG.

Then thus the bride: what fury seiz'd on thee,
Unhappy man! to lose thyself and me?
And now farewell! involv'd in shades of night,
For ever I am ravish'd from thy sight:
In vain I reach my feeble hands to join
In sweet embraces, ah! no longer thine!
DRYDEN.

Constantia was a woman of extraordinary wit and beauty, but very unhappy in a father, who having arrived at great riches by his own industry, took delight in nothing but his money. Theodosius was the younger son of a decayed family, of great parts and learning, improved by a genteel and virtuous education. When he was in the twentieth year of his age he became acquainted with Constantia, who had not then passed her fifteenth. As he lived but a few miles distant from her father's house, he had frequent opportunities of seeing her; and by the advantages of a good person and a pleasing conversation, made such an impression in her heart as it was impossible for time to efface: he was himself no less smitten with Constantia. A long acquaintance made them still discover new beauties in each other, and by degrees raised in them that mutual passion which had an influence on their following lives. It unfortunately happened, that in the midst of this intercourse of love and friendship between Theodosius and Constantia, there broke out an irreparable quarrel between their parents, the one valuing himself too much upon his birth, and the other upon his possessions. The father of Constantia was so much incensed at the father of Theodosius, that he contracted an unreasonable aversion towards his son, insomuch that he forbad him his house, and charged his daughter upon her duty never to see him more. In the mean time, to break off all communication between the two lovers, who he knew entertained secret hopes of some favourable opportunity that should bring them together, he found out a young gentleman of a good fortune and an agreeable person, whom he pitched upon as a husband for his daughter. He soon concerted this affair so well, that he told Constantia it was his design to marry her to such a gentleman, and that her wedding should be celebrated on such a day. Constantia, who was overawed with the authority of her father, and unable to object any thing against so advantageous a match, received the proposal with a profound silence, which her father commended in her, as the most decent manner of a virgin's giving her consent to an overture of that kind. The noise of this intended marriage soon reached Theodosius, who, after a long tumult of passions which naturally rise in a lover's heart on such an occasion, writ the following letter to Constantia.

"The thought of my Constantia, which for some years has been my only happiness, is now become a greater torment to me than I am able to bear. Must I then live to see you another's? The streams, the fields, and meadows, where we have so often talked together, grow painful to me; life itself is become a burden. May you long be happy in the world, but forget that there was ever such a man in it as

"THEODOSIUS."

The letter was conveyed to Constantia that very evening, who fainted at the reading of it; and the next morning she was much more alarmed by two or three messengers that came to her father's house one after another to inquire if they had heard any thing of Theodosius, who it seems had left his chamber about midnight, and could nowhere be found. The deep melancholy which had hung upon his mind some time before, made them apprehend the worst that could befall him. Constantia, who knew that nothing but the report of her marriage could have driven him to such extremities, was not to be comforted: she now accused herself for having so tamely given an ear to the proposal of a husband, and looked upon the new lover as the murderer of Theodosius: in short, she resolved to suffer the utmost effects of her father's displeasure, rather than comply with a marriage which appeared to her so full of guilt and horror. The father seeing himself entirely rid of Theodosius, and likely to keep a considerable portion in his family, was not very much concerned at the obstinate refusal of his daughter, and did not find it very difficult to excuse himself upon that account to his intended son-in-law, who had all along regarded this alliance rather as a marriage of convenience than of love. Constantia had now no relief but in her devotions and exercises of religion, to which her afflictions had so entirely subjected her mind, that after some years had abated the violence of her sorrows, and settled her thoughts in a kind of tranquillity, she resolved to pass the remainder of her days in a convent. Her father was not displeased with a resolution which would save money in his family, and accordingly complied with his daughter's intentions. Accordingly, in the twenty-fifth year of her age, while her beauty was yet in all its height and bloom, he carried her to a neighbouring city, in order to look out a sisterhood of nuns among whom to place his daughter. There was in this place a father of a convent who was very much renowned for his piety and exemplary life; and as it is usual in the Romish church for those who are under any great affliction, or trouble of mind, to apply themselves to the most eminent confessors for pa·don and consolation, our beautiful votary took the opportunity of confessing herself to this celebrated father.

We must now return to Theodosius, who, the very morning that the above-mentioned inquiries had been made after him, arrived at a religious house in the city where now Constantia resided; and desiring that secrecy and concealment of the fathers of the convent, which is very usual upon any extraordinary occasion, he made himself one of the order, with a private vow never to inquire after Constantia, whom he looked upon as given away to his rival upon the day on which, according to common fame, their marriage was to have been solemnized. Having in his youth made a good progress in learning, that he might dedicate himself more entirely to religion, he entered into holy orders, and in a few years became renowned for his sanctity of life, and those pious sentiments which he inspired into all who conversed with him. It was this holy man to whom Constantia had determined to apply herself in confession, though neither she nor any other, besides the prior of the convent, knew any thing of his name or family. The gay, the amiable Theodosius had now taken upon him the name of Father Francis, and was so far concealed in a long beard, a shaven head, and a religious habit, that it was impossible to discover the man of the world in the venerable conventual.

As he was one morning shut up in his confessional, Constantia, kneeling by him, opened the state of her soul to him; and after having given him the history of a life full of innocence, she burst out in tears, and entered upon that part of her story in which he himself had so great a share. My behaviour, says she, has, I fear, been the death of a man who had no other fault but that of loving me too much. Heaven only knows how dear he was to me whilst he lived, and how bitter the remembrance of him has been to me since his death. She here paused, and lifted up her eyes, that streamed with tears, towards the father who was so moved with the sense of her sorrows, that he could only command his voice, which was broke with sighs and sobbing, so far as to bid her proceed. She followed his directions, and in a flood of tears poured out her heart before him. The father could not forbear weeping aloud, insomuch that in the agonies of his grief the seat shook under him. Constantia, who thought the good man was thus moved by his compassion towards her, and by the horror of her guilt, proceeded with the utmost contrition to acquaint him with that vow of virginity in which she was going to engage herself, as the proper atonement for her sins, and the only sacrifice she could make to the memory of Theodosius. The father, who by this time had pretty well composed himself, burst out again in tears upon hearing that name to which he had been so long disused, and upon receiving this instance of an unparalleled fidelity from one who he thought had several years since given herself up to the possession of another. Amidst the interruptions of his sorrow, seeing his penitent overwhelmed with grief, he was only able to bid her from time to time be comforted—to tell her that her sins were forgiven her—that her guilt was not so great as she apprehended—that she should not suffer herself to be afflicted above measure. After which he recovered himself enough to give the absolution in form; directing her at the same time to repair to him again the next day, that he might encourage her in the pious resolutions she had taken, and give her suitable exhortations for her behaviour in it. Constantia retired, and the next morning renewed her applications. Theodosius having manned his soul with proper thoughts and reflections, exerted himself on this occasion in the best manner he could to animate his penitent in the course of life she was entered upon, and wear out of her mind those groundless fears and apprehensions which had taken possession of it: concluding with a promise to her, that he would from time to time continue his admonitions when she should have taken upon her the holy veil. The rules of our respective orders, says he, will not permit that I should see you, but you may assure yourself not only of having a place in my prayers, but of receiving such frequent instructions as I can convey to you by letters. Go on cheerfully in the glorious course you have undertaken, and you will quickly find such a peace and satisfaction in your mind, which it is not in the power of the world to give.

Constantia's heart was so elevated with the discourse of Fatner Francis, that the very next day she entered upon her vow. As soon as the solemnities of her reception were over, she retired, as it is usual, with the abbess into her own apartment.

The abbess had been informed the night before of all that had passed between her noviciate and Father Francis: from whom she now delivered to her the following letter:

"As the first-fruits of those joys and consolations which you may expect from the life you are now engaged in, I must acquaint you that Theodosius, whose death sits so heavy upon your thoughts, is still alive: and that the father, to whom you have confessed yourself, was once that Theodosius whom you so much lament. The love which we have had for one another will make us more happy in its disappointment than it could have done in its success. Providence has disposed of us for our advantage, though not according to our wishes. Consider your Theodosius still as dead, but assure yourself of one who will not cease to pray for you in Father "FRANCIS."

Constantia saw that the handwriting agreed with the contents of the letter: and upon reflecting on the voice of the person, the behaviour, and above all the extreme sorrow of the father during her confession, she discovered Theodosius in every particular. After having wept with tears of joy, It is enough, says she, Theodosius is still in being: I shall live with comfort, and die in peace.

The letters which the father sent her afterward are yet extant in the nunnery where she resided; and are often read to the young religious, in order to inspire them with good resolutions and sentiments of virtue. It so happened, that after Constantia had lived above ten years in the cloister, a violent fever broke out in the place, which swept away great multitudes, and among others Theodosius. Upon his death-bed, he sent his benediction in a very moving manner to Constantia, who at that time was herself so far gone in the same fatal distemper, that she lay delirious. Upon the interval which generally precedes death in sicknesses of this nature, the abbess, finding that the physicians had given her over, told her that Theodosius was just gone before her, and that he had sent her his benediction in his last moments. Constantia received it with pleasure: And now, says she, if I do not ask any thing improper, let me be buried by Theodosius. My vow reaches no farther than the grave. What I ask is, I hope, no violation of it—She died soon after, and was interred according to her request.

Their tombs are still to be seen, with a short Latin inscription over them to the following purpose:

"Here lie the bodies of Father Francis and Sister Constance. They were lovely in their lives, and in their deaths they were not divided." C.

INQUISITIVE PEOPLE.

Percunctatorem fugito, nam garrulus idem est.
HOR.

Shun the inquisitive and curious man;
For what he hears he will relate again.
POOLY.

There is a creature who has all the organs of speech, a tolerable good capacity for conceiving what is said to it, together with a pretty proper behaviour in all the occurrences of common life; but naturally very vacant of thought in itself, and therefore forced to apply itself to foreign assistances. Of this make is that man who is very inquisitive. You may often observe, that though he speaks as good sense as any man upon any thing with which he is well acquainted, he cannot trust to the range of his own fancy to entertain himself upon that foundation, but goes on still to new inquiries. Thus, though you know he is fit for the most polite conversation, you shall see him very well contented to sit by a jockey, giving an account of the many revolutions in his horse's health, what potion he made him take, how that agreed with him, how afterward he came to his stomach, and his exercise, or any the like impertinence; and be as well pleased as if you talked to him on the most important truths. This humour is far from making a man unhappy, though it may subject him to raillery; for he generally falls in with a person who seems to be born for him, which is your talkative fellow. It is so ordered, that there is a secret bent, as natural as the meeting of different sexes, in these two characters, to supply each other's wants. I had the honour the other day to sit in a public room, and saw an inquisitive man look with an air of satisfaction upon the approach of one of these talkers. The man of ready utterance sat down by him, and rubbing his head, leaning on his arm, and making an uneasy countenance, he began; "There is no manner of news to-day, I cannot tell what is the matter with me, but I slept very ill last night; whether I caught cold or no, I know not, but I fancy I do not wear shoes thick enough for the weather, and I have coughed all this week: it must be so, for the custom of washing my head winter and summer with cold water, prevents any injury from the season entering that way: so it must come in at my feet; but I take no notice of it: as it comes, so it goes. Most of our evils proceed from too much tenderness; and our faces are naturally as little able to resist the cold as other parts. The Indian answered very well to an European, who asked him how he could go naked? I am all face."

I observed this discourse was as welcome to my general inquirer as any other of more consequence could have been; but somebody calling our talker to another part of the room, the inquirer told the next man who sat by him, that Mr. Such-a-one, who was just gone from him, used to wash his head in cold water every morning; and so repeated almost *verbatim* all that had been said to him. The truth is, the inquisitive are the funnels of conversation; they do not take in any thing for their own use, but merely to pass it to another: they are the channels through which all the good and evil that is spoken in town are conveyed.

Such as are offended at them, or think they suffer by their behaviour, may themselves mend that inconvenience; for they are not a malicious people, and if you will supply them, you may contradict any thing they have said before by their own mouths. A farther account of a thing is one of the gratefullest goods that can arrive to them: and it is seldom that they are more particular than to say, the town will have it, or I have it from a good hand; so that there is room for the town to know the matter more particularly, and for a better hand to contradict what was said by a good one.

I have not known this humour more ridiculous, than in a father, who has been earnestly solicitous to have an account how his son passed his leisure hours; if it be in a way thoroughly insignificant, there cannot be a greater joy than an inquirer discovers in seeing him follow so hopefully his own steps: but this humour among men is most pleasant when they are saying something which is not wholly proper for a third person to hear, and yet is in itself indifferent. The other day there came in a well-dressed young fellow, and two gentlemen of this species immediately fell a whispering his pedigree. I could overhear, by breaks, She was his aunt; then an answer, Ay, she was of the mother's side: then again in a little lower voice, His father wore generally a darker wig; answer, Not much. But this gentleman wears higher heels to his shoes.

As the inquisitive, in my opinion, are such merely from a vacancy in their own imaginations, there is nothing, methinks, so dangerous as to communicate secrets to them; for the same temper of inquiry makes them as impertinently communicative: but no man, though he converses with them, need put himself in their power, for they will be contented with matters of less moment as well. When there is fuel enough, no matter what it is—thus the ends of sentences in the newspapers, as, "this wants confirmation, this occasions many speculations, and time will discover the event," are read by them, and considered not as mere expletives.

One may see now and then this humour accompanied with an insatiable desire of knowing what passes without turning it to any use in the world but merely their own entertainment. A mind which is gratified this way is adapted to humour and pleasantry, and formed for an unconcerned character in the world; and to be a mere spectator. This curiosity without malice or self-interest, lays up in the imagination a magazine of circumstances which cannot but entertain when they are produced in conversation. If one were to know, from the man of the first quality to the meanest servant, the different intrigues, sentiments, pleasures, and interests of mankind, would it not be the most pleasing entertainment imaginable to enjoy so constant a farce, as the observing mankind much more different from themselves in their secret thoughts and public actions, than in their nightcaps and long periwigs? T.

MELANCHOLY NOT RELIGION.

Ægritudinem laudare, unam rem maxime detestabilem, quorum est tandem philosophorum? CIC.

What kind of philosophy is it, to extol melancholy, the most detestable thing in nature?

About an age ago, it was the fashion in England for every one that would be thought religious, to throw as much sanctity as possible into his face, and, in particular, to abstain from all appearances of mirth and pleasantry, which were looked upon as the marks of a carnal mind. The saint was of a sorrowful countenance, and generally eaten up with spleen and melancholy. A gentleman who was lately a great ornament to the learned world has diverted me more than once with an account of the reception which he met with from a very famous independent minister, who was head of a college in these times. This gentleman was then a young adventurer in the republic of letters, and just fitted out for the university with a good cargo of Latin and Greek. His friends were resolved that he should try his fortune at an election which was drawing near in the college, of which the independent minister whom I have before mentioned was governor. The youth, according to custom, waited on him in order to be examined. He was received at the door by a servant, who was one of that gloomy generation that were then in fashion. He conducted him, with great silence and seriousness, to a long gallery which was darkened at noon-day and had only a single candle burning in it. After a short stay in this melancholy apartment, he was led into a chamber hung with black, where he entertained himself for some time by the glimmering of a taper, till at length the head of the college came out to him, from an inner room, with half a dozen nightcaps upon his head, and religious horror in his countenance. The young man trembled; but his fears increased, when instead of being asked what progress he had made in learning, he was examined how he abounded in grace. His Latin and Greek stood him in little stead; he was to give an account only of the state of his soul, whether he was of the number of the elect; what was the occasion of his conversion; upon what day of the month, and hour of the day it happened; how it was carried on, and when completed. The whole examination was summed up with one short question, namely, whether he was prepared for death? The boy, who had been bred up by honest parents, was frighted out of his wits at the solemnity of the proceeding, and by the last dreadful interrogatory; so that upon making his escape out of the house of mourning, he could never be brought a second time to the examination, as not being able to go through the terrors of it.

Notwithstanding this general form and outside of religion is pretty well worn out among us, there are many persons, who, by a natural uncheerfulness of heart, mistaken notions of piety, or weakness of understanding, love to indulge this uncomfortable way of life, and give up themselves a prey to grief and melancholy Superstitious fears and groundless scruples cut them off from the pleasures of conversation, and all those social entertainments which are not only innocent, but laudable; as if mirth was made for reprobates, and cheerfulness of heart denied those who are the only persons that have a proper title to it.

Sombrius is one of these sons of sorrow. He thinks himself obliged in duty to be sad and disconsolate. He looks on a sudden fit of laughter as a breach of his baptismal vow. An innocent jest startles him like blasphemy. Tell him of one who is advanced to a title of honour, he lifts up his hands and eyes: describe a public ceremony, he shakes his head; show him a gay equipage, he blesses himself. All the little ornaments of life are pomps and vanities. Mirth is wanton, and wit profane. He is scandalized at youth for being lively, and at childhood for being playful. He sits at a christening, or a marriage-feast, as at a funeral; sighs at the conclusion of a merry story, and grows devout when the rest of the company grow pleasant. After all Sombrius is a religious man, and would have behaved himself very properly, had he lived when Christianity was under a general persecution.

I would by no means presume to tax such characters with hypocrisy, as is done too frequently; that being a vice which I think none but he, who knows the secrets of men's hearts, should pretend to discover in another, where the proofs of it do not amount to a demonstration. On the contrary, as there are many excellent persons, who are weighed down by this habitual sorrow of heart, they rather deserve our compassion than our reproaches. I think, however, they would do well to consider whether such a behaviour does not deter men from a religious life, by representing it as an unsociable state, that extinguishes all joy and gladness, darkens the face of nature, and destroys the relish of being itself.

I have, in former papers, shown how great a tendency there is to cheerfulness in religion, and how such a frame of mind is not only most lovely, but the the most commendable in a virtuous person. In short, those who represent religion in so unamiable a light, are like the spies sent by Moses to make a discovery of the Land of Promise, when by their reports they discouraged the people from entering upon it. Those who show us the joy, the cheerfulness, the good humour, that naturally spring up in this happy state, are like the spies bringing along with them the clusters of grapes, and delicious fruits, that might invite their companions into the pleasant country which produced them.

An eminent pagan writer has made a discourse, to show that the atheist, who denies a God, does him less dishonour than the man who owns his being, but at the same time believes him to be cruel, hard to please, and terrible to human nature. For my own part, says he, I would rather it should be said of me, that there was never any such a man as Plutarch, than that Plutarch was ill-natured, capricious, or inhuman.

If we may believe our logicians, man is distinguished from all other creatures by the faculty of laughter. He has an heart capable of mirth, and naturally disposed to it. It is not the business of virtue to extirpate the affections of the mind, but to regulate them. It may moderate and restrain, but was not designed to banish gladness from the heart of man. Religion contracts the circle of our pleasures, but leaves it wide enough for her votaries to expatiate in. The contemplation of the Divine Being, and the exercise of virtue, are in their own nature so far from excluding all gladness of heart, that they are perpetual sources of it. In a word, the true spirit of religion cheers as well as composes the soul; it banishes indeed all levity of behaviour, all vicious and dissolute mirth, but in exchange fills the mind with a perpetual serenity, uninterrupted cheerfulness, and an habitual inclination to please others, as well as to be pleased in itself.

AN HEROIC WOMAN.

Nos decebat
Lugere ubi esset aliquis in lucem editus
Humanæ vitæ varia reputantes mala:
At qui labores morte finisset graves,
Omnes amicos laude et lætitia exequi.

EURIP.

When first an infant draws the vital air,
Officious grief should welcome him to care
But joy should life's concluding scene attend,
And mirth be kept to grace a dying friend.

I KNOW not, whether Madame de Villacerfe's departure out of this life, a man of philosophy will call unfortunate or not, since it was attended with some circumstances as much to be desired as to be lamented. She was her whole life happy in an uninterrupted health, and was always honoured for an evenness of temper and greatness of mind. That lady was taken with an indisposition which confined her to her chamber; but was such as was too slight to make her take a sick bed, and yet too grievous to admit of any satisfaction in being out of it. It is notoriously known, that, some years ago, Monsieur Festeau, one of the most considerable surgeons in Paris, was desperately in love with this lady; her quality placed her above any application to her on the account of his passion; but, as a woman always has some regard to the person whom she believes to be her real admirer, she now took it in her head (upon advice of her physicians to lose some of her blood) to send for Monsieur Festeau on that occasion. I happened to be there at that time, and my near relation gave me the privilege to be present. As soon as her arm was stripped bare, and he began to press it in order to raise the vein, his colour changed, and I observed him seized with a sudden tremour, which made me take the liberty to speak of it to my cousin with some apprehension; she smiled, and said, she knew Mr. Festeau had no inclination to do her injury. He seemed to recover himself, and smiling also, proceeded in his work. Immediately after the operation he cried out, that he was the most unfortunate of all men, for that he had opened an artery instead of a vein. It is as impossible to express the artist's distraction as the patient's composure. I will not dwell on little circumstances, but go on to inform you, that within three days time it was thought necessary to take off her arm. She was so far from using Festeau as it would be natural to one of a lower spirit to treat him, that she would not let him be absent from any consultation about her present condition, and on every occasion asked whether he was satisfied in the measures that were taken about her. Before this last operation she ordered her will to be drawn, and, after having been a quarter of an hour alone, she bid the surgeons, of whom poor Festeau was one, go on in their work. I know not how to give the terms of art; but there appeared such symptoms after the amputation of her arm, that it was visible she could not live four and twenty hours. Her behaviour was so magnanimous throughout this whole affair, that I was particularly curious in taking notice of what passed, as her fate approached nearer and nearer, and took notes of what she said to all about her, particularly word for word what she spoke to Mr. Festeau, which was as follows:

"Sir, you give me inexpressible sorrow for the anguish with which I see you overwhelmed. I am removed to all intents and purposes from the interests of human life, therefore I am to begin to think like one wholly unconcerned in it. I do not consider you as one by whose error I have lost my life; no, you are my benefactor, as you have hastened my entrance into an happy immortality. This is my sense of this accident; but the world in which you live may have thoughts of it to your disadvantage: I have therefore taken care to provide for you in my will, and have placed you above what you have to fear from their ill-nature."

While this excellent woman spoke these words, Festeau looked as if he received a condemnation to die, instead of a pension for his life. Madame de

Villacerfe lived till eight of the clock next night; and, though she must have laboured under the most exquisite torments, she possessed her mind with so wonderful a patience, that one may rather say she ceased to breathe than she died at that hour. You who had not the happiness to be personally known to this lady have nothing but to rejoice in the honour you had of being related to so great merit; but we who have lost her conversation cannot so easily resign our own happincss by reflection upon hers.

There hardly can be a greater instance of an heroic mind, than the unprejudiced manner in which this lady weighed this misfortune. The regard of life itself could not make her overlook the contrition of the unhappy man, whose more than ordinary concern for her was all his guilt. It would certainly be of singular use to human society to have an exact account of this lady's ordinary conduct, which was crowned by so uncommon magnanimity. Such greatness was not to be acquired in the last article, nor is it to be doubted but it was a constant practice of all that is praiseworthy, which made her capable of beholding death, not as the dissolution, but the consummation of her life. T.

EGOTISTS.

—*Præsens, absens ut sies.* TER.

Be present as if absent

"It is a hard and nice subject for a man to speak of himself," says Cowley; "it grates his own heart to say any thing of disparagement, and the reader's ears to hear any thing of praise for him." Let the tenor of his discourse be what it will upon this subject, it generally proceeds from vanity. An ostentatious man will rather relate a blunder or an absurdity he has committed, than be lebarred of talking of his own dear person.

Some very great writers have been guilty of this fault. It is observed of Tully in particular, that his works run very much in the first person, and that he takes all occasions of doing himself justice. "Does he think," says Brutus, "that his consulship deserves more applause than my putting Cæsar to death, because I am not perpetually talking of the Ides of March, as he is of the Nones of December?" I need not acquaint my learned reader, that in the Ides of March, Brutus destroyed Cæsar, and that Cicero quashed the conspiracy of Catiline in the Calends of December. How shocking soever this great man's talking of himself might have been to his contemporaries, I must confess I am never better pleased than when he is on this subject. Such openings of the heart give a man a thorough insight into his personal character, and illustrate several passages in the history of his life: besides that, there is some little pleasure in discovering the infirmity of a great man, and seeing how the opinion he has of himself agrees with what the world entertains of him.

The gentlemen of Port Royal, who were more eminent for their learning and for their humility than any other in France, banished the way of speaking in the first person out of all their works, as rising from vainglory and self-conceit. To show their particular aversion to it, they branded this form of writing with the name of egotism; a figure not to be found among the ancient rhetoricians.

The most violent egotism which I have met with in the course of my reading, is that of Cardinal Wolsey, *Ego et rex meus*, "I and my king;" as perhaps the most eminent egotist that ever appeared in the world, was Montaigne, the author of the celebrated essays. This lively old Gascon has woven all his bodily infirmities into his works, and after having spoken of the faults or virtues of any other men, immediately publishes to the world how it stands with himself in that particular. Had he kept his own counsel, he might have passed for a much better man, though perhaps he would not have been so diverting an author. The title of an essay promises perhaps a discourse upon Virgil or Julius Cæsar; but when you look into it, you are sure to meet with more upon Monsieur Montaigne, than of either of them. The younger Scaliger, who seems to have been no great friend to this author, after having acquainted the world that his father sold herrings, adds these words; *La grand fadaise de Montaigne, qui a ecrit qu'il aimoit mieux le vin blanc—que diable a-t-on a faire de scavoir ce qu'il aime?* "For my part," says Montaigne, "I am a great lover of your white wines."—"What the devil signifies it to the public," says Scaliger, "whether he is a lover of white wines, or of red wines?"

I cannot here forbear mentioning a tribe of egotists for whom I have always had a mortal aversion, I mean the authors of memoirs, who are never mentioned in any works but their own, and who raise all their productions out of this single figure of speech.

Most of our modern prefaces favour very strongly of the egotism. Every insignificant author fancies it of importance to the world, to know that he writ his book in the country, that he did it to pass away some of his idle hours, that it was published at the importunity of friends, or that his natural temper, studies, or conversation, directed him to the choice of his subject.

—*Id populus curat scilicet.*

Such informations cannot but be highly improving to the reader.

In works of humour, especially when a man writes under a fictitious personage, the talking of one's self may give some diversion to the public; but I would advise every other writer, never to speak of himself, unless there be something very considerable in his character: though I am sensible this rule will be of little use in the world, because there is no man who fancies his thoughts worth publishing, that does not look upon himself as a considerable person.

I shall close this paper with a remark upon such as are egotists in conversation: these are generally the vain or shallow part of mankind, people being naturally full of themselves when they have nothing else in them. There is one kind of egotists which is very common in the world, though I do not remember that any writer has taken notice of them; I mean those empty conceited fellows, who repeat as sayings of their own, or some of their particular friends, several jests which were made before they were born, and which every one, who has conversed in the world, has heard a hundred times over. A forward young fellow of my acquaintance was very guilty of this absurdity: he would be always laying a new scene for some old piece of wit, and telling us, that as he and Jack Such-a-one were together, one or t'other of them had such a conceit on such an occasion; upon which he would laugh very heartily, and wonder the company did not join with him. When his mirth was over, I have often reprehended him out of Terence, *Tuumne, obsecro te, hoc dictum erat? vetus credidi.* But finding him still incorrigible, and having a kindness for the young coxcomb, who was otherwise a good-natured fellow, I recommended to his perusal the Oxford and Cambridge jests, with several little pieces of pleasantry of the same nature. Upon the reading of them, he was under no small confusion to find that his jokes had passed through several editions, and that what he thought was a new conceit, and had appropriated to his own use, had appeared in print before he or his ingenious friends were ever heard of. This had so good an effect upon him, that he is content at present to pass for a man of plain sense in his conversation, and is never facetious but when he knows his company.

EPISTOLARY POETICAL WRITING.

——Neque enim concludere versum
Dixeris esse satis : neque siquis scribat, uti nos,
Sermoni propiora, putes hunc esse poetam.

HOR

'Tis not enough the measur'd feet to close ;
Nor will you give a poet's name to those,
Whose humble verse, like mine, approaches prose.

I INTEND to offer some remarks upon the epistolary way of writing in verse. This is a species of poetry by itself; and has not so much as been hinted at in any of the arts of poetry, that have ever fallen into my hands: neither has it in any age, or in any nation, been so much cultivated, as the other several kinds of poesy. A man of genius may, if he pleases, write letters in verse upon all manner of subjects, that are capable of being embellished with wit and language, and may render them new and agreeable by giving the proper turn to them. But in speaking, at present, of epistolary poetry, I would be understood to mean only such writings in this kind, as have been in use among the ancients, and have been copied from them by some moderns. These may be reduced into two classes : in the one I shall range love-letters, letters of friendship, and letters upon mournful occasions : in the other I shall place such epistles in verse as may properly be called familiar, critical, and moral ; to which may be added letters of mirth and humour. Ovid for the first, and Horace for the latter, are the best originals we have left.

He that is ambitious of succeeding in the Ovidian way, should first examine his heart well, and feel whether his passions (especially those of the gentler kind) play easy, since it is not his wit, but the delicacy and tenderness of his sentiments, that will affect his readers. His versification likewise should be soft, and all his numbers flowing and querulous.

The qualifications requisite for writing epistles, after the model given us by Horace, are of a quite different nature. He that would excel in this kind must have a good fund of strong masculine sense: to this there must be joined a thorough knowledge of mankind, together with an insight into the business, and the prevailing humours of the age. Our author must have his mind well seasoned with the finest precepts of morality, and be filled with nice reflections upon the bright and dark sides of human life; he must be a master of refined raillery, and understand the delicacies as well as the absurdities of conversation. He must have a lively turn of wit, with an easy and concise manner of expression: every thing he says must be in a free and disengaged manner. He must be guilty of nothing that betrays the air of a recluse, but appear a man of the world throughout. His illustrations, his comparisons, and the greatest part of his images, must be drawn from common life. Strokes of satire and criticism, as well as panegyric, judiciously thrown in, (and as it were by the by) give a wonderful life and ornament to compositions of this kind. But let our poet, while he writes epistles, though never so familiar, still remember that he writes in verse, and must for that reason have a more than ordinary care not to fall into prose, and a vulgar diction, excepting where the nature and humour of the things does necessarily require it. In this point Horace hath been thought by some critics to be sometimes careless, as well as too negligent of his versification; of which he seems to have been sensible himself.

Both these manners of writing may be made as entertaining in their way, as any other species of poetry, if undertaken by persons duly qualified; and the latter sort may be managed so as to become in a peculiar manner instructive.

Subjects of the most sublime nature are often treated in the epistolary way with advantage, as in the famous epistle of Horace to Augustus. The poet surprises us with his pomp, and seems rather betrayed into his subject, than to have aimed at it by design. He appears, like the visit of a king incognito, with a mixture of familiarity and grandeur. In works of this kind, when the dignity of the subject hurries the poet into descriptions and sentiments, seemingly unpremeditated, by a sort of inspiration; it is usual for him to recollect himself, and fall back gracefully into the natural style of a letter.

VIEW OF THE SEA MAJESTIC.

—Βαθυρρειταο μεγα σθενος 'Ωκεανοιο.

HOM.

The mighty force of ocean's troubled flood.

Of all objects that I have ever seen, there is none which affects my imagination so much as the sea or ocean. I cannot see the heavings of this prodigious bulk of water, even in a calm, without a very pleasing astonishment: but when it is worked up in a tempest, so that the horizon on every side is nothing but foaming billows and floating mountains, it is impossible to describe the agreeable horror that rises from such a prospect. A troubled ocean, to a man who sails upon it, is, I think, the biggest object that he can see in motion, and consequently gives his imagination one of the highest kinds of pleasure that can arise from greatness. I must confess it is impossible for me to survey this world of fluid matter, without thinking on the hand that first poured it out, and made a proper channel for its reception. Such an object naturally raises in my thoughts the idea of an Almighty Being, and convinces me of his existence as much as a metaphysical demonstration. The imagination prompts the understanding, and, by the greatness of the sensible object, produces in it the idea of a being who is neither circumscribed by time nor space.

As I have made several voyages upon the sea, I have often been tossed in storms, and on that occasion have frequently reflected on the descriptions of them in ancient poets. I remember Longinus highly recommends one in Homer, because the poet has not amused himself with little fancies upon the occasion, as authors of an inferior genius, whom he mentions, had done, but because he has gathered together those circumstances which are the most apt to terrify the imagination, and which really happen in the raging of a tempest. It is for the same reason, that I prefer the following description of a ship in a storm, which the psalmist has made, before any other I have ever met with. "They that go down to the sea in ships, that do business in great waters: these see the works of the Lord, and his wonders in the deep. For he commandeth and raiseth the stormy wind, which lifteth up the waters thereof: they mount up to the heaven, they go down again to the depths, their soul is melted because of trouble. They reel to and fro, and stagger like a drunken man, and are at their wit's end. Then they cry unto the Lord in their trouble, and he bringeth them out of their distresses. He maketh the storm a calm, so that the waves thereof are still. Then they are glad, because they be quiet, so he bringeth them unto their desired haven."

By the way, how much more comfortable as well as rational, is this system of the psalmist, than the pagan scheme in Virgil, and other poets, where one deity is represented as raising a storm, and another as laying it? Were we only to consider the sublime in this piece of poetry, what can be nobler than the idea it gives us of the Supreme Being thus raising a tumult among the elements, and recovering them out of their confusion, thus troubling and becalming nature?

Great painters do not only give us landscapes of gardens, groves, and meadows, but very often employ their pencils upon sea-pieces. The following divine Ode has been made by a gentleman upon the conclusion of his travels.

How are thy servants bless'd, O Lord!
How sure is their defence!
Eternal wisdom is their guide
Their help, Omnipotence.

In foreign realms and lands remote,
  Supported by thy care,
Through burning climes I pass'd unhurt,
  And breath'd in tainted air.

Thy mercy sweeten'd every soil,
  Made every region please:
The hoary Alpine hills it warm'd,
  And smooth'd the Tyrrhene seas.

Think, O my soul, devoutly think,
  How with affrighted eyes,
Thou saw'st the wide extended deep
  In all its horrors rise!

Confusion dwelt in every face,
  And fear in every heart;
When waves on waves, and gulfs on gulfs,
  O'ercame the pilot's art.

Yet then from all my griefs, O Lord,
  Thy mercy set me free,
Whilst in the confidence of prayer
  My soul took hold on thee.

For though in dreadful whirls we hung
  High on the broken wave,
I knew thou wert not slow to hear,
  Nor impotent to save.

The storm was laid, the winds retir'd,
  Obedient to thy will;
The sea that roar'd at thy command,
  At thy command was still.

In midst of dangers, fears, and death,
  Thy goodness I'll adore,
And praise thee for thy mercies past,
  And humbly hope for more.

My life, if thou preserv'st my life,
  Thy sacrifice shall be;
And death, if death must be my doom,
  Shall join my soul to thee

A MOONLIGHT CONTEMPLATION.

Frigora mitescunt zephyris, ver proterit æstas
Interitura simul
Pomifer autumnus fruges effuderit, et mox
Bruma recurrit iners. HOR.

The cold grows soft with western gales,
The summer over spring prevails,
But yields to autumn's fruitful rain,
As this to winter storms and hails:
Each loss the hasting moon repairs again.
SIR W. TEMPLE.

There is hardly any thing gives me a more sensible delight, than the enjoyment of a cool still evening after the uneasiness of a hot sultry day. Such a one I passed not long ago, which made me rejoice when the hour was come for the sun to set, that I might enjoy the freshness of the evening in my garden, which then affords me the pleasantest hours I pass in the whole four and twenty. I immediately rose from my couch, and went down into it. You descend at first by twelve stone steps into a large square divided into four grass plots, in each of which is a statue of white marble. This is separated from a large parterre by a low wall, and from thence, through a pair of iron gates, you are led into a long broad walk of the finest turf, set on each side with tall yews, and on either hand bordered by a canal, which on the right divides the walk from a wilderness parted into variety of alleys and arbours, and on the left from a kind of amphitheatre, which is the receptacle of a great number of oranges and myrtles. The moon shone bright, and seemed then most agreeably to supply the place of the sun, obliging me with as much light as was necessary to discover a thousand pleasing objects, and at the same time divested of all power of heat.— The reflection of it in the water, the fanning of the wind rustling on the leaves, the singing of the thrush and nightingale, and the coolness of the walks, all conspired to make me lay aside all displeasing thoughts, and brought me into such a tranquillity of mind, as is I believe the next happiness to that of hereafter. In this sweet retirement I naturally fell into the repetition of some lines out of a poem of Milton's, which he entitles Il Penseroso, the ideas of which were exquisitely suited to my present wandering of thought.

Sweet bird! that shunn'st the noise of folly,
Most musical! most melancholy!
Thee, chantress, oft the woods among
I woo, to hear thy evening song:
And missing thee, I walk unseen
On the dry, smooth-shaven green,
To behold the wand'ring moon,
Riding near her highest noon,
Like one that hath been led astray,
Thro' the Heaven's wide pathless way,
And oft, as if her head she bow'd,
Stooping thro' a fleecy cloud.

Then let some strange mysterious dream
Wave with his wings in airy stream,
Of lively portraiture display'd,
Softly on my eyelids laid;
And as I wake, sweet music breathe
Above, about, or underneath,
Sent by spirits to mortals good,
Or th' unseen genius of the wood.

I reflected then upon the sweet vicissitudes of night and day, on the charming disposition of the seasons, and their return again in a perpetual circle; and, oh! said I, that I could from these my declining years, return again to my first spring of youth and vigour; but that, alas! is impossible; all that remains within my power, is to soften the inconveniencies I feel with an easy contented mind, and the enjoyment of such delights as this solitude affords me. In this thought I sate me down on a bank of flowers and dropped into a slumber, which whether it were the effect of fumes and vapours, or my present thoughts, I know not; but methought the Genius of the garden stood before me, and introduced into the walk where I lay this drama and different scenes of the revolution of the year, which whilst I then saw, even in my dream, I resolved to write down.

The first person whom I saw advancing towards me, was a youth of a most beautiful air and shape, though he seemed not yet arrived at that exact proportion and symmetry of parts which a little more time would have given him; but however, there was such a bloom in his countenance, such satisfaction and joy, that I thought it the most desirable form that I had ever seen. He was clothed in a flowing mantle of green silk, interwoven with flowers: he had a chaplet of roses on his head, and a narcissus in his hand; primroses and violets sprang up under his feet, and all nature was cheered at his approach. Flora was on one hand, and Vertumnus on the other in a robe of changeable silk. After this I was surprised to see the moonbeams reflected with a sudden glare from armour, and to see a man completely armed advancing with his sword drawn. I was soon informed by the Genius it was Mars, who had long usurped a place among the attendants of the Spring. He made way for a softer appearance, it was Venus, without any ornament but her own beauties, not so much as her own cestus, with which she had encompassed a globe, which she held in her right hand, and in her left she had a sceptre of gold. After her followed the Graces with their arms entwined within one another, their girdles were loosed, and they moved to the sound of soft music, striking the ground alternately with their feet: then came up the three months which belong to this season. As March advanced towards me, there was methought in his look a louring roughness, which ill befitted a month which was ranked in so soft a season; but as he came forwards his features became insensibly more mild and gentle: he smoothed his brow, and looked with so sweet a countenance that I could not but lament his departure, though he made way for April. He appeared in the greatest gayety imaginable, and had a thousand pleasures to attend him: his look was frequently clouded, but immediately returned to its first composure and remained fixed in a smile. Then came May attended by Cupid, with his bow strung, and in a posture to let fly an arrow: as he passed by methought I heard a confused noise or soft complaints, gentle ecstasies, and tender sighs of lovers; vows of constancy, and as many complainings of perfidiousness: all which the winds wafted away as soon as they had reached my hearing. After these I saw a man advance in the full prime and vigour of his age, his complexion was sanguine and ruddy, his hair black, and fell down in beautiful ringlets beneath his shoulders; and a mantle of hair-coloured silk hung loosely upon him: he advanced with a hasty step after the Spring, and sought out the shade and cool fountains which played in the garden. He was particularly well pleased when a troop of Zephyrs fanned him with their wings: he had two companions who walked on each side, that made him appear the most agreeable, the one was Aurora with fingers of roses, and her feet dewy, attired in gray; the other was Vesper in a robe of azure beset with drops of gold, whose breath he caught whilst it passed over a bundle of honeysuckles and tuberoses which he held in his hand. Pan and Ceres followed them with four reapers, who danced a morrice to the sound of oaten pipes and cymbals. Then came the attendant months. June retained still some small likeness of the Spring; but the other two seemed to step with a less vigorous tread, especially August, who seemed almost to faint, whilst for half the steps he took the dog-star levelled his rays full at his head; they passed on and made way for a person that seemed to bend a little under the weight of years: his beard and hair, which were full grown, were composed of an equal number of black and gray; he wore a robe which he had girt round him of a yellowish cast, not unlike the colour of fallen leaves, which he walked upon. I thought he hardly made amends for expelling the foregoing scene by the large quantity of fruits which he bore in his hands. Plenty walked by his side with an healthy fresh countenance, pouring out from a horn all the various products of the year. Pomona follow ed with a glass of cider in her hand, with Bacchus in a chariot drawn by tigers, accompanied by a whole troop of Satyrs, Fauns, and Sylvans. September, who came next, seemed in his looks to promise a new spring, and wore the livery of those months. The succeeding month was all soiled with the juice of grapes, as if he had just come from the winepress. November, though he was in this division, yet, by the many stops he made, seemed rather inclined to the Winter, which followed close at his heels. He advanced in the shape of an old man in the extremity of age; the hair he had was so very white it seemed a real snow; his eyes were red and piercing, and his beard hung with a great quantity of icicles; he was wrapt up in furs, but yet so pinched with excess of cold that his limbs were all contracted, and his body bent to the ground, so that he could not have supported himself had it not been for Comus the god of Revels, and Necessity the mother of Fate, who sustained him on each side. The shape and mantle of Comus was one of the things that most surprised me; as he advanced towards me his countenance seemed the most desirable I had ever seen: on the forepart of his mantle was pictured joy, delight, and satisfaction, with a thousand emblems of merriment, and jests with faces looking two ways at once; but as he passed from me I was amazed at a shape so little correspondent to his face: his head was bald, and all the rest of his limbs appeared old and deformed. On the hinder part of his mantle was represented Murder, with dishevelled hair and a dagger all bloody. Anger in a robe of scarlet, and Suspicion squinting with both eyes; but above all, the most conspicuous was the battle of the Lapithæ and the Centaurs. I detested so hideous a shape, and turned my eyes upon Saturn, who was stealing away behind him with a scythe in one hand and an hour-glass in t'other unobserved. Behind Necessity was Vesta the goddess of Fire, with a lamp which was perpetually supplied with oil, and whose flame was eternal. She cheered the rugged brow of Necessity, and warmed her so far as almost to make her assume the features and likeness of Choice. December, January, and February, passed on after the rest all in furs; there was little distinction to be made amongst them, and they were more or less displeasing as they discerned more or less haste towards the grateful return of Spring. Z.

ON TRAGEDY.

Ac ne forte putes me que facere ipse recusem
Cum recte tractant alii, laudare maligne;
Ille per extentum funem mihi posse videtur
Ire poeta, meum qui pectus inaniter angit,
Irritat, mulcet, falsis terroribus implet
Ut magus; et modo me Thebis, modo ponit Athenis.
HOR.

IMITATED

Yet lest you think I rally more than I teach,
Or praise, malignant, arts I cannot reach,
Let me for once presume t' instruct the times,
To know the poet from the man of rhymes;
'Tis he, who gives my breast a thousand pains,
Can make me feel each passion that he feigns;
Enrage, compose, with more than magic art,
With pity, and with terror, tear my heart;
And snatch me o'er the earth, or thro' the air,
To Thebes, to Athens, when he will and where.
POPE.

As a perfect tragedy is the noblest production of human nature, so it is capable of giving the mind one of the most delightful and most improving entertainments. A virtuous man (says Seneca) struggling with misfortunes, is such a spectacle as gods might look upon with pleasure; and such a pleasure it is which one meets with in the representation of a well-written tragedy. Diversions of this kind wear out of our thoughts every thing that is mean and little. They cherish and cultivate that humanity which is the ornament of our nature. They soften insolence, sooth affliction, and subdue the mind to the dispensations of Providence.

D

It is no wonder therefore that in all the polite nations of the world, this part of the drama has met with public encouragement.

The modern tragedy excels that of Greece and Rome, in the intricacy and disposition of the fable; but, what a Christian writer would be ashamed to own, falls infinitely short of it in the moral part of the performance.

This I may show more at large hereafter; and in the mean time, that I may contribute something towards the improvement of the English tragedy, I shall take notice, in this and in other following papers, of some particular parts in it that seem liable to exception.

Aristotle observes, that the iambic verse in the Greek tongue was the most proper for tragedy; because at the same time that it lifted up the discourse from prose, it was that which approached nearer to it than any other kind of verse. For, says he, we may observe that men, in ordinary discourse, very often speak iambics, without taking notice of it. We may make the same observation of our Euglish blank verse, which often enters into our common discourse, hough we do not attend to it, and is such a due medium between rhyme and prose, that it seems wonderfully adapted to tragedy. I am therefore very much offended when I see a play in rhyme, which is as absurd in English, as a tragedy of hexameters would have been in Greek or Latin. The solecism is, I think, still greater in those plays that have some scenes in rhyme and some in blank verse, which are to be looked upon as two several languages; or where we see some particular simies dignified with rhyme, at the same time that every thing about them lies in blank verse. I would not however debar the poet from concluding his tragedy, or, if he pleases, every act of it, with two or three couplets, which may have the same effect as an air in the Italian opera after a long recitativo, and give the actor a graceful exit. Besides that we see a diversity of numbers in some parts of the old tragedy, in order to hinder the ear from being tired with the same continued modulation of voice. For the same reason, I do not dislike the speeches in our English tragedy that close with an hemistich, or half verse, notwithstanding the person who speaks after it begins a new verse, without filling up the preceding one: nor with abrupt pauses and breakings off in the middle of a verse, when they humour any passion that is expressed by it.

Since I am upon this subject, I must observe that our English poets have succeeded much better in the style, than in the sentiments of their tragedies. Their language is very often noble and sonorous, but the sense either very trifling, or very common. On the contrary, in the ancient tragedies, and indeed in those of Corneille and Racine, though the expressions are very great, it is the thought that bears them up, and swells them. For my own part, I prefer a noble sentiment that is depressed with homely language, infinitely before a vulgar one that is blown up with all the sound and energy of expression. Whether this defect in our tragedies may arise from want of genius, knowledge, or experience in the writers, or from their compliance with the vicious taste of their readers, who are better judges of the language than of the sentiments, and consequently relish the one more than the other, I cannot determine. But I believe it might rectify the conduct both of the one and of the other, if the writer laid down the whole contexture of his dialogue in plain English, before he turned it into blank verse; and if the reader, after the perusal of a scene, would consider the naked thought of every speech in it, when divested of all its tragic ornaments. By these means, without being imposed upon by words, we may judge impartially of the thought, and consider whether it be natural or great enough for the person that utters it; whether it deserves to shine in such a blaze of eloquence, or show itself in such a variety of lights as are generally made use of by the writers of our English tragedy.

I must in the next place observe, that when our thoughts are great and just, they are often obscured by the sounding phrases, hard metaphors, and forced expressions in which they are clothed. Shakspeare is often very faulty in this particular. There is a fine observation in Aristotle to this purpose, which I have never seen quoted. "The expression," says he, "ought to be very much laboured in the unactive parts of the fable, as in descriptions, similitudes, narrations, and the like; in which the opinions, manners, and passions of men are not represented; for these (namely the opinions, manners, and passions,) are apt to be obscured by pompous phrases and elaborate expressions." Horace, who copied most of his criticisms after Aristotle, seems to have had his eye on the foregoing rule, in the following verses:

> *Et tragicus plerumque dolet sermone pedestri*
> *Telephus et Peleus, cum pauper et exul uterque,*
> *Projicit ampullas et sesquipedalia verba,*
> *Si curat cor spectantis tetigisse querela.*
>
> Ars. Poet. ver. 95.

> "Tragedians too lay by their state to grieve,
> Peleus and Telephus, exiled and poor,
> Forget their swelling and gigantic words."
>
> ROSCOMMON.

Among our modern English poets, there is none who was better turned for tragedy than Lee; if instead of favouring the impetuosity of his genius, he had restrained it, and kept it within its proper bounds. His thoughts are wonderfully suited to tragedy, but frequently lost in such a cloud of words, that it is hard to see the beauty of them. There is an infinite fire in his works, but so involved in smoke, that it does not appear in half its lustre. He frequently succeeds in the passionate parts of the tragedy, but more particularly where he slackens his efforts, and eases the style of those epithets and metaphors, in which he so much abounds. What can be more natural, more soft, or more passionate, than that line in Statira's speech, where she describes the charms of Alexander's conversation?

Then he would talk—Good gods! how he would talk."

That unexpected break in the line, and turning the description of his manner of talking into an admiration of it, is inexpressibly beautiful, and wonderfully suited to the fond character of the person that speaks it. There is a simplicity in the words, that outshines the utmost pride of expression.

Otway has followed nature in the language of his tragedy, and therefore shines in the passionate parts, more than any of our English poets. As there is something familiar and domestic in the fable of his tragedy, more than in those of any other poet, he has little pomp, but great force in his expressions. For which reason, though he has admirably succeeded in the tender and melting part of his tragedies, he sometimes falls into too great a familiarity of phrase in those parts, which, by Aristotle's rule, ought to have been raised and supported by the dignity of expression.

It has been observed by others, that this poet has founded his tragedy of Venice Preserved on so wrong a plot, that the greatest characters in it are those of rebels and traitors. Had the hero of his play discovered the same good qualities in the defence of his country, that he showed for its ruin and subversion, the audience could not enough pity and admire him: but as he is now represented, we can only say of him what the Roman historian says of Catiline, that his fall would have been glorious (*si pro patria sic concidisset*) had he so fallen in the service of his country.

* * * *

The English writers of tragedy are possessed with a notion, that when they represent a virtuous or innocent person in distress, they ought not to leave him till they have delivered him out of his troubles, or made him triumph over his enemies. This error they have been led into by a ridiculous doctrine in modern criticism, that they are obliged to an equal distribution of rewards and punishments, and an impartial execution of poetical justice. Who were the first that established this rule I know not; but I am sure it has no foundation in nature, in reason, or in the practice of the ancients. We find that good and evil happen alike to all men on this side the grave; and as the principal design of tragedy is to raise commiseration and terror in the minds of the audience, we shall defeat this great end, if we always make virtue and innocence happy and successful. Whatever crosses and disappointments a good man suffers in the body of the tragedy, they will make but small impression on our minds, when we know that in the last act he is to arrive at the end of his wishes and desires. When we see him engaged in the depth of his afflictions, we are apt to comfort ourselves, because we are sure he will find his way out of them, and that his grief, how great soever it may be at present, will soon terminate in gladness. For this reason, the ancient writers of tragedy treated men in their plays, as they are dealt with in the world, by making virtue sometimes happy and sometimes miserable, as they found it in the fable which they made choice of, or as it might affect their audience in the most agreeable manner. Aristotle considers the tragedies that were written in either of these kinds, and observes, that those which ended unhappily had always pleased the people, and carried away the prize in the public disputes of the stage, from those that ended happily. Terror and commiseration leave a pleasing anguish in the mind; and fix the audience in such a serious composure of thought, as is much more lasting and delightful than any little transient starts of joy and satisfaction. Accordingly we find, that more of our English tragedies have succeeded, in which the favourites of the audience sink under calamities, than those in which they recover themselves out of them.

The best plays of this kind are, The Orphan, Venice Preserved, Alexander the Great, Theodosius, All for Love, Oedipus, Oroonoko, Othello, &c. King Lear is an admirable tragedy of the same kind, as Shakspeare wrote it; but as it is reformed according to the chimerical notion of poetical justice, in my humble opinion it has lost half its beauty. At the same time I must allow, that there are very noble tragedies, which have been framed upon the other plan, and have ended happily; as indeed most of the good tragedies which have been written since the starting of the above-mentioned criticism, have taken this turn; as The Mourning Bride, Tamerlane, Ulysses, Phædra and Hippolitus, with most of Mr. Dryden's. I must also allow that many of Shakspeare's, and several of the celebrated tragedies of antiquity, are cast in the same form. I do not therefore dispute against this way of writing tragedies, but against the criticism that would establish this as the only method; and by that means would very much cramp the English tragedy, and perhaps give a wrong bent to the genius of our writers.

The tragi-comedy, which is the product of the English theatre, is one of the most monstrous inventions that ever entered into a poet's thoughts. An author might as well think of weaving the adventures of Æneas and Hudibras into one poem, as of writing such a motley piece of mirth and sorrow. But the absurdity of these performances is so very visible, that I shall not insist upon it.

The same objections which are made to tragi-comedy, may in some measure be applied to all tragedies that have a double plot in them, which are likewise more frequent upon the English stage, than upon any other; for though the grief of the audience, in such performances, be not changed into another passion, as in tragi-comedies; it is diverted upon another object, which weakens their concern for the principal action, and breaks the tide of sorrow, by throwing it into different channels. This inconvenience, however, may in a great measure be cured, if not wholly removed, by the skilful choice of an under-plot, which may bear such a near relation to the principal design, as to contribute towards the completion of it, and be concluded by the same catastrophe.

There is also another particular, which may be reckoned among the blemishes, or rather the false beauties of our English tragedy: I mean those particular speeches which are commonly known by the name of *rants*. The warm and passionate parts of a tragedy are always the most taking with the audience; for which reason we often see the players pronouncing, in all the violence of action, several parts of the tragedy which the author writ with great temper, and designed that they should have been so acted. I have seen Powell very often raise himself a loud clap by this artifice. The poets that were acquainted with this secret, have given frequent occasion for such emotions in the actor, by adding vehemence to words where there was no passion, or inflaming a real passion into fustian. This hath filled the mouths of our heroes with bombast; and given them such sentiments, as proceed rather from a swelling than a greatness of mind. Unnatural exclamations, curses, vows, blasphemies, a defiance of mankind, and an outraging of the gods, frequently pass upon the audience for towering thoughts, and have accordingly met with infinite applause.

I shall here add a remark, which I am afraid our tragic writers may make an ill use of. As our heroes are generally lovers, their swelling and blustering upon the stage very much recommends them to the fair part of their audience. The ladies are wonderfully pleased to see a man insulting kings, or affronting the gods, in one scene, and throwing himself at the feet of his mistress in another. Let him behave himself insolently towards the men, and abjectly towards the fair one, and it is ten to one but he proves a favourite of the boxes. Dryden and Lee, in several of their tragedies, have practised this secret with good success.

But to show how a rant pleases beyond the most just and natural thought that is not pronounced with vehemence, I would desire the reader, when he sees the tragedy of Oedipus, to observe how quietly the hero is dismissed at the end of the third act, after having pronounced the following lines, in which the thought is very natural, and apt to move compassion:

"To you, good gods, I make my last appeal;
Or clear my virtues, or my crimes reveal.
If in the maze of fate I blindly run,
And backward trod those paths I sought to shun;
Impute my errors to your own decree:
My hands are guilty, but my heart is free."

Let us then recollect with what thunder-claps of applause he leaves the stage, after the impieties and execrations at the end of the fourth act; and you will wonder to see an audience so cursed and so pleased at the same time.

"O that, as oft I have at Athens seen,
[*Where, by the way, there was no stage till many years after Oedipus*]
The stage arise, and the big clouds descend;
So now, in very deed, I might behold
This pond'rous globe, and all yon marble roof,
Meet like the hands of Jove, and crush mankind:
For all the elements," &c. C.

ENTHUSIASM AND SUPERSTITION.

Religentem esse oportet, religiosu nefas.
Incerti Autoris apud Aul. Gell.

A man should be religious, not superstitious.

It is of the last importance to season the passions of a child with devotion, which seldom dies in a mind that has received an early tincture of it. Though it may seem extinguished for a while by the cares of the world, the heats of youth, or the allurements of vice, it generally breaks out and discovers itself again as soon as discretion, consideration, age, or misfortunes, have brought the man to himself. The fire may be covered and overlaid, but cannot be entirely quenched and smothered.

A state of temperance, sobriety, and justice, without devotion, is a cold, lifeless, insipid condition of virtue: and is rather to be styled philosophy than religion. Devotion opens the mind to great conceptions, and fills it with more sublime ideas than any that are to be met with in the most exalted science: and at the same time warms and agitates the soul more than usual pleasure.

It has been observed by some writers, that man is more distinguished from the animal world by devotion than by reason, as several brute creatures discover in their actions something like a faint glimmering of reason, though they betray in no single circumstance of their behaviour any thing that bears the least affinity to devotion. It is certain the propensity of the mind to religious worship, the natural tendency of the soul to fly to some superior Being for succour in dangers and distresses, the gratitude to an invisible superintendent which arises in us upon receiving any extraordinary and unexpected good fortune, the acts of love and admiration with which the thoughts of men are so wonderfully transported in meditating upon the divine perfections, and the universal concurrence of all the nations under heaven in the great article of adoration, plainly show that devotion or religious worship must be the effect of tradition from some first founder of mankind, or that it is conformable to the natural light of reason, or that it proceeds from instinct implanted in the soul itself. For my part, I look upon all these to be the concurrent causes; but whichever of them shall be assigned as the principle of divine worship, it manifestly points to a Supreme Being as the first author of it.

I may take some other opportunity of considering those particular forms and methods of devotion which are taught us by Christianity; but shall here observe into what errors even this divine principle may sometimes lead us, when it is not moderated by that right reason which was given us as the guide of all our actions.

The two great errors into which a mistaken devotion may betray us, are enthusiasm and superstition.

There is not a more melancholy object than a man who has his head turned with religious enthusiasm. A person that is crazed, though with pride or malice, is a sight very mortifying to human nature; but when the distemper arises from any indiscreet fervours of devotion, or too intense an application of the mind to its mistaken duties, it deserves our compassion in a more particular manner. We may however learn this lesson from it, that since devotion itself (which one would be apt to think could not be too warm) may disorder the mind, unless its heats are tempered with caution and prudence, we should be particularly careful to keep our reason as cool as possible, and to guard ourselves in all parts of life against the influence of passion, imagination, and constitution.

Devotion, when it does not lie under the check of reason, is very apt to degenerate into enthusiasm. When the mind finds herself very much inflamed with her devotions, she is too much inclined to think they are not of her own kindling, but blown up by something divine within her. If she indulges this thought too far, and humours the growing passion, she at last flings herself into imaginary raptures and ecstasies; and when once she fancies herself under the influence of a divine impulse, it is no wonder if she slights human ordinances, and refuses to comply with any established form of religion, as thinking herself directed by a much superior guide.

As enthusiasm is a kind of excess in devotion, superstiton is the excess not only of devotion, but of religion in general, according to an old heathen saying, quoted by Aulus Gellius, *Rel gentem esse oportet, religiosum nefas;* a man should be religious, not superstitious; for as the author tells us, Nigidius observed upon this passage, that the Latin words which terminate in *osus* generally imply vicious characters, and the having of any quality to an excess.

An enthusiast in religion is like an obstinate clown, a superstitious man like an insipid courtier. Enthusiasm has something in it of madness, superstition, or folly. Most of the sects that fall short of the church of England have in them strong tinctures of enthusiasm, as the Roman Catholic religion is one huge overgrown body of childish and idle superstitions.

The Roman Catholic church seems indeed irrecoverably lost in this particular. If an absurd dress or behaviour be introduced in the world, it will soon be found out and discarded: on the contrary, a habit or ceremony, though never so ridiculous, which has taken sanctuary in the church, sticks in it for ever. A Gothic bishop, perhaps, thought it proper to repeat such a form in such particular shoes or slippers; another fancied it would be very decent if such a part of public devotions were performed with a mitre on his head, and a crosier in his hand. To this a brother Vandal, as wise as the others, adds an antic dress, which he conceived would allude very aptly to such and such mysteries, until by degrees the whole office has degenerated into an empty show.

Their successors see the vanity and inconvenience of these ceremonies; but instead of reforming, perhaps add others, which they think more significant, and which take possession in the same manner, and are never to be driven out after they have been once admitted. I have seen the Pope officiate at St. Peter's, where for two hours together, he was busied in putting on or off his different accoutrements, according to the different parts he was to act in them.

Nothing is so glorious in the eyes of mankind, and ornamental to human nature, setting aside the infinite advantages which arise from it, as a strong, steady, masculine piety; but enthusiasm and superstition are the weakness of human reason, that expose us to the derision and scorn of infidels, and sink us even below the beasts that perish.

Idolatry may be looked upon as another error arising from mistaken devotion; but because reflections on that subject would be of no use to an English reader, I shall not enlarge upon it.

L.

THOUGHTS

UPON THE

DEATH OF A FRIEND.

Quis desiderio sit pudor, aut modus
Tam chari capitis? HOR

——Who can grieve too much, what time shall end
Our mourning for so dear a friend. CREECH.

THERE is a sort of delight which is alternately mixed with terror and sorrow, in the contemplation of death. The soul has its curiosity more than ordinarily awakened, when it turns its thoughts upon the subject of such who have behaved themselves with an equal, a resigned, a cheerful, a generous, or heroic temper in that extremity. We are affected with these respective manners of behaviour, as we secretly believe the part of the dying person imitable by ourselves, or such as we imagine ourselves more particularly capable of. Men of exalted minds march before us like princes, and are, to the ordinary race of mankind, rather subjects for their admiration than example. Innocent men who have suffered as criminals, though they were benefactors to human society, seem to be persons of the highest distinction, amongst the vastly great number of human race, the dead. When the iniquity of the times brought Socrates to his execution, how great and wonderful is it to behold him, unsupported by any thing but the testimony of his own conscience and conjectures of hereafter, receive the poison with an air of mirth and good humour; and, as if going on an agreeable journey, bespeak some deity to make it fortunate?

When Phocion's good actions had met with the like reward from his country, and he was led to death with many others of his friends, they bewailing their fate, he walking composedly toward the place of execution, how gracefully does he support his illustrious character to the very last instant! One of the rabble spitting at him as he passed, with his usual authority he called to know if no one was ready to teach this fellow how to behave himself. When a poor-spirited creature that died at the same time bemoaned himself unmanfully he rebuked him with this question, Is it no consolation to such a man as thou art to die with Phocion ? At the instant when he was to die, they asked what commands he had for his son: he answered, to forget this injury of the Athenians. Niocles, his friend, under the same sentence, desired he might drink the potion before him; Phocion said, because he never had denied him any thing he would not even this, the most difficult request he had ever made.

These instances were very noble and great, and the reflections of those sublime spirits had made death to them what it is really intended to be by the author of nature, a relief from a various being ever subject to sorrows and difficulties.

Epaminondas the Theban general, having received in fight a mortal stab with a sword, which was left in his body, lay in that posture until he had intelligence that his troops had obtained the victory, and then permitted it to be drawn out, at which instant he expressed himself in this manner, "This is not the end of my life, my fellow-soldiers; it is now your Epaminondas is born, who dies in so much glory."

It were an endless labour to collect the accounts with which all ages have filled the world of noble and heroic minds that have resigned this being, as if the termination of life were but an ordinary occurrence of it.

This common-place way of thinking I fell into from an awkward endeavour to throw off a real and fresh affliction, by turning over books in a melancholy mood; but it is not easy to remove griefs which touch the heart, by applying remedies which only entertain the imagination. As therefore this paper is to consist of any thing which concerns human life, I cannot help letting the present subject regard what has been the last object of my eyes, though an entertainment of sorrow.

I went this evening to visit a friend with a design to rally him upon a story I had heard of his intending to steal a marriage without the privity of us his intimate friends and acquaintance. I came into his apartment with that intimacy which I have done for very many years, and walked directly into his bed-chamber, where I found my friend in the agonies of death. What could I do? The innocent mirth in my thoughts struck upon me like the most flagitious wickedness: I in vain called upon him; he was senseless, and too far spent to have the least knowledge of my sorrow, or any pain in himself. Give me leave then to transcribe my soliloquy, as I stood by his mother, dumb with the weight of grief for a son who was her honour and her comfort, and never until that hour since his birth had been an occasion of a moment's sorrow to her.

"How surprising is this change! from the possession of vigorous life and strength, to be reduced in a few hours to this fatal extremity! Those lips which look so pale and livid, within these few days gave delight to all who heard their utterance; it was the business, the purpose of his being, next to obeying him to whom he is going, to please and instruct, and that for no other end but to please and instruct. Kindness was the motive of his actions, and with all the capacity requisite for making a figure in a contentious world, moderation, good nature, affability, temperance, and chastity, were the arts of his excellent life. There, as he lies in helpless agony, no wise man who knew him so well as I, but would resign all the world can bestow to be so near the end of such a life. Why does my heart so little obey my reason as to lament thee, thou excellent man? Heaven receive him, or restore him! Thy beloved mother, thy obliged friends, thy helpless servants, stand around thee without distinction. How much wouldst thou, hadst thou thy senses, say to each of us?

"But now that good heart bursts, and he is at rest—with that breath expired a soul who never indulged a passion unfit for the place he has gone to: where are now thy plans of justice, of truth, of honour? Of what use the volumes thou hast collated, the arguments thou hast invented, the examples thou hast followed? Poor were the expectations of the studious, the modest, and the good, if the reward of their labours were only to he expected from man. No, my friend, thy intended pleadings, thy intended good offices to thy friends, thy intended services to thy country, are already performed, as to thy concern in them, in his sight before whom the past, the present, and future, appear at one view. While others with thy talents were tormented with ambition, with vain-glory, with envy, with emulation, how well didst thou turn thy mind to its own improvement, in things out of the power of fortune; in probity, in integrity, in the practice and study of justice, how silent thy passage, how private thy journey, how glorious thy end! many have I known more famous, some more knowing, not one so innocent" *L.*

ABUSE OF THE UNDERSTANDING.

Credebant hoc grande nefas, et morte piandum
Si juvenis vetulo non assurrexerat— JUV.

'Twas impious then; (so much was age rever'd)
For youth to keep their seat, when an old man appear'd.

I KNOW no evil under the sun so great as the abuse of the understanding, and yet there is no one vice more common. It has diffused itself through both sexes and all qualities of mankind; and there is hardly that person to be found, who is not more concerned for the reputation of wit and sense, than honesty and virtue. But this unhappy affection of being wise rather than honest, witty than good natured, is the source of most of the ill habits of life. Such false impressions are owing to the abandoned writings of men of wit, and the awkward imitation of the rest of mankind.

The reflections of men of fine parts are so delicate upon all occurrences which they are concerned in, that they should be exposed to more than ordinary infamy and punishment for offending against such quick admonitions as their own souls give them, and blunting the fine edge of their minds in such a manner that they are no more shocked at vice and folly, than men of slower capacities. There is no greater monster in being, than a very ill man of great parts: he lives like a man in a palsy with one side of him dead. While perhaps he enjoys the satisfaction of luxury, of wealth, of ambition, he has lost the taste of good-will, of friendship, of innocence. Scarecrow, the beggar in Lincoln's Inn Fields, who disabled himself in his right leg, and asks alms all day to get himself a warm supper and a trull at night, is not half so despicable a wretch as such a man of sense. The beggar has no relish above sensations; he finds rest more agreeable than motion; and while he has a warm fire and his doxy, never reflects that he deserves to be whipped. Every man who terminates his satisfactions and enjoyments within the supply of his own necessities and passions, is, in my eye, as poor a rogue as Scarecrow. But, for the loss of public and private virtue, we are beholden to your men of parts forsooth; it is with them no matter what is done, so it is done with an air. But to him, who in a corrupt age acts according to nature and reason, a selfish man, in the most shining circumstance and equipage, appears in the same condition with the fellow above mentioned, but more contemptible, in proportion to what more he robs the public of and enjoys above him. I lay it down therefore for a rule, that the whole man is to move together; that every action of any importance, is to have a prospect of public good; and that the general tendency of our indifferent actions, ought to be agreeable to the dictates of reason, of religion, of good breeding: without this, a man, as I before have hinted, is hopping instead of walking, he is not in his entire and proper motion.

I am of opinion, that to polish our understandings

and neglect our manners, is of all things the most inexcusable. Reason should govern passion, but instead of that, you see, it is often subservient to it; and as unaccountable as one would think it, a wise man is not always a good man. This degeneracy is not only the guilt of particular persons, but also at some times of a whole people; and perhaps it may appear upon examination, that the most polite ages are the least virtuous. This may be attributed to the folly of admitting wit and learning as merit in them selves, without considering the application of them By this means it becomes a rule, not so much to regard what we do, as how we do it. But this false beauty will not pass upon men of honest minds and true taste: Sir Richard Blackmore says, with as much good sense as virtue, It is a mighty dishonour and shame to employ excellent faculties and abundance of wit, to humour and please men in their vices and follies. The great enemy of mankind, notwithstanding his wit and angelic faculties, is the most odious being in the whole creation. He goes on soon after to say very generously, that he undertook the writing of his poem to rescue the Muses out of the hands of ravishers, to restore them to their sweet and chaste mansions, and to engage them in an employment suitable to their dignity. This certainly ought to be the purpose of every man who appears in public; and whoever does not proceed upon that foundation, injures his country as fast as he succeeds in his studies. When modesty ceases to be the chief ornament of one sex, and integrity of the other, society is upon a wrong basis, and we shall be ever after without rules to guide our judgment in what is really becoming and ornamental. Nature and reason direct one thing, passion and humour another; to follow the dictates of the two latter, is going into a road that is both endless and intricate; when we pursue the other, our passage is delightful, and what we aim at easily attainable.

I do not doubt but England is at present as polite a nation as any in the world; but any man who thinks, can easily see, that the affectation of being gay and in fashion, has very near eaten up our good sense and our religion. Is there any thing so just, as that mode and gallantry should be built upon exerting ourselves in what is proper and agreeable to the institutions of justice and piety among us? and yet is there any thing more common, than that we run in perfect contradiction to them? all which is supported by no other pretension, than that it is done with what we call a good grace.

Nothing ought to be held laudable or becoming, but what nature itself should prompt us to think so. Respect to all kinds of superiors is founded, methinks, upon instinct; and yet what is so ridiculous as age? I make this abrupt transition to the mention of this vice more than any other, in order to introduce a little story, which I think a pretty instance that the most polite age is in danger of being the most vicious.

"It happened at Athens, during a public representation of some play exhibited in honour of the commonwealth, that an old gentleman came too late for a place suitable to his age and quality. Many of the young gentlemen who observed the difficulty and confusion he was in, made signs to him that they would accommodate him if he came where they sate: the good man bustled through the crowd accordingly: but when he came to the seats to which he was invited, the jest was to sit close and expose him, as he stood out of countenance, to the whole audience. The frolic went round all the Athenian benches. But on those occasions there were also particular places assigned for foreigners: when the good man skulked towards the boxes appointed for the Lacedemonians, that honest people, more virtuous than polite, rose up all to a man, and with the greatest respect received him among them. The Athenians being suddenly touched with a sense of the Spartan virtue and their own degeneracy, gave a thunder of applause; and the old man cried out, 'the Athenians understand what is good, but the Lacedemonians practise it.'"

R.

NECESSITY OF FOLLOWING NATURE.

—— *Non omnia possumus omnes.* VIRG.

With various talents form'd, we variously excel.

NATURE does nothing in vain; the Creator of the universe has appointed every thing to a certain use and purpose, and determined it to a settled course and sphere of action, from which, if it in the least deviates, it becomes unfit to answer those ends for which it was designed. In like manner it is in the dispositions of society, the civil economy is formed in a chain as well as the natural; and in either case the breach but of one link puts the whole in some disorder. It is, I think, pretty plain, that most of the absurdity and ridicule we meet with in the world, is generally owing to the impertinent affectation of excelling in characters men are not fit for, and for which nature never designed them.

Every man has one or more qualities which may make him useful both to himself and others: Nature never fails of pointing them out, and while the infant continues under her guardianship, she brings him on in his way, and then offers herself for a guide in what remains of the journey; if he proceeds in that course, he can hardly miscarry: Nature makes good her engagements; for as she never promises what she is not able to perform, so she never fails of performing what she promises. But the misfortune is, men despise what they may be masters of, and affect what they are not fit for; they reckon themselves already possessed of what their genius inclined them to, and so bend all their ambition to excel in what is out of their reach. Thus they destroy the use of their natural talents, in the same manner as covetous men do their quiet and repose; they can enjoy no satisfaction in what they have, because of the absurd inclination they are possessed with for what they have not.

Cleanthes had good sense, a great memory, and a constitution capable of the closest application: in a word, there was no profession in which Cleanthes might not have made a very good figure; but this won't satisfy him; he takes up an unacountable fondness for the character of a fine gentleman: all his thoughts are bent upon this, instead of attending a dissection, frequenting the courts of justice, or studying the fathers. Cleanthes reads plays, dances, dresses, and spends his time in drawing-rooms, instead of being a good lawyer, divine, or physician; Cleanthes is a downright coxcomb, and will remain to all that knew him a contemptible example of talents misapplied. It is to this affectation the world owes its whole race of coxcombs: Nature, in her whole drama, never drew such a part; she has sometimes made a fool, but a coxcomb is always of a man's own making, by applying his talents otherwise than Nature designed, who ever bears an high resentment for being put out of her course, and never fails of taking her revenge on those that do so. Opposing her tendency in the application of a man's parts, has the same success as declining from her course in the production of vegetables, by the assistance of art and an hot-bed: we may possibly extort an unwilling plant, or an untimely salad; but how weak, how tasteless, and insipid! Just as insipid as the poetry of Valerio: Valerio had an universal character, was genteel, had learning, thought justly, spoke correctly; 'twas believed there was nothing in which Valerio did not excel; and 'twas so far true, that there was but one: Valerio had no genius for poetry, yet he's resolved to be a poet; he writes verses, and takes great pains to convince the town, that Valerio is not that extraordinary person he was taken for.

If men would be content to graft upon nature, and assist her operations, what mighty effects might we expect? Tully would not stand so much alone in oratory, Virgil in poetry, or Cæsar in war. To build upon nature, is laying the foundation upon a rock; every thing disposes itself into order as it were of course, and the whole work is half done as soon as undertaken. Cicero's genius inclined him to oratory; Virgil's to fol low the train of the Muses; they piously obeyed the admonition, and were rewarded. Had Virgil attended the bar, his modest and ingenuous virtue would surely have made but a very indifferent figure; and Tully's declamatory inclination would have been as useless in poetry. Nature, if left to herself, leads us on in the best course, but will do nothing by compulsion and constraint; and if we are not satisfied to go her way, we are always the greatest sufferers by it.

Wherever Nature designs a production, she always disposes seeds proper for it, which are as absolutely necessary to the formation of any moral or intellectual excellence, as they are to the being and growth of plants; and I know not by what fate and folly it is, that men are taught not to reckon him equally absurd that will write verses in spite of Nature, with that gardener that should undertake to raise a jonquil or tulip without the help of their respective seeds.

As there is no good or bad quality that does not affect both sexes, so it is not to be imagined but the fair sex must have suffered by an affectation of this nature, at least as much as the other: the ill effect of it is in none so conspicuous as in the two opposite characters of Cælia and Iras; Cælia has all the charms of person, together with an abundant sweetness of nature, but wants wit, and has a very ill voice; Iras is ugly and ungenteel, but has wit and good sense: if Cælia would be silent, her beholders would adore her; if Iras would talk, her hearers would admire her; but Cælia's tongue runs incessantly, while Iras gives herself silent airs and soft languors; so that 'tis difficult to persuade one's self that Cælia has beauty and Iras wit; each neglects her own excellence, and is ambitious of the other's character; Iras would be thought to have as much beauty as Cælia, and Cælia as much wit as Iras.

The great misfortune of this affectation is, that men not only lose a good quality, but also contract a bad one: they not only are unfit for what they were designed, but they assign to themselves what they are not fit for; and instead of making a very good figure one way, make a very ridiculous one another. If Semanthe would have been satisfied with her natural complexion, she might still have been celebrated by the name of the olive beauty; but Semanthe has taken up an affectation to white and red, and is now distinguished by the character of the lady that paints so well. In a word, could the world be reformed to the obedience of that famed dictate, Follow Nature, which the Oracle of Delphos pronounced to Cicero when he consulted what course of studies he should pursue, we should see almost every man as eminent in his proper sphere as Tully was in his, and should, in a very short time, find impertinence and affectation banished from among the women, and coxcombs and false characters from among the men. For my part, I could never consider this preposterous repugnancy to Nature any otherwise, than not only as the greatest folly, but also one of the most heinous crimes, since it is a direct opposition to the disposition of Providence, and, as Tully expresses it, like the sin of the giants, an actual rebellion against Heaven. Z.

THE PARADISE OF FOOLS.

A VISION.

Decipimur specie recti. HOR.

Deluded by a seeming excellence.
ROSCOMMON.

METHOUGHT I was transported to a hill, green, flowery, and of an easy ascent. Upon the broad top of it resided squint-eyed Error, and popular Opinion with many heads; two that dealt in sorcery, and were famous for bewitching people with the love of themselves. To these repaired a multitude from every side, by two different paths which lead toward each of them. Some who had the most assuming air, went directly of themselves to Error, without expecting a conductor; others of a softer nature went first to popular Opinion, from whence, as she influenced and engaged them with their own praises, she delivered them over to his government.

When we had ascended to an open part of the summit where Opinion abode, we found her entertaining several who had arrived before us. Her voice was pleasing; she breathed odours as she spoke: she seemed to have a tongue for every one: every one thought he heard something that was valuable in himself, and expected a paradise which she promised as the reward of his merit. Thus were we drawn to follow her, till she should bring us where it was to be bestowed: and it was observable, that all the way we went, the company was either praising themselves in their qualifications, or one another for those qualifications which they took to be conspicuous in their own characters, or dispraising others for wanting theirs, or vying in the degrees of them.

At last we approached a bower, at the entrance of which Error was seated. The trees were thick woven, and the place where he sat artfully contrived to darken him a little. He was disguised in a whitish robe, which he had put on, that he might appear to us with a nearer resemblance to Truth: and as she has a light whereby she manifests the beauties of nature to the eyes of her adorers, so he had provided himself with a magical wand, that he might do something in imitation of it, and please with delusions. This he lifted solemnly, and muttering to himself, bid the glories which he kept under enchantment to appear before us. Immediately we cast our eyes on that part of the sky to which he pointed, and observed a thin blue prospect, which cleared as mountains in a summer morning when the mists go off, and the palace of Vanity appeared to sight.

The foundation hardly seemed a foundation, but a set of curling clouds, which it stood upon by magical contrivance. The way by which we ascended was painted like a rainbow; and as we went, the breeze that played about us bewitched the senses. The walls were gilded all for show; the lowest set of pillars were of the slight fine Corinthian order, and the top of the building being rounded, bore so far the resemblance of a bubble.

At the gate the travellers neither met with a porter nor waited till one should appear; every one thought his merits a sufficient passport, and pressed forward. In the hall we met with several phantoms, that roved among us, and ranged the company according to their sentiments. There was decreasing Honour, that had nothing to show in but an old coat of his ancestor's achievements. There was Ostentation, that made himself his own constant subject, and Gallantry strutting upon his tip-toes At the upper end of the hall stood a throne, whose canopy glittered with all the riches that gayety could contrive to lavish on it; and between the gilded arms sat Vanity, decked in the peacock's feathers, and acknowledged for another Venus by her votaries. The boy who stood beside her for a Cupid, and who made the world to bow before her, was called Self-Conceit. His eyes had every now and then a cast inward, to the neglect of all objects about him: and the arms which he made use of for conquest, were borrowed from those against whom he had a design. The arrow which he shot at the soldier, was fledged from his own plume of feathers; the dart he directed against the man of wit, was winged from the quills he writ with; and that which he sent against those who presumed upon their riches, was headed with gold out of their treasuries: he made nets for statesmen from their own contrivances; he took fire from the eyes of ladies, with which he melted their hearts: and lightning from the tongues of the eloquent, to inflame them with their own glories. At the foot of the throne sat three false graces: Flattery with a shell of paint, Affectation with a mirror to practise at, and Fashion ever changing the posture of her clothes. These applied themselves to secure the conquests which Self-Conceit had gotten, and had each of them their particular polities. Flattery gave new colours and complexions to all things, Affectation new airs and appearances, which, as she said, were not vulgar, and Fashion both concealed some home defects, and added some foreign external beauties.

As I was reflecting upon what I saw, I heard a voice in the crowd bemoaning the condition of mankind, which is thus managed by the breath of Opinion, deluded by Error, fired by Self-Conceit, and given up to be trained in all the courses of Vanity, till Scorn or Poverty come upon us. These expressions were no sooner handed about, but I immediately saw a general disorder, till at last there was a parting in one place, and a grave old man, decent and resolute, was led forward to be punished for the words he had uttered. He appeared inclined to have spoken in his own defence, but I could not observe that any one was willing to hear him. Vanity cast a scornful smile at him; Self-Conceit was angry; Flattery, who knew him for Plain-Dealing, put on a vizard, and turned away; Affectation tossed her fan, made mouths, and called him Envy or Slander; and Fashion would have it, that at least he must be Ill-Manners. Thus slighted and despised by all, he was driven out for abusing people of merit and figure; and I heard it firmly resolved, that he should be used no better wherever they met with him hereafter.

I had already seen the meaning of most part of that warning which he had given, and was considering how the latter words would be fulfilled, when a mighty noise was heard without, and the door was blackened by a numerous train of harpies crowding in upon us. Folly and Broken-Credit were seen in the house before they entered, Trouble, Shame, Infamy, Scorn, and Poverty, brought up the rear. Vanity, with her Cupid and Graces, disappeared; her subjects ran into holes and corners; but many of them were found and carried off (as I was told by one who stood near me) either to prisons or cellars, solitude or little company, the mean arts or the viler crafts of life. But these, added he, with a disdainful air, are such who would fondly live here, when their merits neither matched the lustre of the place, nor their riches its expenses. We have seen such scenes as these before now; the glory you saw will all return when the hurry is over. I thanked him for his information, and believing him so incorrigible as that he would stay till it was his turn to be taken, I made off to the door, and overtook some few, who, though they would not hearken to Plain-Dealing, were now terrified to good purpose by the example of others; but when they had touched the threshold, it was a strange shock to them to find that the delusion of Error was gone, and they plainly discerned the building to hang a little up in the air without any real foundation. At first we saw nothing but a desperate leap remained for us, and I a thousand times blamed my unmeaning curiosity that had brought me into so much danger. But as they began to sink lower in their own minds, methought the palace sunk along with us, till they were arrived at the due point of Esteem which they ought to have for themselves; then the part of the building in which they stood touched the earth, and we departing out, it retired from our eyes. Now, whether they who stayed in the palace were sensible of this descent, I cannot tell; it was then my opinion that they were not. However it be, my dream broke up at it, and has given me occasion all my life to reflect upon the fatal consequences of following the suggestions of Vanity.

PHYSIOGNOMY THE MIRROR OF THE SOUL.

Heu quam difficile est crimen non prodere vultu!
OVID.

How in the looks does conscious guilt appear.
ADDISON.

There are several arts which all men are in some measure masters of, without having been at the pains of learning them. Every one that speaks or reasons is a grammarian and a logician, though he may be wholly unacquainted with the rules of grammar or logic, as they are delivered in books and systems. In the same manner, every one is in some degree a master of that art which is generally distinguished by the name of Physiognomy:* and naturally forms to himself the character or fortune of a stranger, from the features and lineaments of his face. We are no sooner presented to any one we never saw before, but we are immediately struck with the idea of a proud, a reserved, an affable, or a good-natured man; and upon our first going into a company of strangers, our benevolence or aversion, awe or contempt, rises naturally towards several particular persons, before we have heard them speak a single word, or so much as know who they are.

Every passion gives a particular cast to the countenance, and is apt to discover itself in some feature or other. I have seen an eye curse for half an hour together, and an eyebrow call a man a scoundrel. Nothing is more common than for lovers to complain, resent, languish, despair, and die in dumb show. For my own part, I am so apt to frame a notion of every man's humour or circumstances by his looks, that I have sometimes employed myself from Charing-cross to the Royal Exchange in drawing the characters of

* The English reader will find this subject very ingeniously discussed in Dr Hunter's translation of Lavater.

those who have passed by me. When I see a man with a sour rivelled face, I cannot forbear pitying his wife: and when I meet with an open ingenuous countenance, I think on the happiness of his friends, his family, and relations. I cannot recollect the author* of a famous saying to a stranger who stood silent in his company, "Speak, that I may see thee." But, with submission, I think we may be better known by our looks than by our words, and that a man's speech is much more easily disguised than his countenance. In this case, however, I think the air of the whole face is much more expressive than the lines of it. The truth of it is, the air is generally nothing else but the inward disposition of the mind made visible.

Those who have established physiognomy into an art, and laid down rules of judging men's tempers by their faces, have regarded the features much more than the air. Martial has a pretty epigram on this subject:

Crine ruber, niger ore, brevis pede, lumine læsus
Rem magnum præstas, Zoile, si bonus es.
Epig. liv. 12.

"Thy beard and head are of a different dye;
Short of one foot, distorted in an eye:
With all these tokens of a knave complete,
Should'st thou be honest, thou'rt a devlish cheat."

I have seen a very ingenious author on this subject, who founds his speculations on the supposition, that as a man hath in the mould of his face a remote likeness to that of an ox, a sheep, a lion, a hog, or any other creature; he hath the same resemblance in the frame of his mind, and is subject to those passions which are predominant in the creature that appears in his countenance. Accordingly he gives the prints of several faces that are of a different mould, and by a little overcharging the likeness, discovers the figures of these several kinds of brutal faces in human fea-

* Socrates.—*Loquere ut te videam.* Apul. Flor. 1 Pr.

tures. I remember, in the Life of the famous Prince of Conde, the writer observes, the face of that prince was like the face of an eagle, and that the prince was very well pleased to be told so. In this case therefore we may be sure, that he had in his mind some general implicit notion of this art of physiognony which I have just now mentioned; and that when his courtiers told him his face was made like an eagle's, he understood them in the same manner as if they had told him, there was something in his looks which showed him to be strong, active, piercing, and of a royal descent. Whether or no the different motions of the animal spirits, in different passions, may have any effect on the mould of the face when the lineaments are pliable and tender, or whether the same kind of souls require the same kind of habitations, I shall leave to the consideration of the curious. In the mean time, I think nothing can be more glorious than for a man to give the lie to his face, and to be an honest, just, good-natured man, in spite of all those marks and signatures which nature seems to have set upon him for the contrary. This very often happens among those, who, instead of being exasperated by their own looks, or envying the looks of others, apply themselves entirely to the cultivating of their minds, and getting those beauties which are more lasting and more ornamental. I have seen many an amiable piece of deformity; and have observed a certain cheerfulness in as bad a system of features as ever was clapped together, which hath appeared more lovely than all the blooming charms of an insolent beauty. There is a double praise due to virtue, when it is lodged in a body that seems to have been prepared for the reception of vice; in many such cases the soul and the body do not seem to be fellows.

Socrates was an extraordinary instance of this nature. There chanced to be a great physiognomist in his time at Athens, who had made strange discoveries of men's tempers and inclinations by their outward appearances. Socrates's disciples, that they might put this artist to the trial, carried him to their master, whom he had never seen before, and did not know he was then in company with him. After a short examination of his face, the physiognomist pronounced him the most lewd, libidinous, drunken old fellow that he had ever met with in his whole life. Upon which the disciples all burst out a laughing, as thinking they had detected the falsehood and vanity of his art. But Socrates told them, that the principles of his art might be very true, notwithstanding his present mistake; for that he himself was naturally inclined to those particular vices which the physiognomist had discovered in his countenance, but that he had conquered the strong dispositions he was born with by the dictates of philosophy.

He are indeed told by an ancient author, that Socrates very much resembled Silenus in his face; which we find to have been very rightly observed from the statues and busts of both, that are still extant; as well as on several antique seals and precious stones, which are frequently enough to be met with in the cabinets of the curious. But however observations of this nature may sometimes hold, a wise man should be particularly cautious how he gives credit to a man's outward appearance. It is an irreparable injustice we are guilty of toward one another, when we are prejudiced by the looks and features of those whom we do not know. How often do we conceive hatred against a person of worth, or fancy a man to be proud or ill-natured by his aspect, whom we think we cannot esteem too much when we are acquainted with his real character? Dr. Moore, in his admirable System of Ethics, reckons this particular inclination to take a prejudice against a man for his looks, among the smaller vices in morality, and, if I remember, gives it the name of a Prosopolepsia. L.

COMPLIMENTARY STYLE.

——— *Sibi quivis*
Speret idem sudet multum frustraque laboret
Ausus idem — HOR.

All men will try, and hope to write as well,
And not, without much pains, be undeceiv'd.
ROSCOMMON.

"—AMONG* too many other instances of the great corruption and degeneracy of the age wherein we live, the great and general want of sincerity in conversation is none of the least, the world is grown so full of dissimulation and compliment, that men's words are hardly any signification of their thoughts; and if any man measure his words by his heart, and speak as he thinks, and do not express more kindness to every man, than men usually have for any man, he can hardly escape the censure of want of breeding. The old English plainness and sincerity, that generous integrity of nature, and honesty of disposition, which always argues true greatness of mind, and is usually accompanied with undaunted courage and resolution, is in a great measure lost among us. There hath been a long endeavour to transform us into foreign manners and fashions, and to bring us to a servile imitation of none of the best of our neighbours, in some of the worst of their qualities. The dialect of conversation is now-a-days so swelled with vanity and compliment, and so surfeited (as I may say) of expressions of kindness and respect, that if a man that lived an age or two ago should return into the world again, he would really want a dictionary to help him to understand his own language, and to know the true intrinsic value of the phrase in fashion, and would hardly at first believe at what a low rate the highest strains and expressions of kindness imaginable do commonly pass in current payment: and when he should come to understand it, it would be a great while before he could bring him-

* Tillotson's Sermon on Sincerity.

self with a good countenance and a good conscience to converse with men upon equal terms, and in their own way.

"And in truth it is hard to say, whether it should more provoke our contempt or our pity to hear what solemn expressions of respect and kindness will pass between men, almost upon no occasion; how great honour and esteem they will declare for one whom perhaps they never saw before, and how entirely they are all on the sudden devoted to his service and interest, for no reason; how infinitely and eternally obliged to him, for no benefit; and how extremely they will be concerned for him, yea and afflicted too, for no cause. I know it is said, in justification of this hollow kind of conversation, that there is no harm, no real deceit in compliment, but the matter is well enough, so long as we understand one another; *et verba valent ut nummi*, 'words are like money;' and when the current value of them is generally understood, no man is cheated by them. This is something, if such words were any thing; but being brought into the account, they are mere ciphers. However, it is still a just matter of complaint, that sincerity and plainness are out of fashion, and that our language is running into a lie; that men have almost quite perverted the use of speech, and made words to signify nothing; that the greatest part of the conversation of mankind is little else but driving a trade of dissimulation; insomuch that it would make a man heartily sick and weary of the world, to see the little sincerity that is in use and practice among men."

When the vice is placed in this contemptible light, he argues unanswerably against it, in words and thoughts so natural, that any man who reads them would imagine he himself could have been the author of them.

"If the show of any thing be good for any thing, I am sure sincerity is better: for why does any man dissemble, or seem to be that which he is not, but because he thinks it good to have such a quality as he pretends to? For to counterfeit and dissemble, is to put on the appearance of some real excellency. Now the best way in the world to seem to be any thing, is really to be what he would seem to be. Besides, that it is many times as troublesome to make good the pretence of a good quality, as to have it; and if a man have it not, it is ten to one but he is discovered to want it; and then all his pains and labour to seem to have it, is lost."

In another part of the same discourse he goes on to show, that all artifice must naturally tend to the disappointment of him that practises it.

"Whatsoever convenience may be thought to be in falsehood and dissimulation, it is soon over; but the inconvenience of it is perpetual, because it brings a man under an everlasting jealousy and suspicion, so that he is not believed when he speaks the truth, nor trusted when perhaps he means honestly. When a man hath once forfeited the reputation of his integrity, he is set fast, and nothing will then serve his turn, neither truth nor falsehood." *R.*

A FEMALE DEVOTEE.

——— *Cum magnis virtutibus affers*
Grande supercilium.———

JUV. Sat. 5. v. 168.

We own thy virtues; but we blame beside
Thy mind elate with insolence and pride.

A Devotee is one of those who disparage religion by their indiscreet and unseasonable introduction of the mention of virtue on all occasions; she professes she is what nobody ought to doubt she is; and betrays the labour she is put to, to be what she ought to be with cheerfulness and alacrity. She lives in the world, and denies herself none of the diversions of it, with a constant declaration how insipid all things in it are to her. She is never herself but at church: there she displays her virtue, and is so fervent in her devotions, that I have frequently seen her pray herself out of breath. While other young ladies in the house are dancing, or playing at questions and commands, she reads aloud in her closet. She says, all love is ridiculous except it be celestial; but she speaks of the passion of one mortal to another, with too much bitterness, for one that had no jealousy mixed with her contempt of it. If at any time she sees a man warm in his addresses to his mistress, she will lift up her eyes to heaven, and cry, What nonsense is that fool talking? Will the bell never ring for prayers? We have an eminent lady of this stamp in our country, who pretends to amusements very much above the rest of her sex. She never carries a white shock-dog, with bells under her arm, nor a squirrel or dormouse in her pocket, but always an abridged piece of morality to steal out when she is sure of being observed. When she went to the famous ass-race, (which I must confess was but an odd diversion to be encouraged by people of rank and figure) it was not, like other ladies, to hear those poor animals bray, nor to see fellows run naked, or to hear country squires in bob-wigs and white girdles make love at the side of a coach, and cry, 'Madam, this is dainty weather.' Thus she described the diversion; for she went only to pray heartily that nobody might be hurt in the crowd, and to see if the poor fellow's face, which was distorted with grinning might any way be brought to itself again. She never chats over her tea, but covers her face, and is supposed in an ejaculation before she tastes a sup. This ostentatious behaviour is such an offence to true sanctity, that it disparages it, and makes virtue not only unamiable, but also ridiculous. The sacred writings are full of reflections which abhor this kind of conduct; and a devotee is so far from promoting goodness, that she deters others by her example. Folly and vanity in one of these ladies, is like vice in a clergyman; it does not only debase him, but makes the inconsiderate part of the world think the worse of religion.

T.

EULOGY ON NEEDLEWORK.

—— *longum cantu salato laborem*
Arguta conjux percurrit pectine telas. VIRG.

—— mean time at home
The good wife singing plies the various loom.

What a delightful entertainment must it be to the fair sex, whom their native modesty and the tenderness of men toward them, exempt from public business, to pass their hours in imitation fruits and flowers, and transplanting all the beauties of nature into their own dress, or raising a new creation in their closets and apartments. How pleasing is the amusement of walking among the shades and groves planted by themselves, in surveying heroes slain by their needle, or little Cupids which they have brought into the world without pain!

This is, methinks, the most proper way wherein a lady can show a fine genius, and I cannot forbear wishing, that several writers of that sex had chosen to apply themselves rather to tapestry than to rhyme. Your pastoral poetesses may vent their fancy in rural landscapes, and place despairing shepherds under silken willows, or drown them in a stream of mohair. The heroic writers may work up battles as successfully, and inflame them with gold or stain them with crimson. Even those who have only a turn to a song or an epigram, may put many valuable stitches into a purse, and crowd a thousand graces into a pair of garters.

If I may without breach of good manners, imagine that any pretty creature is void of genius, and would perform her part therein very awkwardly, I must nevertheless insist upon her working, if it be only to keep her out of harm's way.

Another argument for busying good women in works of fancy, is, because it takes them off from scandal, the usual attendant of tea-tables, and all other unactive scenes of life. While they are forming their birds and beasts, their neighbours will be allowed to be fathers of their own children: and Whig and Tory will be but seldom mentioned, where the great dispute is, whether blue or red is the more proper colour. How much greater glory would Sophronia do the general, if she would choose rather to work the Battle of Blenheim in tapestry, than signalize herself with so much vehemence against those who are Frenchmen in their hearts.

A third reason that I shall mention, is the profit that is brought to the family where these pretty arts are encouraged. It is manifest that this way of life not only keeps fair ladies from running out into expenses, but is at the same time an actual improvement. How memorable would that matron be, who shall have it subscribed upon her monument, "That she wrought out the whole Bible in tapestry, and died in a good old age, after having covered three hundred yards of wall in the mansion house."

The premises being considered, I humbly submit the following proposals to all mothers in Great Britain.

I. That no young virgin whatsoever be allowed to receive the addresses of her first lover, but in a suit of her own embroidering.

II. That before every fresh humble servant, she be obliged to appear with a new stomacher at the least.

III. That no one be actually married until she hath the child-bed, pillows, &c. ready stitched, as likewise the mantle for the boy quite finished.

These laws, if I mistake not, would effectually restore the decayed art of needlework, and make the virgins of Great Britain exceedingly nimble-fingered in their business.

There is a memorable custom of the Grecian ladies in this particular, preserved in Homer, which I hope will have a good effect with my country-women. A widow, in ancient times, could not without indecency receive a second husband, until she had woven a shroud for her deceased lord, or the next of kin to him. Accordingly, the chaste Penelope, having, as she thought, lost Ulysses at sea, she employed her time in preparing a winding sheet for Laertes, the father of her husband. The story of her web being very famous, and yet not sufficiently known in its several circumstances, I shall give it to my reader, as Homer makes one of her wooers relate it.

"Sweet hope she gave to every youth apart,
With well-taught looks, and a deceitful heart:
A web she wove of many a slender twine,
Of curious texture, and perplex'd design;
My youths, she cried, my lord but newly dead,
Forbear awhile to court my widow'd bed,
Till I have wov'n, as solemn vows require,
This web, a shroud for poor Ulysses' sire.
His limbs, when fate the hero's soul demands,
Shall claim this labour of his daughter's hands·
Lest all the dames of Greece my name despise,
While the great king without a covering lies.
"Thus she. Nor did her friends mistrust the guile,
All day she sped the long laborious toil:
But when the burning lamps supplied the sun,
Each night unravell'd what the day begun.
Three live-long summers did the fraud prevail:
The fourth her maidens told th' amazing tale:
These eyes beheld, as close I took my stand,
The backward labours of her faithless hand:
Till watch'd at length, and press'd on every side,
Her task she ended, and commenced a bride."

CLUBS.

—— *Tigris agit rabida cum tigride pacem*
Perpetuam, sævis inter se convenit ursis. JUV

Tiger with tiger, bear with bear you'll find
In leagues offensive and defensive join'd. TATE.

Man is said to be a sociable animal, and as an instance of it, we may observe, that we take all occasions and pretences of forming ourselves into those little nocturnal assemblies, which are commonly known by the name of Clubs. When a set of men find themselves agree in any particular, though never so trivial, they establish themselevs into a kind of fraternity, and meet once or twice a week, upon the account of such a fantastic resemblance. I know a considerable market-town, in which there was a club of fat men, that did not come together (as you may well suppose) to entertain one another with sprightliness and wit, but to keep one another in countenance: the room where the club met was something of the largest, and had two entrances, the one by a door of a moderate size, and the other by a pair of folding-doors. If a candidate for this corpulent club could make his entrance through the first, he was looked upon as unqualified; but if he stuck in the passage, and could not force his way through it, the folding-doors were immediately thrown open for his reception, and he was saluted as a brother. I have heard that this club, though it consisted but of fifteen persons, weighed above three tons.

In opposition to this society, there sprung up another, composed of scare-crows and skeletons, who being very meagre and envious, did all they could to thwart the designs of their bulky brethren, whom they represented as men of dangerous principles; till at length they worked them out of the favour of the people, and consequently out of the magistracy. These factions tore the corporation in pieces for several years, till at length they came to this accommodation; that the two bailiffs of the town should be annually chosen out of the two clubs; by which means the principal magistrates are at this day coupled like rabbits, one fat and one lean.

Every one has heard of the club, or rather the confederacy, of the Kings. This grand alliance was formed a little after the return of King Charles the Second, and admitted into it men of all qualities and professions, provided they agreed in this surname of King which, as they imagined, sufficiently declared the owners of it to be altogether untainted with republican and anti-monarchical principles.

A christian name has likewise been often used as a badge of distinction, and made the occasion of a club. That of the George's, which used to meet the sign of the George, on St. George's day an swear before George, is still fresh in every one' memory.

There are at present in several parts of this city what they call Street-Clubs, in which the chief inhabitants of the street converse together every night. I remember, upon my inquiring after lodgings in Ormond-street, the landlord, to recommend that quarter of the town, told me, there was at that time a very good club in it; he also told me, upon further discourse with him, that two or three noisy country squires, who were settled there the year before, had considerably sunk the price of house-rent; and that the club (to prevent the like inconveniences for the future) had thoughts of taking every house that became vacant into their own hands, till they had found a tenant for it, of a sociable nature and good conversation.

The Hum-drum Club, of which I was formerly an unworthy member, was made up of very honest gentlemen, of peaceable dispositions, that used to sit together, smoke their pipes, and say nothing till midnight. The Mum Club (as I am informed) is an institution of the same nature, and as great an enemy to noise.

After these two innocent societies, I cannot forbear mentioning a very mischievous one, that was erected in the reign of King Charles the Second; I mean, the Club of Duellists, in which none was to be admitted that had not fought his man. The president of it was said to have killed half a dozen in single combat; and as for the other members, they took their seats according to the number of their slain. There was likewise a side-table, for such as had only drawn blood, and shown a laudable ambition of taking the first opportunity to qualify themselves for the first table. This club, consisting only of men of honour, did not continue long, most of the members of it being put to the sword, or hanged, a little after its institution.

Our modern celebrated clubs are founded upon eating and drinking, which are points wherein most men agree, and in which the learned and illiterate, the dull and the airy, the philosopher and the buffoon, can all of them bear a part. The Kit-Cat itself is said to have taken its original from a mutton-pie. The Beef-steak and October clubs are neither of them averse to eating and drinking, if we may form a judgment of them from their respective titles.

When men are thus knit together, by a love of society, not a spirit of faction, and do not meet to censure or annoy those that are absent, but to enjoy one another; when they are thus combined for their own improvement, or for the good of others, or at least to relax themselves from the business of the day, by an innocent and cheerful conversation, there may be something very useful in these little institutions and establishments.

FATAL EFFECTS

OF

A FURIOUS PARTY SPIRIT

Ne, pueri, ne tanta animis assuescite bella :
Nec patriæ validas in viscera vertite vires. VIRG.

Embrace again, my sons, be foes no more ;
Nor stain your country with her children's gore.
DRYDEN.

THERE cannot be a greater judgment befall a country than a dreadful spirit of division, which rends a government into two distinct people, and makes them greater strangers and more averse to one another, than if they were actually two different nations. The effects of such a division are pernicious to the last degree, not only with regard to those advantages which they give the common enemy, but to those private evils which they produce in the heart of almost every particular person. This influence is very fatal both to men's morals and their understandings; it sinks the virtue of a nation, and not only so, but destroys even common sense.

F

A furious party spirit, when it rages in its full violence, exerts itself in civil war and bloodshed; and when it is under greatest restraints, naturally breaks out in falsehood, detraction, calumny, and a partial administration of justice. In a word, it fills a nation with spleen and rancour, and extinguishes all the seeds of good-nature, compassion, and humanity.

Plutarch says very finely, that a man should not allow himself to hate even his enemies, because, says he, if you indulge this passion on some occasions, it will rise of itself in others; if you hate your enemies, you will contract such a vicious habit of mind, as by degrees will break out upon those who are your friends, or those who are indifferent to you. I might here observe how admirably this precept of morality, which derives the malignity of hatred from the passion itself, and not from its object, answers to that great rule which was dictated to the world about an hundred years before this philosopher wrote; but instead of that, I shall only take notice, with a real grief of heart, that the minds of many good men among us appear soured with party-principles, and alienated from one another in such a manner as seems to me altogether inconsistent with the dictates either of reason or religion. Zeal for a public cause is apt to breed passions in the hearts of virtuous persons, to which the regard of their own private interest would never have betrayed them.

If this party-spirit has so ill an effect on our morals, it has likewise a very great one upon our judgments. We often hear a poor insipid paper or pamphlet cried up, and sometimes a noble piece depreciated, by those who are of a different principle from the author. One who is actuated by this spirit is almost under an incapacity of discerning either real blemishes or beauties. A man of merit in a different principle, is like an object seen in two different mediums, that appears crooked or broken, however straight and entire it may be in itself. For this reason there is scarce a person of any figure in England, who does not go by two contrary characters, as opposite to one another as light and darkness. Knowledge and learning suffer in a particular manner from this strange prejudice, which at present prevails amongst all ranks and degrees in the British nation. As men formerly became eminent in learned societies by their parts and acquisitions, they now distinguish themselves by the warmth and violence with which they espouse their respective parties. Books are valued upon the like consideration; an abusive scurrilous style passes for satire, and a dull scheme of party-notions is called fine writing.

There is one piece of sophistry practised by both sides, and that is the taking any scandalous story that has been ever whispered or invented of a private man, for a known undoubted truth, and raising suitable speculations upon it. Calumnies that have been never proved, or have been often refuted, are the ordinary postulatums of those infamous scribblers, upon which they proceed as upon first principles granted by all men, though in their hearts they know they are false, or at best very doubtful. When they have laid these foundations of scurrility, it is no wonder that their superstructure is every way answerable to them. If this shameless practice of the present age endures much longer, praise and reproach will cease to be motives of action in good men.

There are certain periods of time in all governments when this inhuman spirit prevails. Italy was long torn in pieces by the Guelfes and Gibellines, and France by those who were for and against the league; but it is very unhappy for a man to be born in such a stormy and tempestuous season. It is the restless ambition of artful men that thus breaks a people into factions, and draws several well-meaning persons to their interest by a specious concern for their country. How many honest minds are filled with uncharitable and barbarous notions, out of their zeal for the public good! What cruelties and outrages would they not commit against men of an adverse party whom they would honour and esteem, if, instead of considering them as they are represented, they knew them as they are! Thus are persons of the greatest probity seduced into shameful errors and prejudices, and made bad men even by that noblest of principles, the love of their country. I cannot here forbear mentioning the famous Spanish proverb, 'If there were neither fools nor knaves in the world, all people would be of one mind.'

For my own part, I could heartily wish that all honest men would enter into an association, for the support of one another against the endeavours of those whom they ought to look upon as their common enemies, whatsoever side they may belong to. Were there such an honest body of neutral forces, we should never see the worst of men in great figures of life, because they are useful to a party: nor the best unregarded, because they are above practising those methods which would be grateful to their faction. We should then single every criminal out of the herd, and hunt him down, however formidable and overgrown he might appear: on the contrary, we should shelter distressed innocence, and defend virtue, however beset with contempt or ridicule, envy or defamation. In short, we should not any longer regard our fellow-subjects as Whigs or Tories, but should make the man of merit our friend, and the villain our enemy.

* * * *

Were there a combination of honest men, who without any regard to places, would endeavour to extirpate all such furious zealots as would sacrifice one half of their country to the passion and interest of the other; as also such infamous hypocrites, that are for promoting their own advantage under colour of the public good; with all the profligate immoral retainers to each side, that have nothing to recommend them but an implicit submission to their leaders; we should soon see that furious party-spirit extinguished, which may in time expose us to the derision and contempt of all the nations about us.

A member of this society, that would thus carefully employ himself in making room for merit, by throwing down the worthless and depraved part of mankind from those conspicuous stations of life to which they have been sometimes advanced, and all this without any regard to his private interest, would be no small benefactor to his country.

I remember to have read in Diodorus Siculus an account of a very little active animal, which I think he calls the little ichneumon, that makes it the whole business of its life to break the eggs of the crocodile, which he is always in search after. This instinct is the more remarkable, because the ichneumon never feeds upon the eggs he has broken, nor any other way finds his account in them. Were it not for the incessant labours of this industrious animal, Egypt, says the historian, would be overrun with crocodiles; for the Egyptians are so far from destroying those pernicious creatures, that they worship them as gods.

If we look into the behaviour of ordinary partisans, we shall find them far from resembling this disinterested animal and rather acting after the example of the wild Tartars, who are ambitious of destroying a man of the most extraordinary parts and accomplishments, as thinking that upon his decease the same talents, whatever post they qualified him for, enter of course into his destroyer.

I observe that the spirit of party reigns more in the country than in the town. It here contracts a kind of brutality and rustic fierceness, to which men of a politer conversation are wholly strangers. It extends itself even to the return of the bow and the hat; and at the same time that the heads of parties preserve towards one another an outward show of good-breeding, and keep up a perpetual intercourse of civilities, their tools that are dispersed in these outlying parts will not so much as mingle together at a cock-match. This humour fills the country with several periodical meetings of whig jockeys and tory fox-hunters; not to mention the innumerable curses, frowns, and whispers, it produces at a quarter-sessions.

It gives a serious concern to see such a spirit of dissention in the country; not only as it destroys virtue and common sense, and renders us in a manner barbarians towards one another, but as it perpetuates our animosities, widens our breaches, and transmits our present passions and prejudices to our posterity. I am sometimes afraid that I discover the seeds of a civil war in these our divisions; and therefore cannot but bewail, as in their first principles, the miseries and calamities of our children.

C.

WORLDLY PURSUITS.

Audire, atque togam jubeo componere, quisquis
Ambitione mala, aut argenti pallet amore,
Quisquis luxaria——— HOR.

Sit still and hear, those whom proud thoughts do swell,
Those look pale by loving coin too well;
Whom luxury corrupts. CREECH.

MANKIND is divided into two parts, the busy and the idle. The busy world may be divided into the virtuous and the vicious. The vicious again into the covetous, the ambitious, and the sensual. The idle part of mankind are in a state inferior to any one of these. All the other are engaged in the pursuit of happiness, though often misplaced, and are therefore more likely to be attentive to such means as shall be proposed to them for that end. The idle, who are neither wise for this world nor the next, are emphatically called, by Doctor Tillotson, fools at large. They propose themselves no end, but run adrift with every wind. Advice therefore would be but thrown away upon them, since they would scarce take the pains to read it. I shall not fatigue any of this worthless tribe with a long harangue; but will leave them with this short saying of Plato, that "labour is preferable to idleness, as brightness to rust."

The pursuits of the active part of mankind are either in the paths of religion or virtue; or, on the other hand, in the roads to wealth, honours, or pleasure. I shall, therefore, compare the pursuits of avarice, ambition, and sensual delight, with their opposite virtues; and shall consider which of those principles engages men in a course of the greatest labour, suffering, and assiduity. Most men, in their cool reasonings, are willing to allow that a course of virtue will in the end be rewarded the most amply; but represent the way to it as rugged and narrow. If therefore it can be made appear, that men struggle through as many troubles to be made miserable, as they do to be happy, my readers may perhaps be persuaded to be good, when they find they shall lose nothing by it.

First, for avarice. The miser is more industrious than the saint: the pains of getting, the fears of losing, and the inability of enjoying his wealth, have been the mark of satire in all ages. Were his repentance upon his neglect of a good bargain, his sorrow for being overreached, his hope of improving a sum, and his fear of falling into want, directed to their proper objects, they would make so many different Christian graces and virtues. He may apply to himself a great part of St. Paul's catalogue of sufferings. "In journeying often; in perils of waters, in perils of robbers, in perils among false brethren. In weariness and painfulness, in watchings often, in hunger and thirst, in fastings often." At how much less expense might he "lay up to himself treasures in heaven?" or if I may, in this place, be allowed to add the saying of a great philosopher, he may "provide such possessions, as fear neither arms, nor men, nor Jove himself."

In the second place, if we look upon the toils of ambition, in the same light as we have considered those of avarice, we shall readily own that far less trouble is requisite to gain lasting glory, than the power and reputation of a few years; or in other words, we may with more ease deserve honour, than obtain it. The ambitous man should remember Cardinal Wolsey's complaint: "Had I served God with the same application wherewith I served my king, he would not have forsaken me in my old age." The Cardinal here softens his ambition by the specious pretence of "serving his king;" whereas his words, in the proper construction, imply, that if, instead of being actuated by ambition, he had been actuated by religion, he should now have felt the comforts of it, when the whole world turned its back upon him.

Thirdly, let us compare the pains of the sensual, with those of the virtuous, and see which are heavier in the balance. It may seem strange, at the first view, that the men of pleasure should be advised to change their course, because they lead a painful life. Yet when we see them so active and vigilant in quest of delight; under so many disquiets, and the sport of such various passions; let them answer, as they can, if the pains they undergo do not outweigh their enjoyments. The infidelities on the one part between the two sexes, and the caprices on the other, the debasement of reason, the pangs of expectation, the disappointments in possession, the stings of remorse, the vanities and vexations attending even the most refined delights that make up this business of life, render it so silly and uncomfortable, that no man is thought wise until he hath got over it, or happy, but in proportion as he hath cleared himself from it.

The sum of all is this: Man is made an active being. Whether he walks in the paths of virtue or vice, he is sure to meet with many difficulties to prove his patience and excite his industry. The same, if not greater labour, is required in the service of vice and folly, as of virtue and wisdom; and he hath this easy choice left him, whether, with the strength he is master of, he will purchase happiness or repentance.

INVECTIVE AGAINST BACHELORS.

Dum potuit, solita gemitum virtute repressit.
OVID, Met. l. ix. v. 163.

With wonted fortitude she bore the smart,
And not a groan confess'd her burning heart. GAY.

"Sir,

"I AM a woman loaded with injuries, and the aggravation of my misfortune is, that they are such which are overlooked by the generality of mankind, and though the most afflicting imaginable, not regarded as such in the general sense of the world. I have hid my vexation from all mankind; but have now taken pen, ink, and paper, and am resolved to unbosom myself to you, and lay before you what grieves me and all the sex. Why have you not in any one speculation directly pointed at the partial freedom men take, the unreasonable confinement women are obliged to, in the only circumstance in which we are necessarily to have a commerce with them, that of love? The case of celibacy is the great evil of our nation; and the indulgence of the vicious conduct of men in that state, with the ridicule to which women are exposed, though ever so virtuous, if long unmarried, is the root of the greatest irregularities of this nation. To show you that I read good books of my own choosing, I shall insert on this occasion a paragraph or two out of Echard's Roman History. In the 44th page of the second volume the author observes that Augustus, upon his return to Rome at the end of a war, received complaints that too great a number of the young men of quality were unmarried.

The Emperor thereupon assembled the whole equestrian order; and having separated the married from the single, did particular honours to the former, but he told the latter, that is to say, sir, he told the Bachelors, 'That their lives and actions had been so peculiar, that he knew not by what name to call them; not by that of men, for they performed nothing that was manly; not by that of citizens, for the city might perish notwithstanding their care; nor by that of Romans, for they designed to extirpate the Roman name.' Then proceeding to show his tender care and hearty affection for his people, he further told them, 'That their course of life was of such pernicious consequence to the glory and grandeur of the Roman nation, that he could not choose but tell them, that all other crimes put together could not equalise theirs: for they were guilty of murder, in not suffering those to be born which should proceed from them; of impiety, in causing the name and honours of their ancestors to cease; and of sacrilege, in destroying their kind, which proceeded from the immortal gods, and human nature, the principal thing consecrated to them: therefore in this respect they dissolved the government, in disobeying its laws; betrayed their country, by making it barren and waste; nay, and demolished their city, in depriving it of inhabitants. And he was sensible that all this proceeded not from any kind of virtue or abstinence, but from a looseness and wantonness, which ought never to be encouraged in any civil government.' There are no particulars dwelt upon that let us into the conduct of these young worthies, whom this great Emperor treated with so much justice and indignation; but any one who observes what passes in this town, may very well frame to himself a notion of their riots and debaucheries all night, and their apparent preparations for them all day. It is not to be doubted but these Romans never passed any of their time innocently but when they were asleep, and never slept but when they were weary and heavy with excesses, and slept only to prepare themselves for the repetition of them. I have not patience to proceed gravely on this abominable libertinism; for I cannot but reflect, as I am writing to you, upon a certain lascivious manner which all our young gentlemen use in public, and examine our eyes with a petulancy in their own, which is a downright affront to modesty. A disdainful look on such an occasion is returned with a countenance rebuked, but by averting their eyes from the woman of honour and decency to some flippant creature, who will, as the phrase is, be kinder. I must set down things as they come into my head, without standing upon order. Ten thousand to one but the gay gentleman who stared, at the same time is an housekeeper: for you must know they have got into a humour of late of being very regular in their sins, and a young fellow shall keep his four maids and three footmen with the greatest gravity imaginable. There are no less than six of these venerable housekeepers of my acquaintance. This humour among young men of condition is imitated by all the world below them, and a general dissolution of manners arises from this one source of libertinism, without shame or reprehension in the male youth. It is from this one fountain that so many beautiful helpless young women are sacrificed and given up to lewdness, shame, poverty, and disease. It is to this also that so many excellent young women, who might be patterns of conjugal affection, and parents of a worthy race, pine under unhappy passions for such as have not attention enough to observe. or virtue enough to prefer them to their common wenches. Now sir, I must be free to own to you, that I myself suffer a tasteless insipid being, from a consideration I have for a man who would not, as he has said in my hearing, resign his liberty, as he calls it, for all the beauty and wealth the whole sex is possessed of. Such calamities as these would not happen, if it could possibly be brought about, that by fining bachelors as papists convict, or the like, they were distinguished to their disadvantage from the rest of the world, who fall in with the measures of civil societies. Lest you should think I speak this as being, according to the senseless rude phrase, a malicious old maid, I shall acquaint you I am a woman of condition, not now three-and-twenty, and have had proposals from at least ten different men, and the greater number of them have upon the upshot refused me. Something or other is always amiss when the lover takes to some new wench: a settlement is easily excepted against, and there is very little recourse to avoid the vicious part of our youth, but throwing one's self away upon some lifeless blockhead, who, though he is without vice, is also without virtue. Now-a-days we must be contented if we can get creatures which are not bad, good are not to be expected. I hope you'll take notice of these evils, and print this memorial, dictated from the disdainful heavy heart of,

"Sir,
"Your most obedient
"humble servant,
T. "RACHEL WELLADAY."

JOURNAL OF A SOBER CITIZEN.

——*fruges consumere nati.* HOR.

—— Born to drink and eat. CREECH.

AUGUSTUS, a few moments before his death, asked his friends who stood about him, if they thought he had acted his part well; and upon receiving such an answer as was due to his extraordinary merit, Let me then, says he, go off the stage with your applause; using the expression with which the Roman actors made their exit at the conclusion of a dramatic piece. I could wish that men, while they are in health, would consider well the nature of the part they are engaged in, and what figure it will make in the minds of those they leave behind them: whether it was worth coming into the world for; whether it be suitable to a reasonable being; in short, whether it appears graceful in this life, or will turn to an advantage in the next. Let the sycophant or buffoon, the satirist or the good companion, consider with himself, when his body shall be laid in the grave, and his soul pass into another state of existence, how much it will redound to his praise to have it said of him, that no man in England ate better, that he had an admirable talent at turning his friends into ridicule, that nobody out-did him at an ill-natured jest, or that he never went to bed before he had despatched his third bottle. These are, however, very common funeral orations and eulogiums on deceased persons who have acted among mankind with some figure and reputation.

But if we look into the bulk of our species, they are such as are not likely to be remembered a moment after their disappearance. They leave behind them no traces of their existence, but are forgotten as though they had never been. They are neither wanted by the poor, regretted by the rich, nor celebrated by the learned. They are neither missed in the commonwealth, nor lamented by private persons. Their actions are of no significancy to mankind, and might have been performed by creatures of much less dignity than those who are distinguished by the faculty of reason. An eminent French author speaks somewhere to the following purpose: I have often seen from my chamber window two noble creatures, both of them of an erect countenance, and endowed with reason. These two intellectual beings are employed from morning to night, in rubbing two smooth stones one upon another; that is, as the vulgar phrase is, in polishing marble.

My friend, Sir Andrew, gave me an account of a sober citizen, who died a few days since. This honest man being of greater consequence in his own thoughts, than in the eye of the world, had for some years past kept a journal of his life. Sir Andrew showed me one week of it. Since the occurrences set down in it mark out such a road of action as that I have been speaking of, I shall present my reader with a faithful copy of it: after having first informed him, that the deceased person had in his youth been bred to trade, but finding himself not so well turned for business, he had for several years last past lived altogether upon a moderate annuity.

Monday, eight o'clock. I put on my clothes and walked into the parlour.

Nine a-clock ditto. Tied my knee-strings, and washed my hands.

Hours ten, eleven and twelve. Smoked three pipes of Virginia. Read the Supplement and Daily Courant. Things go ill in the north. Mr. Nisby's opinion thereupon.

One a-clock in the afternoon. Chid Ralph for mislaying my tobacco-box.

Two a-clock. Sat down to dinner. Mem. Too many plums, and no suet.

From three to four. Took my afternoon's nap.

From four to six. Walked into the fields. Wind S. S. E.

From six to ten. At the club. Mr. Nisby's opinion about the peace.

Ten a-clock. Went to bed, slept sound.

Tuesday, being holyday, eight a-clock. Rose as usual.

Nine a-clock. Washed hands and face, shaved, put on my double soaled shoes.

Ten, eleven, twelve. Took a walk to Islington.

One. Took a pot of mother Cob's mild.

Between two and three. Returned, dined on a knuckle of veal and bacon. Mem. Sprouts wanting.

Three. Nap as usual.

From four to six. Coffee-house. Read the news. A dish of twist. Grand Vizier strangled.

From six to ten. At the club. Mr. Nisby's account of the Great Turk.

Ten. Dream of the Grand Vizier. Broken sleep.

Wednesday, eight a-clock. Tongue of my shoe buckle broke. Hands but not face.

Nine. Paid off the butcher's bill. Mem. To be allowed for the last leg of mutton.

Ten, eleven. At the coffee-house. More work in the north. Stranger in a black wig asked me how stocks went.

From twelve to one. Walked in the fields. Wind to the south.

From one to two. Smoked a pipe and a half.

Two. Dined as usual. Stomach good.

Three. Nap broke by the falling of a pewter dish. Mem. Cook-maid in love, and grown careless.

From four to six. At the coffee-house. Advice from Smyrna, that the Grand Vizier was first of all strangled, and afterward beheaded.

Six a-clock in the evening. Was half an hour in the club before any body else came. Mr. Nisby of opinion that the Grand Vizier was not strangled the sixth instant.

Ten at night. Went to bed. Slept without waking till nine next morning.

Thursday, nine a-clock. Staid within till two a-clock for Sir Timothy: who did not bring me my annuity according to his promise.

Two in the afternoon. Sat down to dinner. Loss of appetite. Small-beer sour. Beef over-corned.

Three. Could not take my nap.

Four and five. Gave Ralph a box on the ear. Turned off my cook-maid. Sent a messenger to Sir Timothy. Mem. I did not go to the club to-night. Went to bed at nine o'clock.

Friday, passed the morning in meditation upon Sir Timothy, who was with me a quarter before twelve.

Twelve a-clock. Bought a new head to my cane, and tongue to my buckle. Drank a glass of purl to recover appetite.

Two and three. Dined, and slept well.

From four to six. Went to the coffee-house. Met Mr. Nisby there. Smoked several pipes. Mr. Nisby of opinion that laced coffee is bad for the head.

Six a-clock. At the club as steward. Sat late.

Twelve a-clock. Went to bed, dreamt that I drank small beer with the Grand Vizier.

Saturday, waked at eleven, walked in the fields. Wind N. E.

Twelve. Caught in a shower.

One in the afternoon. Returned home, and dried myself.

Two. Mr. Nisby dined with me. First course marrow-bones; second, ox-cheek, with a bottle of Brooks and Hellier.

Three a-clock Overslept myself.

SIX. Went to the club. Like to have fallen into a gutter. Grand Vizier certainly dead, &c.

I question not but the reader will be surprised to find the above-mentioned journalist taking so much care of a life that was filled with such inconsiderable actions, and received so very small improvements; and yet, if we look into the behaviour of many whom we daily converse with, we shall find the most of their hours are taken up in those three important articles of eating, drinking, and sleeping. I do not suppose that a man loses his time, who is not engaged in public affairs, or in an illustrious course of action. On the contrary, I believe our hours may very often be more profitably laid out in such transactions as make no figure in the world, than in such as are apt to draw upon them the attention of mankind. One may become wiser and better by several methods of employing one's self in secrecy and silence, and do what is laudable without noise or ostentation. I would, however, recommend to every one of my readers, the keeping a journal of their lives for one week, and setting down punctually their whole series of employments during that space of time. This kind of self-examination would give them a true state of themselves, and incline them to consider seriously what they are about. One day would rectify the omissions of another, and make a man weigh all those indifferent actions, which, though they are easily forgotten, must certainly be accounted for. L.

DRUNKENNESS.

Reges dicuntur multis urgere cululli
Et torquere mero, quem perspexisse laborent,
An sit amicitia dignus—— HOR.

Wise were the kings, who never chose a friend,
Till with full cups they had unmask'd his soul,
And seen the bottom of his deepest thoughts.
ROSCOMMON.

No vices are so incurable as those which men are apt to glory in. One would wonder how drunkenness should have the good luck to be of this number. Anacharsis, being invited to a match of drinking at Corinth, demanded the prize very humorously, because he was drunk before any of the rest of the company; for, says he, when we run a race, he who arrives at the goal first is entitled to the reward: on the contrary, in this thirsty generation, the honour falls upon him who carries off the greatest quantity of liquor, and knocks down the rest of the company. I was the other day with honest Will Funnell, the West-Saxon, who was reckoning up how much liquor had passed through him in the last twenty years of his life, which, according to his computation, amounted to twenty-three hogsheads of October, four tun of port, half a kilderkin of small beer, nineteen barrels of cider, and three glasses of champaigne; besides which he had assisted at four hundred bowls of punch, not to mention sips, drams, and whets without number. I question not but every reader's memory will suggest to him several ambitious young men, who are as vain in this particular as Will Funnell, and can boast of as glorious exploits.

Our modern philosophers observe that there is a general decay of moisture in the globe of the earth. This they chiefly ascribe to the growth of vegetables, which incorporate into their own substance many fluid bodies that never return again to their former nature: but with submission, they ought to throw into their account those innumerable rational beings which fetch their nourishment chiefly out of liquids; especially when we consider that men, compared with their fellow-creatures, drink much more than comes to their share.

But however highly this tribe of people may think of themselves, a drunken man is a greater monster than any that is to be found among all the creatures which God has made; as indeed there is no character which appears more despicable and deformed, in the eyes of all reasonable persons, than that of a drunkard. Bonosus, one of our own countrymen, who was addicted to this vice, having set up for a share in the Roman empire, and being defeated in a great battle, hanged himself. When he was seen by the army in this melancholy situation, notwithstanding he had behaved himself very bravely, the common jest was, that the thing they saw hanging upon the tree before them, was not a man but a bottle.

This vice has very fatal effects on the mind, the body, and fortune of the person who is devoted to it.

In regard to the mind, it first of all discovers every flaw in it. The sober man, by the strength of reason, may keep under and subdue every vice or folly to which he is most inclined; but wine makes every latent seed sprout up in the soul, and show itself; gives fury to the passions, and force to those objects which are apt to produce them. When a young fellow complained to an old philosopher that his wife was not handsome; Put less water in your wine, says the philosopher, and you will quickly make her so. Wine heightens indifference into love, love into jealousy, and jealousy into madness. It often turns the good-natured man into an idiot, and the choleric into an assassin. It gives bitterness to resentment, it makes vanity insupportable, and displays every little spot of the soul in its utmost deformity.

Nor does this vice only betray the hidden faults of a man, and show them in the most odious colours, but often occasions faults to which he is not naturally subject. There is more of turn than of truth in a saying of Seneca, that drunkenness does not produce but discover faults. Common experience teaches the contrary. Wine throws a man out of himself, and infuses qualities into the mind, which she is a stranger to in her sober moments. The person you converse with, after the third bottle, is not the same man who at first sat down at table with you. Upon this maxim is founded one of the prettiest sayings I ever met with, which is ascribed to Publius Syrus, *Qui ebrium ludificat, lædit absentem:* "He who jests upon a man that is drunk, injures the absent."

Thus does drunkenness act in a direct contradiction to reason, whose business it is to clear the mind of every vice which is crept into it, and to guard it against all the approaches of any that endeavours to make its entrance. But besides these ill effects which this vice produces in the person who is actually under its dominion, it has also a bad influence on the mind even in its sober moments, as it insensibly weakens the understanding, impairs the memory, and makes those faults habitual which are produced by frequent excesses.

MISCHIEFS BY GIPSY VAGRANTS.

————Semperque recentes
Convectare juvat prædas, et vivere rapto.
VIRG.

Hunting their sport, and plund'ring was their trade.
DRYDEN.

As I was yesterday riding out in the fields with my friend Sir Roger, we saw a little distance from us a troop of Gipsies: upon the first discovery of them, my friend was in some doubt whether he should not exert the Justice of the Peace upon such a band of lawless vagrants, but not having his clerk with him, who is a necessary counsellor on these occasions, and fearing that his poultry might fare the worse for it, he let the thought drop; but at the same time gave me a particular account of the mischiefs they do in the country, in stealing people's goods and spoiling their servants. If a stray piece of linen hangs upon a hedge, says Sir Roger, they are sure to have it; if the hog loses his way in the fields, it is ten to one but he becomes their prey; our geese cannot live in peace for them; if a man prosecutes them with severity, his hen-roost is sure to pay for it; they generally straggle into these parts about this time of the year; and set the heads of our servant maids so agog for husbands, that we do not expect to have any business done as it should be, whilst they are in the country. I have an honest dairy-maid who crosses their hands with a piece of silver every summer, and never fails being promised the handsomest young fellow in the parish for her pains. The butler has been fool enough to be seduced by them; and though he is sure to lose a knife, a fork, or a spoon, every time his fortune is told him, generally shuts himself up in the pantry with an old gipsy for above half an hour once in a twelvemonth. Sweethearts are the things they live upon, which they bestow very plentifully upon all those that apply themselves to them. You see now and then some handsome young jades among them; the sluts have very often white teeth and black eyes.

I might here entertain my reader with historical remarks on this idle profligate people, who infest all the countries of Europe, and live in the midst of governments in a kind of commonwealth by themselves. But instead of entering into observations of this nature, I shall fill the remaining part of my paper with a story which is still fresh in Holland, and was printed in one of our monthly accounts about twenty years ago. "As the Trekschuyt, or hackney-boat, which carries passengers from Leyden to Amsterdam, was putting off, a boy running along the side of the canal desired to be taken in; which the master of the boat refused, because the lad had not quite money enough to pay the usual fare. An eminent merchant being pleased with the looks of the boy, and secretly touched with compassion towards him, paid the money for him, and ordered him to be taken on board. Upon talking with him afterward, he found that he could speak readily in three or four languages, and learned upon further examination that he had been stolen away when he was a child by a gipsy, and had rambled ever since with a gang of strollers up and down several parts of Europe. It happened that the merchant, whose heart seems to have inclined toward the boy by a secret kind of instinct, had himself lost a child some years before. The parents, after a long search for him, gave him up for drowned in one of the canals with which that country abounds; and the mother was so afflicted at the loss of a fine boy, who was her only son, that she died for grief of it. Upon laying together all particulars, and examining the several moles and marks by which the mother used to describe the child when he was first missing, the boy proved to be the son of the merchant whose heart had so unaccountably melted at the sight of him. The lad was very well pleased to find a father who was so rich, and likely to leave him a good estate; the father, on the other hand, was not a little delighted to see a son return to him, whom he had given up for lost, with such a strength of constitution, sharpness of understanding, and skill in languages." Here the printed story leaves off; but if I may give credit to reports, our linguist having received such extraordinary rudiments towards a good education, was afterward trained up in every thing that becomes a gentleman; wearing off by little and little all the vicious habits and practices that he had been used to in the course of his peregrinations: nay, it is said, that he has since been employed in foreign courts upon national business with great reputation to himself, and honour to those who sent him, and that he has visited several countries as a public minister, in which he formerly wandered as a gipsy.*

* Since the purchase of Norwood Common in 1806 Gipsies are unknown in the environs of London; and in another generation it is expected there will be none in England.

DISSECTION OF A COQUETTE'S HEART

Pectoribus inhians cpirantia consulit exta.
VIRG.

Anxious the reeking entrails he consults.

I SHALL here enter upon the dissection of a Coquette's heart, and communicate to the public such particularities as we observed in that curious piece of anatomy.

I should perhaps have waived this undertaking, had not I been desired to do it by several of my unknown correspondents, who are very importunate with me to make an example of the coquette. It is therefore in compliance with the request of friends, that I have looked over the minutes of my dream, in order to give the public an exact relation of it, which I shall enter upon without further preface.

Our operator, before he engaged in this visionary dissection, told us, that there was nothing in his art more difficult than to lay open the heart of a coquette, by reason of the many labyrinths and recesses which are to be found in it, and which do not appear in the heart of any other animal.

He desired us first of all to observe the pericardium, or outward case of the heart, which we did very attentively; and by the help of our glasses discerned in it millions of little scars, which seemed to have been occasioned by the points of innumerable darts and arrows, that from time to time had glanced upon the outward coat; though we could not discover the smallest orifice, by which any of them had entered and pierced the inward substance.

Every smatterer in anatomy knows that this pericardium, or case of the heart, contains in it a thin reddish liquor, supposed to be bred from the vapours which exhale out of the heart, and being stopped here, are condensed into this watery substance. Upon examining this liquor, we found that it had in it all the qualities of that spirit which is made use of in the thermometer, to show the change of weather.

Nor must I here omit an experiment one of the company assured us he himself had made with this liquor, which he found in great quantity about the heart of a coquette whom he had formerly dissected. He affirmed to us, that he had actually enclosed it in a small tube made after the manner of a weather-glass; but that instead of acquainting him with the variations of the atmosphere, it showed him the qualities of those persons who entered the room where it stood. He affirmed also, that it rose at the approach of a plume of feathers, an embroidered coat, or a pair of fringed gloves; and that it fell as soon as an ill-shaped periwig, a clumsy pair of shoes, or an unfashionable coat, came into his house: nay, he proceeded so far as to assure us, that upon his laughing aloud when he stood by it, the liquor mounted very sensibly, and immediately sunk again upon his looking serious. In short, he told us, that he knew very well by this invention whenever he had a man of sense or a coxcomb in his room.

Having cleared away the pericardium, or the case and liquor above-mentioned, we came to the heart itself. The outward surface of it was extremely slippery, and the mucro, or point, so very cold withal, that upon endeavouring to take hold of it, it glided through the fingers like a smooth piece of ice.

The fibres were turned and twisted in a more intricate and perplexed manner than they are usually found in other hearts; insomuch that the whole heart was wound up together in a Gordian knot, and must have had very irregular and unequal motions, whilst it was employed in its vital function.

One thing we thought very observable, namely, that upon examining all the vessels which came into it, or issued out of it, we could not discover any communication that it had with the tongue.

We could not but take notice, likewise, that several of those little nerves in the heart which are affected by the sentiments of love, hatred, and other passions, did not descend to this before us from the brain, but from the muscles which lie about the eye.

Upon weighing the heart in my hand, I found it to be extremely light, and consequently very hollow, which I did not wonder at, when, upon looking into the inside of it, I saw multitudes of cells and cavities running one within another, as our historians describe the apartments of Rosamond's bower. Several of these little hollows were stuffed with innumerable sorts of trifles, which I shall forbear giving any particular account of, and shall therefore only take notice of what lay first and uppermost, which upon our unfolding it and applying our microscopes to it, appeared to be a flame-coloured hood.

We were informed that the lady of this heart, when living, received the addresses of several who made love to her, and did not only give each of them encouragement, but made every one she conversed with believe that she regarded him with an eye of kindness; for which reason we expected to have seen the impression of multitudes of faces among the several plaits and foldings of the heart, but to our great surprise not a single print of this nature discovered itself till we came into the very core and centre of it. We there observed a little figure, which, upon applying our glasses to it, appeared dressed in a very fantastic manner. The more I looked upon it, the more I thought I had seen the face before, but could not possibly recollect either the place or time; when, at length one of the company, who had examined this figure more nicely than the rest, showed us plainly by the make of its face, and the several turns of its features, that the little idol which was thus lodged in the very middle of the heart was a deceased beau.

As soon as we had finished our dissection, we resolved to make an experiment of the heart, not being able to determine among ourselves the nature of its substances, which differed in so many particulars from that of the heart in other females. Accordingly we laid it into a pan of burning coals, when we observed in it a certain salamandrine quality, that made it capable of living in the midst of fire and flame, without being consumed, or so much as singed.

As we were admiring this strange phenomenon, and standing round the heart in a circle, it gave a most prodigious sigh, or rather crack, and dispersed all at once in smoke and vapour. This imaginary noise, which methought was louder than the burst of a cannon, produced such a violent shake in my brain, that it dissipated the fumes of sleep, and left me in an instant broad awake. *L.*

THE NATURE OF THE SUPREME BEING.

Qui mare et terras variisque mundum
Temperat horis:
Unde nil majus generatur ipso,
Nec viget quicquam simile aut secundum

HOR.

Who guides below and rules above,
The great Disposer and the mighty King,
Than he none greater, next him none
That can be, is, or was;
Supreme he singly fills the throne.

CREECH.

SIMONIDES being asked by Dionysius the Tyrant what God was, desired a day's time to consider of it before he made his reply. When the day was expired, he desired two days; and afterward, instead of returning his answer, desired still double time to consider of it. This great poet and philosopher, the more he contemplated the Nature of the Deity, found that he waded but the more out of his depth: and that he lost himself in the thought, instead of finding an end of it.

If we consider the idea which wise men, by the light of reason, have framed of the Divine Being, it amounts to this: That he has in him all the perfection of a spiritual nature; and since we have no notion of any kind of spiritual perfection but what we discover in our own souls, we join infinitude to each kind of these perfections, and what is a faculty in an human soul becomes an attribute in God. We exist in place and time the Divine Being fills the immensity of space with his presence, and inhabits eternity. We are possessed of a little power and a little knowledge, the Divine Being is almighty and omniscient. In short, by adding infinity to any kind of perfection we enjoy, and by joining all these different kinds of perfections in one being, we form our idea of the great Sovereign of Nature.

Though every one who thinks must have made this observation, I shall produce Mr. Locke's authority to the same purpose, out of his Essay on Human Understanding. "If we examine the idea we have of the incomprehensible Supreme Being, we shall find, that we come by it the same way; and that the complex ideas we have both of God and separate spirits, are made up of the simple ideas we receive from reflection, *v. g.* having, from what we experiment in ourselves, got the ideas of existence and duration, of knowledge and power, of pleasure and happiness, and of several other qualities and powers, which it is better to have than to be without; when we would frame an idea the most suitable we can to the Supreme Being, we enlarge every one of these with our idea of infinity; and so putting them together, make our complex idea of God."

It is not impossible that there may be many kinds of spiritual perfection, besides those which are lodged in a human soul; but it is impossible that we should have ideas of any kinds of perfection, except those of which we have some small rays and short imperfect strokes in ourselves. It would be therefore, a very high presumption to determine whether the Supreme Being has not many more attributes than those which enter into our conceptions of him. This is certain, that if there be any kind of spiritual perfection which is not marked out in a human soul, it belongs in its fulness to the Divine Nature.

Several eminent philosophers have imagined that the soul, in her separate state, may have new faculties springing up in her, which she is not capable of exerting during her present union with the body and whether these faculties may not correspond with other attributes in the Divine Nature, and open to us hereafter new matter of wonder and adoration, we are altogether ignorant This, as I have said before, we ought to acquiesce in, that the Sovereign Being, the great Author of Nature, has in him all possible perfection, as well in kind as in degrees; to speak according to our methods of conceiving. I shall only add under this head, that when we have raised our notion of this infinite Being as high as it is possible for the mind of man to go, it will fall infinitely short of what he really is. There is no end of his greatness: the most exalted creature he has made is only capable of adoring it, none but himself can comprehend it.

The advice of the son of Sirach is very just and sublime in this light. "By his word all things consist. We may speak much, and yet come short: wherefore in sum, he is all. How shall we be able to magnify him? For he is great above all his works. The Lord is terrible and very great; and marvellous in his power. When you glorify the Lord, exalt him as much as you can: for even yet will he far exceed. And when you exalt him, put forth all your strength, and be not weary; for you can never go far enough. Who hath seen him, that he might tell us? And who can magnify him as he is? There are yet hid greater things than these be, for we have seen but a few of his works."

I have here only considered the Supreme Being by the light of reason and philosophy. If we would see him in all the wonders of his mercy, we must have recourse to revelation, which represents him to us, not only as infinitely great and glorious, but as infinitely good and just in his dispensations toward man. But as this is a theory which falls under every one's consideration, though indeed it can never be sufficiently considered, I shall here only take notice of that habitual worship and veneration which we ought to pay to this Almighty Being. We should often refresh our minds with the thought of him, and annihilate ourselves before him, in the contemplation of our own worthlessness, and of his transcendent excellency and perfection. This would imprint in our minds such a constant and uninterrupted awe and veneration as that which I am here recommending, and which is in reality a kind of incessant prayer, and reasonable humiliation of the soul before him who made it.

This would effectually kill in us all the little seeds of pride, vanity, and self-conceit which are apt to shoot up in the minds of such whose thoughts turn more on those comparative advantages which they enjoy over some of their fellow-creatures, than on that infinite distance which is placed between them and the supreme model of all perfection. It would likewise quicken our desires and endeavours of uniting ourselves to him by all the acts of religion and virtue.

Such an habitual homage to the Supreme Being would, in a particular manner, banish from among us that prevailing impiety of using his name on the most trivial occasions.

I find the following passage in an excellent sermon, preached at the funeral of a gentleman who was an honour to his country, and a more diligent as well as successful inquirer into the works of nature, than any other our nation has ever produced: "He had the profoundest veneration for the great God of heaven and earth that I have ever observed in any person. The very name of God was never mentioned by him without a pause, and a visible stop in his discourse; in which, one that knew him most particularly above twenty years, has told me, that he was so exact, that he does not remember to have observed him once to fail in it."

Every one knows the veneration which was paid by the Jews to a Name so great, wonderful, and holy. They would not let it enter even into their religious discourses. What can we then think of those who make use of so tremendous a Name in the ordinary expressions of their anger, mirth, and most impertinent passions? Of those who admit it into the most familiar questions and assertions, ludicrous phrases and works of humour; not to mention those who violate it by solemn perjuries? It would be an affront to reason to endeavour to set forth the horror and profaneness of such a practice. The very mention of it exposes it sufficiently to those in whom the light of Nature, not to say religion, is not utterly extinguished.

O.

AFFECTATION OF FASHION.

Nitor in adversum; nec me, qui cætera, vincit
Impetus; et rapido contrarius evehor orbi.

OVID.

I steer against their motions, nor am I
Borne back by all the current of the sky.

ADDISON

I REMEMBER a young man of very lively parts, and of a sprightly turn in conversation, who had only one fault, which was an inordinate desire of appearing fashionable. This ran him into many amours, and consequently into many distempers. He never went to bed until two o'clock in the morning, because he would not be a queer fellow, and was every now and then knocked down by a constable, to signalize his vivacity. He was initiated into half a dozen clubs before he was one-and-twenty, and so improved in them his natural gayety of temper, that you might frequently trace him to his lodging by a range of broken windows, and other like monuments of wit and gallantry. To be short, after having fully established his reputation of being a very agreeable rake, he died of old age at five-and-twenty.

There is indeed nothing which betrays a man into so many errors and inconveniences, as the desire of not appearing singular; for which reason it is very necessary to form a right idea of singularity, that we may know when it is laudable, and when it is vicious. In the first place, every man of sense will agree with me, that singularity is laudable, when, in contradiction to a multitude, it adheres to the dictates of conscience, morality, and honour In these cases we ought to consider, that it is not custom, but duty, which is the rule of action; and that we should be only so far sociable, as we are reasonable creatures. Truth is never the less so, for not being attended to: and it is the nature of actions, not the number of actors, by which we ought to regulate our behaviour. Singularity in concerns of this kind is to be looked upon as heroic bravery, in which a man leaves the species only as he soars above it. What greater instance can there be of a weak and pusillanimous temper, than for a man to pass his whole life in opposition to his own sentiments? or not to dare to be what he thinks he ought to be?

Singularity, therefore, is only vicious when it makes men act contrary to reason, or when it puts them upon distinguishing themselves by trifles. As for the first of these, who are singular in any thing that is irreligious, immoral, or dishonourable, I believe every one will give them up. I shall therefore only speak of those who are remarkable for their singularity in things of no importance, as in dress, behaviour, conversation, and all the little intercourses of life In these cases there is a certain deference due to custom; and notwithstanding there may be a colour of reason to deviate from the multitude in some particulars, a man ought to sacrifice his private inclinations and opinions to the practice of the public. It must be confessed that good sense often makes a humorist; but then it unqualifies him for any moment in the world, and renders him ridiculous to persons of a much inferior understanding.

I have heard of a gentleman in the north of England, who was a remarkable instance of this foolish singularity. He had laid it down as a rule within himself, to act in the most indifferent parts of life according to the most abstracted notions of reason and good sense, without any regard to fashion or example. This humour broke out at first in many little oddnesses; he had never any stated hours for his dinner, supper, or sleep; because, said he, we ought to attend the calls of nature, and not set our meals, but bring our meals to our appetites. In his conversation with country gentlemen, he would not make use of a phrase that was not strictly true: he never told any of them, that he was his humble servant, but that he was his well-wisher, and would be rather thought a malecontent, than drink the king's health when he was not dry. He would thrust his head out at the chamber-window every morning, and after having gaped for fresh air about half an hour, repeat fifty verses as loud as he could bawl them for the benefit of his lungs; to which end he generally took them out of Homer; the Greek tongue, especially in that author, being more deep and sonorous, and more conducive to expectoration, than any other. He had many other particularities, for which he gave sound and philosophical reasons. As this humour still grew upon him, he chose to wear a turban instead of a periwig; concluding very justly, that a bandage of clean linen about his head was much more wholesome, as well as cleanly, than the caul of a wig, which is soiled with frequent perspirations. He afterward judiciously observed, that the many ligatures in the English dress, must naturally check the circulation of the blood; for which reason, he made his breeches and his doublet of one continued piece of cloth, after the manner of the Hussars. In short, by following the pure dictates of reason, he at length departed so much from the rest of his countrymen, and indeed from his whole species, that his friends would have clapped him into Bedlam, and have begged his estate; but the judge being informed that he did no harm, contented himself with issuing out a commission of lunacy against him, and putting his estate into the hands of proper guardians.

The fate of this philosopher puts me in mind of a remark in Monsieur Fontenelle's Dialogues of the Dead. "The ambitious and the covetous," says he, "are madmen to all intents and purposes, as much as those who are shut up in dark rooms: but they have the good luck to have numbers on their side; whereas the frenzy of one who is given up for a lunatic, is a frenzy *hors d'œuvre ;*" that is, in other words, something which is singular in its kind, and does not fall in with the madness of the multitude.

PLANTING.

Ipse thymum pinosque ferens de montibus altis,
Tecta serat late circum, cui talia curæ :
Ipse labore manum duro terat ; ipse feraces
Figat humo plantas, et amicos irriget imbres.
VIRG

With his own hand, the guardian of the bees,
For slips of pines may search the mountain trees
And with wild thyme and sav'ry plant the plain,
Till his hard horny fingers ache with pain ;
And deck with fruitful trees the fields around,
And with refreshing waters drench the ground.
DRYDEN.

EVERY station of life has duties which are proper to it. Those who are determined by choice to any particular kind of business are indeed more happy than those who are determined by necessity, but both are under an equal obligation of fixing on employments, which may be either useful to themselves, or beneficial to others : no one of the sons of Adam ought to think themselves exempt from that labour and industry which were denounced to our first parent, and in him to all his posterity. Those to whom birth or fortune may seem to make such an application unnecessary, ought to find out some calling or profession for themselves, that they may not lie as a burden on the species, and be only the useless part of the creation.

Many of our country gentlemen in their busy hours apply themselves wholly to the chase, or to some other diversion which they find in the fields and woods. This gave occasion to one of our most eminent English writers to represent every one of them as lying under a kind of curse pronounced to them in the words of Goliath, "I will give thee to the fowls of the air, and to the beasts of the field."

Though exercises of this kind, when indulged with moderation, may have a good influence both on the mind and body, the country affords many other amusements of a more noble kind.

Among these I know none more delightful in itself, and beneficial to the public, than that of planting. I could mention a nobleman, whose fortune has placed him in several parts of England, and who has always left these visible marks behind him, which show he has been there: he never hired a house in his life, without leaving all about it the seeds of wealth, and bestowing legacies on the posterity of the owner. Had all the gentlemen of England made the same improvements upon their estates, our whole country would have been at this time as one great garden. Nor ought such an employment to be looked upon as too inglorious for men of the highest rank. There have been heroes in this art, as well as in others. We are told in particular of Cyrus the Great, that he planted all the Lesser Asia. There is indeed something truly magnificent in this kind of amusement: it gives a nobler air to some parts of nature; it fills the earth with a variety of beautiful scenes, and has something in it like creation. For this reason the pleasure of one who plants is something like that of a poet, who, as Aristotle observes, is more delighted with his productions than any other writer or artist whatsoever.

Plantations have one advantage in them which is not to be found in most other works, as they give a pleasure of a more lasting date, and continually improve in the eye of the planter. When you have finished a building, or any other undertaking of the like nature, it immediately decays upon your hands; you see it brought to the utmost point of perfection, and from that time hastening to its ruin. On the contrary, when you have finished your plantations, they are still arriving at greater degrees of perfection as long as you live, and appear more delightful in every succeeding year, than they did in the foregoing

But I do not only recommend this art to men of estates as a pleasing amusement, but as it is a kind of virtuous employment, and may therefore be inculcated by moral motives; particularly from the love which we ought to have for our country, and the regard which we ought to bear to our posterity. As for the first, I need only mention what is frequently observed by others, that the increase of forest-trees does by no means bear a proportion to the destruction of them, insomuch that in a few ages the nation may be at a loss to supply itself with timber sufficient for the fleets of England. I know when a man talks of posterity in matters of this nature, he is looked upon with an eye of ridicule by the cunning and selfish part of mankind. Most people are of the humour of an old fellow of a college, who, when he was pressed by the society to come into something that might redound to the good of their successors, grew very peevish; "We are always doing," says he, "something for posterity, but I would fain see posterity do something for us."

But I think men are inexcusable, who fail in a duty of this nature, since it is so easily discharged. When a man considers, that the putting a few twigs into the ground, is doing good to one who will make his appearance in the world about fifty years hence, or that he is perhaps making one of his own descendants easy or rich, by so inconsiderable an expense, if he finds himself averse to it, he must conclude that he has a poor and base heart, void of all generous principles and love to mankind.

There is one consideration, which may very much enforce what I have here said. Many honest minds that are naturally disposed to do good in the world, and become beneficial to mankind, complain within themselves, that they have not talents for it. This, therefore, is a good office, which is suited to the meanest capacities, and which may be performed by multitudes, who have not abilities sufficient to deserve well of their country, and to recommend themselves to their posterity, by any other method. It is the phrase of a friend of mine, when any useful country neighbour

www.ingramcontent.com/pod-product-compliance
Lightning Source LLC
LaVergne TN
LVHW020241110826
845151LV00003B/991

* 9 7 8 1 4 2 5 5 3 0 2 5 9 *